Towards Relational Soc

Towards Relational Sociology argues that social worlds comprise networks of interaction and relations. Crossley argues that relations are lived trajectories of iterated interaction, built up through a history of interaction, but also entailing anticipation of future interaction. In addition, he demonstrates how networks comprise multiple dyadic relations which are mutually transformed through their combination. On this conceptual basis he builds a relational foundation for sociology.

Over the course of the book, three central sociological dichotomies are addressed – individualism/holism, structure/agency and micro/macro – and utilized as a foil against which to construct the case for relational sociology. Through this, Crossley is able to argue that neither individuals nor 'wholes' – in the traditional sociological sense – should take precedence in sociology. Rather sociologists should focus upon evolving and dynamic networks of interaction and relations.

The book covers many of the key concepts and concerns of contemporary sociology, including identity, power, exchange and meaning. As such it is an invaluable reference tool for postgraduate students and researchers alike.

Nick Crossley is a Professor of Sociology at the University of Manchester, UK. He has published on a wide range of issues in sociology, and most recently on social network analysis.

International Library of Sociology
Founded by Karl Mannheim
Editor: John Urry, *Lancaster University*

Recent publications in this series include:

Risk and Technological Culture
Towards a sociology of virulence
Joost Van Loon

Reconnecting Culture, Technology and Nature
Mike Michael

Advertising Myths
The strange half lives of images and commodities
Anne M. Cronin

Adorno on Popular Culture
Robert R. Witkin

Consuming the Caribbean
From arkwarks to zombies
Mimi Sheller

Between Sex and Power
Family in the world, 1900–2000
Goran Therborn

States of Knowledge
The co-production of social science and social order
Sheila Jasanoff

After Method
Mess in social science research
John Law

Brands
Logos of the global economy
Celia Lury

The Culture of Exception
Sociology facing the camp
Bülent Diken and Carsten Bagge Laustsen

Visual Worlds
John Hall, Blake Stimson and Lisa Tamiris Becker

Time, Innovation and Mobilities
Travel in technological cultures
Peter Frank Peters

Complexity and Social Movements
Multitudes acting at the edge of chaos
Ian Welsh and Graeme Chesters

Qualitative Complexity
Ecology, cognitive processes and the re-emergence of structures in post-humanist social theory
Chris Jenks and John Smith

Theories of the Information Society, 3rd Edition
Frank Webster

Crime and Punishment in Contemporary Culture
Claire Grant

Mediating Nature
Nils Lindahl Elliot

Haunting the Knowledge Economy
Jane Kenway, Elizabeth Bullen, Johannah Fahey and Simon Robb

Global Nomads
Techno and new age as transnational countercultures in Ibiza and Goa
Anthony D'Andrea

The Cinematic Tourist
Explorations in globalization, culture and resistance
Rodanthi Tzanelli

Non-Representational Theory
Space, politics, affect
Nigel Thrift

Urban Fears and Global Terrors
Citizenship, multicultures and belongings after 7/7
Victor J. Seidler

Sociology Through the Projector
Bülent Diken and Carsten Bagge Laustsen

Multicultural Horizons
Diversity and the limits of the civil nation
Anne-Marie Fortier

Sound Moves
iPod culture and urban experience
Michael Bull

Jean Baudrillard
Fatal theories
David B. Clarke, Marcus A. Doel, William Merrin and Richard G. Smith

Aeromobilities
Theory and method
Saulo Cwerner, Sven Kesselring and John Urry

Social Transnationalism
Steffen Mau

Mobile Lives
Anthony Elliott and John Urry

Towards Relational Sociology
Nick Crossley

Forthcoming in the series:

Global China
Lash Scott, Keith Michael, Arnoldi Jakob and Rooker Tyler

Unintended Outcomes of Social Movements
The 1989 Chinese student movement
Fang Deng

Stillness in a Mobile World
David Bissell and Gillian Fuller

Revolt, Revolution, Critique
The paradox of society
Bulent Diken

Towards Relational Sociology

Nick Crossley

 Routledge
Taylor & Francis Group

LONDON AND NEW YORK

First published 2011
by Routledge
2 Park Square, Milton Park, Abingdon, Oxon, OX14 4RN

Simultaneously published in the USA and Canada
by Routledge
711 Third Avenue, New York, NY 10017

First issued in paperback 2012

Routledge is an imprint of the Taylor & Francis Group, an informa business

© 2011 Nick Crossley

The right of Nick Crossley to be identified as author of this work has been
asserted by him in accordance with sections 77 and 78 of the Copyright,
Designs and Patents Act 1988.

Typeset in Times New Roman by
Keystroke, Tettenhall, Wolverhampton

British Library Cataloguing in Publication Data
A catalogue record for this book is available from the British Library

Library of Congress Cataloging-in-Publication Data
Crossley, Nick, 1968–
Towards relational sociology / by Nick Crossley.
p. cm.
Includes bibliographical references and index.
1. Sociology–Philosophy. I. Title.
HM585.C77 2010
302–dc22
2010006469

ISBN13: 978-0-415-48014-7 (hbk)
ISBN13: 978-0-415-53427-7 (pbk)
ISBN13: 978-0-203-88706-6 (ebk)

For Michele and Jake

Contents

Figures

Acknowledgements

Although the spirit of this book and even some of its arguments reflect a central thread in my academic work which goes back to its beginnings, much also bears the hallmarks of a hive of activity that has centred upon the Manchester sociology department over the last few years. Manchester has become, not for the first time, a key focus for work on social networks and network analysis in the UK. Whilst I like to think that I have played a role in engineering this state of affairs, I have equally been swept along and transformed by it. As a node in this network of intellectual production I have been inspired, persuaded, converted, sometimes irritated (productively!) and always supported by many colleagues. I would like to thank Mike Savage, Alan Warde, Fiona Devine, Mark Tranmer, Gindo Tampubolon and Mark Elliot for their help and inspiration, at different points, and for getting networks going at Manchester, in every sense. John Scott belongs to this group too and has always offered help and support for which I am very grateful.

More recently, the impact of Elisa Bellotti and Martin Everett has been tremendous and has boosted both my knowledge of and enthusiasm for network analysis, as indeed has the impact of all members of the Mitchell Centre for Social Network Analysis (formerly the Manchester Social Networks Group). There are too many members of the group to name but I should give special mention to those amongst the group who are also my PhD students (past and present) and who often teach me more than I teach them: Yulia Zemlinskaya, Daniela D'Andretta, Fay Bradley, Susan O'Shea, Suzanne Vaughan, Adriana Aguila and Yvonne Thorne. Of course it's sometimes nice, even a relief, to work with students who aren't quite so involved with networks! For that respite I should thank Raphael Schlembach, Gillian Martin and Shantel Ehrenberg.

James Rhodes has long since ceased to be a student and in truth we talk far more about music than 'work' and probably always did, even when he was a student. But he's a good friend and a brilliant 'broker', connecting me to bands and artists that I am nowhere near cool enough to discover for myself these days. Where this book would have gone without his musical input doesn't bear thinking about.

Many of the ideas expressed in the book have emerged in the context of other projects and bear the imprint of my co-workers on those projects. I am especially grateful therefore to Yousaf Ibrahim, Rachel Stevenson, Gemma Edwards, Wendy

Bottero and Ellie Harries. I am very lucky to have had the opportunity to work with you all.

Finally I would like to thank my wife, Michele, and my son, Jake, for their love, support and stimulation. Michele has made sacrifices for me and for us. For this I am deeply grateful. Jake has kept my feet on the ground (barring the incident with the skateboard!) and his grin and humour are truly energizing. Without them none of this would have happened. Thank you both. I promise to chill now!

1 Introduction

Society exists where a number of individuals enter into interaction. This interaction always arises on the basis of certain drives or for the sake of certain purposes.

(Simmel 1971: 23)

Society has for its substratum the mass of associated individuals. The system which they form by uniting together, and which varies according to their geographical disposition and the nature and number of their channels of communication is the basis from which social life is raised. The representations which form the network of social life arise from the relations between individuals thus combined or the secondary groups that are between the individuals and the total society.

(Durkheim 1974: 24)

Society does not consist of individuals, but expresses the sum of interrelations, the relations within which these individual stand.

(Marx 1973: 265)

Mind can never find expression, and could never have come into existence at all, except in terms of . . . an organized set or pattern of social relations and inter-actions . . .

(Mead 1967: 223)

What is the proper unit of analysis for sociology? Should we be 'atomists', also known as 'individualists', and reduce the social world to the actors who compose it? Or should we be 'holists', treating societies as wholes greater than the sum of these individual parts, wholes with laws, a logic and *telos* independent of those of individual actors? The question will be familiar enough to anyone with even the remotest acquaintance with the discipline. The argument of this book is that both alternatives are equally problematic but that there is a third, much preferable option. The most appropriate analytic unit for the scientific study of social life is the network of social relations and interactions between actors (both human and corporate).

Networks of relations and interaction involve actors who interact and form relations. Actors collectively drive interactions and networks. But not qua individual atoms. They are entangled and precisely inter-act. Furthermore, interactions, relations and networks each manifest properties which are irreducible to the actors involved in them and, over (historical) time, generate further emergent properties, including such fundamentals as languages and moral systems, which are similarly irreducible. Even the actors involved in them, at least in the fully developed sense of 'the actor', emerge in and through processes of interaction. The key properties of social actors, as identified in much social science and philosophy, are not primordial properties of the biological organism but rather capacities and dispositions acquired in and sustained through interaction. Not only do moral and linguistic agency presuppose histories of networks of interaction that have generated the morals and languages in question, for example, they also presuppose interactions, usually in childhood, through which those structures have been acquired and mastered, along with a sense of self (Mead 1967), various identities (ibid.), body techniques (Mauss 1979; Crossley 1995; 2004a,b, 2005a, 2007) and many other forms of social competence. And they presuppose continued inter-action through which these skills and dispositions are perpetuated, modified, transformed etc.

In addition, how actors act is shaped on various levels by the situations in which they find themselves, the others involved and the relations they enjoy with those others. Action is always oriented to other actions and events within the networks in which the actor is embedded. And how the actor responds to these actions and events is influenced by both their impact upon her and by the opportunities and constraints afforded her within her networks, networks comprising other actors. Even private contemplation is a process of 'inner conversation', an interaction which, as Mead (1967) notes, both presupposes a conversational competence acquired by way of interaction with others and engages with internalized repre-sentations of the perspectives of significant others. Our private worlds of thought are simulated interactions involving a virtual network of those who matter to us. And they are private only to the extent that we have acquired a sufficient level of interactional competence and social awareness to make them so, that we have mastered speech to the point that we can speak silently and 'to ourselves', for example, and have acquired a social sensibility sufficient to be aware of and bothered about the awareness that others have of us. Privacy is a practice which positions us in relation to others from whom we wish to keep things private. It is both impossible and meaningless in the absence of others.

Actors are important then but we are not self-contained, self-sufficient atoms. We are 'movers' in the social drama but not prime, unmoved movers. We are always agents-in-relation. There is no exception, no Robinson Crusoe[1] moment. In phylogenetic terms, our primate ancestors lived in groups and group life was amongst the environmental conditions that shaped their evolution into human beings (Hirst and Wooley 1982; Levins and Lewontin 1985; Lewontin 1993). The context of group life selected for certain qualities. It was an environmental con-dition to which those actors best 'fit' would have had a greater chance of survival. We were social before we were human and perhaps only ever became the type of organism that we now call 'human' because we were social.

In ontogenetic terms, we take shape within the womb of our mother, as a parasite upon her, and we are born helpless and incomplete, relying upon others to sustain and impart to us the dispositions and skills which will allow us to emerge as relatively autonomous actors within the networks of interdependence and interaction which comprise our social world. At a sociogenetic level, the dispositions and skills imparted to emergent actors vary across time and both geographical and social space, as an effect of networks and interactions. And the shape and demands of those interactions and networks vary similarly. Life in the networks and interactions of the feudal court, to take a well-documented example, was different to that in contemporary capitalism (Elias 1984). And it will be different again as the networks that constitute the ever-evolving fabric of social life, and the culture that grows within those networks, changes again, as indeed it is different for actors in the present who are positioned at different points in those networks.

Even the consciousness which, for some, defines human beings is, as I discuss in Chapter 5, best conceived in relational terms. Consciousness is not, as Descartes (1969) famously suggests, a 'substance'. It is, at least in its primordial, perceptual form, a relation, a connection between a sensuous organism and objects within its environment. To be conscious is always necessarily to be *conscious of* something or other and thereby to be connected to it by way of a sensuous awareness (Merleau-Ponty 1962, 1965; Mead 1967). As such, consciousness is not 'in our heads' but rather lies between, in the relation of a being who is conscious and the being of which they are conscious (ibid.). Consciousness is not a private theatre, an inner simulation of an outer world. It arises in the interaction between the organism and its environment and comprises the grasp which the former achieves upon the latter.

My point is not only that actors are formed within and inseparable from inter-actions and relations, however, but also, in a more methodological vein, that we can identify *mechanisms* within interaction, relations and networks which help to explain and understand events in the social world. That is, to borrow Hedstrom's definition of mechanisms, we can identify constellations 'of entities and activities that are organized such that they regularly bring about a particular type of outcome' (Hedström 2005: 25). There is a growing and important literature on mechanisms and the concept should, I believe, be central to relational sociology. Much of the existing literature derives from rational action theory (see Elster 2007; Hedström and Swedberg 1998; see Abbott 2007a,b for a critique), which is 'methodologically individualistic' and thus tends towards atomism (see Chapter 2). This is not true of all of it, however. Some is relational in orientation (e.g. Tilly 2002, 2006; McAdam, Tarrow and Tilly 2001). And even much of the supposedly 'methodologically individualistic' work, which is often focused upon patterns of interaction, is relational in focus or at least not irreconcilable with a relational approach[2] (especially Hedström 2005). We must claim 'mechanisms' for relational sociology and seek them out in the context of interactions, relations and networks.

To reiterate, however, networks of interaction do not enjoy the independence from agency, the independent *telos* and self-determinacy, which certain strands of holistic sociology, not least crude variants of functionalism and Marxism, have attributed to it. Versions of holism which explain what goes on within a society by reference to the determinate power and requirements of society itself or invariant laws of historical destiny, are no less flawed than the individualism which they oppose. The mantra of holism, that the whole is greater than the sum of its parts, is open to various interpretations. There is a sense in which it is correct but there are also many senses in which it is not. Specifically, it is correct in the respect that networks of interaction, as noted above, manifest irreducible properties and generate further emergent properties, including the very agents who interact within them. But it is deeply flawed if it is taken as a licence to invoke 'society' or its laws or needs as explanations of social activities and outcomes. There are social logics and mechanisms which steer (inter)action but these are logics and mechanisms of interaction, logics and mechanisms which refer us to historically situated agents-in-relation, not mysterious societal forces which compel agents, from behind their backs, to act in particular ways.

Relational sociology is not my idea, even if I do hope to advance its cause and put my own spin upon it. It is 'in the air' at the moment, circulating within sociological networks in a variety of forms, some of which are closer to what I am suggesting than others (e.g. Emirbayer 1997; White 1992, 2008; Tilly 2006; Gould 1993a, 1995; Abbott 1997, 2001, 2007a,b; Strauss 1993; Bourdieu 1998, 2000; Bourdieu and Wacquant 1992; Elias 1978, 1984). Indeed, as the quotations at the start of this chapter indicate, one can identify approximations of it right back through the history of sociology to the founders. I am not calling for yet another revolution or 'turn' in sociology therefore. I am engaging with a current concern in the discipline and also returning to what I take to be certain basic and fundamental sociological ideas in an effort to revive and revise them. In doing so I will draw freely from those other relational sociologists whose version of relationalism is most similar to my own. The point is not to start afresh but rather to achieve some much needed clarity in relation to what some sociologists have, in my view, been striving for all along.

I begin to make my case, in Chapter 2, by way of closer examination of the individualism/holism dichotomy outlined briefly above. The book addresses three sociological dichotomies in total, the other two being the agency/structure (Chapter 8) and micro/macro (Chapter 10) dichotomies respectively, but the individualism/holism dichotomy is the most fundamental, as an 'epistemological obstacle' (Bachelard 2002), from the point of view of establishing a relational approach to sociology.

Having identified relationalism as a potential alternative to both individualism and holism, in Chapter 2, I seek in Chapter 3 to lay out some of the basic concepts of the relational approach. I begin with a reflection upon the concept of 'relations', which leads to a brief discussion of 'interaction' and then 'networks'. These three concepts, 'interaction', 'relations' and 'networks', are in some respects the most fundamental to my approach. Any adequate discussion of them inevitably draws upon other key concepts, such as power, resources and conventions, however, and my conception of networks, whilst heavily indebted to the narrower and more technical version posited in social network analysis (e.g. Wasserman and Faust 1994; Scott 2000), seeks to build upon this basis, adding in a consideration of conventions, resources and overlapping interests, such that a 'network', as I understand it, is akin to what some symbolic interactionists refer to as 'a social world' (see also Crossley 2010a,b), that is to say, something broader than what the concept of 'network' might initially suggest.

Chapter 3 identifies a number of dimensions which are evident to varying degrees within most interactions and relations. Specifically, it identifies strategic, symbolic, affective, conventional (or institutionalized) and exchange dimensions. In Chapters 4, 5, 6 and 7 I draw these aspects out and analyse them in more detail. Chapter 4 takes 'strategic interaction' and game theory as its point of departure but quickly diverts into a discussion which incorporates many other key aspects of and possibilities within interaction, including cooperation, trust, duty and empathy. Chapters 5 and 6 pick up on the theme of intersubjectivity which is raised in this context and discuss it in some detail, elaborating upon the symbolic and affective aspects of interaction which often run parallel to and become entangled in strategic interaction. Chapter 7 concludes this part of the book with a discussion of exchange relations and the power which emerges within them.

The discussion in Chapters 4 through 7 repeatedly bangs up against the concepts 'networks', 'conventions' and 'resources'. Chapters 8 through 10 build upon this, making these concepts central. This begins, in Chapters 8 and 9, with a discussion of the interpenetration of networks, conventions and resources in the context of 'social worlds'. These concepts, it is argued, are crucial for a properly relational investigation of social life and, indeed, to an adequate conception of 'social structure'. In this context the merits of 'convention' relative to 'rules' (Giddens 1984) and 'habitus' (Bourdieu 1992) are also discussed.

The much debated agency/structure dichotomy is also discussed in this context. I argue that, unlike individualism and holism, which constitute incompatible principles of reduction, agency and structure are effectively co-existing aspects of the social world which assume greater or lesser salience in different contexts. We cannot resolve this dichotomy because there is nothing to resolve or at least nothing that can be resolved in general. The job of sociology and especially relational sociology, I suggest, is to examine how, paraphrasing Marx, inter-actors make history (agency) but not in circumstances of their choosing (structure). There is not much else to be said regarding structure and agency than this.

Finally, I turn to the question of whether the position outlined in the book and the concepts invoked are sufficient to engage with the dynamics and structure of the social macro-cosm. I suggest that they are, seeking to demonstrate how different conceptions of 'actors', 'relations' and network structures map onto bigger objects of enquiry than might usually be assumed. Ironically it is sometimes more difficult to appreciate the relational configuration of the social macro-cosm than it is the micro-cosm, and to slip either into an unhelpful holism, with a hypostatized conception of 'society' as a solid and pre-given thing, or into atomism, treating societies as nothing more than aggregates of individuals. Chapter 10 suggests a way in which we might avoid this and find a more theoretically satisfying way of doing macro-sociology, a relational approach which treats 'micro' and 'macro' as two ends of a continuum along which sociologists must learn to move (in both directions).

2 Individualism, holism and beyond

In this chapter I clear the way for a relational approach to sociology through a more extensive discussion of the dichotomy of individualism and holism introduced in the previous chapter. I begin by defining holism. This is followed by a brief outline of the individualist critique of holism and the proposed alternative. I then outline my own criticisms of both holism and, more especially, individualism.

To some extent these criticisms hinge upon my claim that there is a better and persuasive alternative to both holism and individualism, a claim which will only be fully supported over the course of the book. In a number of instances I gesture towards arguments that I will make more fully later or offer only a skeleton of a position which requires filling out. In this respect the chapter should be read as an opening round in a battle that will run through the book rather than a self-contained account. In particular, the claims of the chapter are very closely tied to those of Chapter 3, which originally formed the second half of this one and complements it by elaborating upon such key concepts as 'relations', 'interaction' and 'networks'. As noted, however, the argument begun in this chapter is not really over until the last full stop of the final chapter.

Rational action theory (RAT) is used throughout as a key example of methodological individualism in contemporary sociology and some of my criticism is specifically focused upon it. I concede that some versions of RAT, namely those informed by either game theory or exchange theory, make considerable steps towards a relational position and for this, amongst other reasons, constitute useful resources for relational sociology. I insist, however, that we have good reasons to move further in a relational direction than RATs, qua methodological individualists, are inclined to travel. This argument, which focuses upon the emergence and reproduction of actors within the context of interactions, relations and networks, comprises the final section of the chapter.

Holism defined

The holist believes that we can only understand and explain the 'parts' of the social world by reference to their fit within the whole. The whole is said to be greater than the sum of its parts and more specifically is attributed a systemic nature which the parts are destined to serve. Functional explanations, which account for institutionalized aspects of the social world by reference to the functions which they perform in wider social systems are one obvious example. Radcliffe-Brown (1952a), whose work is in other respects useful from a relational point of view, exemplifies this line of thought, at least in some of his theoretical work. And much of the later work of Parsons (1951, 1979) is similarly exemplary. Parsons identifies key 'functional prerequisites' of social systems which, he argues, must be met if social systems are to survive and flourish, and his examination of social institutions appears to suggest not only that various institutions fulfil these prerequisites but that identifying this fact amounts to an explanation of the institutions in question. For Parsons we explain social institutions by observing the functions which they perform for the wider social system(s) to which they belong.

Historicist theories, in Karl Popper's (2002) sense, which claim that societies or social systems evolve or transform according to fixed 'laws' and therefore follow necessary historical trajectories is another example of holism and its logic of explanation. Historicist theories suggest that history is necessarily moving in a particular direction, towards a particular end, such that individual actions and events cannot be understood and explained except by reference to their furthering that end. There is a tendency and direction in history which is irreducible to individual actions and intentions and to which they are subordinated.

Holist theories are reductive in the respect that their explanations subordinate the behaviour of the parts of the social world, however they are conceived, to the requirements of either a systemic whole or an imagined future–historical destiny. The parts are thereby denied any autonomy. For this reason holism is also deterministic. It precludes an account of human agency because it cannot allow actors to make a difference. Either history is destined to move towards a particular end or it is not. Institutions are either explained by their function within the whole or they are not. There are no half measures, and actors, when they figure at all in genuinely holistic accounts, are therefore necessarily subordinated to the demands of the whole.

Defined thus there may be many theories which invoke 'the whole', 'systems' or indeed 'functions' which are not holistic. Holism, as I am defining it, is necessarily teleological or eschatological in form. It goes beyond a description or specification of functions by invoking functions as causes: x happens because of the function that it fulfils for y. And it goes beyond the identification of 'plot lines' in history to stipulate the inevitability of a particular denouement. In both cases the present is, so to speak, shaped by the future, by a *telos* towards which is it is necessarily propelled.

Durkheim (1965) was mindful of the distinction that I am drawing here when, in *The Rules of Sociological Method*, he distinguished between explaining social facts and describing their functions. For Durkheim, to describe the function of a social institution such as religion is not to explain it. To explain it we must examine its history, identifying the various contingent events, actions and consequences of actions (both intended and unintended) that gave rise to it.

As such, Durkheim is not a holist, as I am using that term, and does not succumb to the problems of holism outlined here – which is not to deny that there are problems with functional descriptions of the kind he offers (Habermas 1988; Hirst 1979).

I doubt that many contemporary sociologists would own up to being a holist in this strict sense. I am constructing a 'straw model' to do battle with. Even within sociological functionalism, Merton (1957) had criticized and rejected teleological explanation before Parsons (1951), who cites him in *The Social System*, had written that seminal work. Teleological and related holistic conceptions are still sneaked into sociological accounts, however. It is by no means uncommon to hear that something happens because capitalism, the system, the symbolic or some such holistic abstraction 'demands it' – a claim which would not necessarily be objectionable if it were not left at that, without further specification of the mechanisms which translate the requirements of the system into actions which meet those requirements. Furthermore, even if the holism I am opposing had no takers at all it is still a useful foil which allows us to clarify more precisely what relationalism involves and what it does not involve.

The individualist critique of holism

Individualists reject holism absolutely. The purpose of sociology, they argue, is to explain. Holism either fails to do this altogether, resorting to mere storytelling (about how everything fits together) and re-description of everyday social observations in high sounding but analytically useless vocabulary, or else it resorts to functional explanations which are deeply flawed (Homans 1973; Hollis 1994; Elster 1989, 2007). Explaining some part of the social world by reference to its functions, they argue, turns a consequence into a cause. The function of an action or institution is its effect, so when we invoke its function to explain an action/institution we are saying that its effect is also its cause. This doesn't make any sense. It contradicts our rationally justifiable belief that causes precede their consequences. And holists give us no reason to revise this belief.

In addition, individualist critics of holism note that teleology has been rejected as a legitimate mode of explanation in the other sciences where it once played a role (ibid.). Attempts to explain events by reference to their functions have repeatedly been undermined by superior and more parsimonious explanations which break the whole down into parts and, reversing the logic of functional explanation, invoke those parts to explain the whole. The parts explain the whole, for the individualist, and science has only advanced to the extent that it has recognized this fact.

Individualists are not necessarily averse to the notion of social systems but they insist that such systems can only be explained by reference to the individuals who comprise them. Indeed, they are often happy with the notion of 'functions' as long as the latter are not invoked as explanations. Jon Elster's (1985) reading of Marxism and the work of James Coleman (e.g. 1990) are good illustrations of a systems focus within the individualist camp.

Popper's (2002) critique of historicism offers an equally robust individualist refutation of holism. Knowledge of any 'laws of history', Popper argues, must inevitably change our behaviour. And this, in turn, must change the direction or plotline of history itself, refuting the notion that such 'laws' are laws at all. The obvious example, close to Popper's own agenda, is Marxism. Marx's prediction of the collapse of capitalism and its replacement by communism has mobilized any number of political actors into both 'revolutionary' and 'counter-revolutionary' actions, actions which have affected the course of history. Marx's work has made an enormous impact upon the history of societies throughout the world. But that fact, in itself, confounds Marx's own attempt to predict the trajectory of history on the basis of inevitable 'laws of development' (if that is what he was attempting to do[1]). It points to the importance of ideas, reflexivity, agency and, indeed, of such key historical players as Marx himself.

In addition, on a more political level, many individualists (Popper 1992) and also relationalists (Merleau-Ponty 1964, 1973) argue that belief in historical inevitability and the laws and needs of society have been used to suppress democracy and support oppressive political regimes, most notably in the formative stages of the former USSR. Somewhat paradoxically, those convinced that society necessarily will, by force of mechanical necessity, develop in certain ways have in some instances resorted to sustained violence to ensure that it does, all the time justifying their violence by reference to the truth of history. Holism, so the argument goes, is antithetic to what Popper (1992) calls the 'open society'.

Individualism defined

Individualists shift the focus of explanatory accounts away from social wholes. The parts explain the whole for individualists and in the case of the social world those parts are individual human actors. Some individualists, whom we might call *ontological individualists*, maintain a very strict formulation of this theory in which, to paraphrase[2] the words of ex-British Prime Minister, Margaret Thatcher (1987), 'there is no such thing as society, just individuals'; or as Jeremy Bentham puts it, 'The Community is a fictitious body, composed of the individual persons who are considered as constituting as it were its members' (Bentham 1988: 3). Individual human beings and their individual actions and properties are the only real elements in the social world and thus the only legitimate analytic focus for social science according to ontological individualists.

It is seldom clear why ontological individualists believe that human beings are the only entities existing in the social world. The position is often informed by a liberal political commitment which emphasizes the sacrosanct nature of the individual but commitments are not ontological arguments and tend rather to presuppose them. In Chapter 3 I consider some potential critiques of the concept of 'relations' which, if they were correct, might inform an individualistic position (I will argue that they are not correct). For now, however, it must suffice to say that individualism derives plausibility for some in virtue of an empiricist conviction that all that exists, or at least all we can know, is that which is given directly to our senses. Some people are individualists, in other words, because human organisms are visible, tangible objects in a way that 'social relations', 'cultures', 'societies' etc. are not, and they are inclined to believe that only perceptible entities exist.

I will offer a critique of this rationale for ontological individualism shortly. First, however, note that not all individualists are ontological individualists. *Methodological individualists* accept that the social world has properties of its own, so-called *emergent properties*, which are distinct from and irreducible to the properties of individuals (qua individuals), but maintain that emergent properties are, at most, a framework and set of resources with and within which individuals operate. They insist that individuals (and their actions and properties) are the only active agents in the social world and thus the only legitimate focus for sociological explanation. Emergent properties don't do anything. Only individuals do things and thus it is individuals we should focus upon. Moreover, most methodological individualists insist that the emergent properties of the social world can, in the final analysis, be explained by reference to, and thus be reduced to, the actions and properties of individuals. The British legal system, for example, is not my invention or the invention of anybody else alive today but, the methodological individualist insists, every aspect of that system can be explained, in principle, by reference to the actions of (multiple) individuals.

A further argument for methodological individualism centres upon the fact that human actors are purposive beings, that is, beings whose actions are oriented to the achievement of self-determined ends. Humans act *in order to* achieve certain goals not *because*[3] of the play of antecedent forces upon them. This necessitates a specific explanatory strategy, it is argued. If human beings pursue goals then we cannot hope to explain their actions in the same way that we might explain the behaviour of inanimate objects or even more basic life forms. However, if we adopt a purposive mode of explanation then we can only legitimately apply that to individual human actors. Only human individuals have intentions, form plans etc. Hence we focus upon human individuals.

There is a potential problem with this argument, as James Coleman (1990), an advocate of it, acknowledges. Purposive explanations might be deemed teleological and thus fall foul of one of the key criticisms that individualists level against holists. This is not the place to discuss this point. Note, however, that there are important differences between purposive accounts of agency and teleological or historicist accounts of social systems which prevent critiques of the latter from being applied to the former. In the first instance, individualists are not seeking to explain parts by reference to a whole. They are not positing functional explanations. They are simply saying that actors have goals which direct their actions in an environment. Second, actors' goals and purposes precede their actions and, as such, do not raise the peculiar difficulties associated with functional explanation. To say that actors act in pursuit of goals is not to say that the consequences of their actions are also the cause of those actions because goals are not consequences. More importantly, unlike consequences, goals precede the actions which they mobilize and may therefore legitimately enter into an explanation of those actions, as a mobilizing force.

Rational action theory (RAT)

The most influential manifestation of methodological individualism in recent sociology has come in the form of rational action theory (RAT). RAT is an economic approach to social behaviour. It argues that human action is governed by cost–benefit principles such that actors seek out the most efficient way of realizing their goals, pursuing the greatest return for the lowest 'expenditure' (whether of money, time, physical effort or whatever). In the classical version, most common in economics, actors are selfish and profit maximizing; they have access to all of the relevant information which might inform their choices; and they act as if capable of performing the fantastically complex calculations that economists perform when seeking to predict how they will act. Even in economics, however, it is sometimes acknowledged that this model is neither empirically plausible nor sufficient to model and predict actual human behaviour. Thus it is sometimes argued that actors seek to *satisfice*[4] rather than maximize utility; sometimes pursue *altruistic* ends; work with *limited information* which it would not be worth their while trying to improve upon; and rely upon *rules of thumb* which *bound* their rationality in various ways. Moreover, in recent discussions of 'bounded rationality' it has been argued that much human action is rooted in intuition rather than the conscious calculation presupposed in traditional RAT accounts (for a review see Kahneman 2003). Intuitive reasoning is said to depart from the idealized rationality of RAT in many significant respects and is much more interpretive and socially–contextually sensitive.

Sociological appropriations of RAT vary in interesting ways (Goldthorpe 2000) but most relax the assumptions of the traditional economic formulation, employing a bounded and more empirically plausible version, and all, importantly, are insistent in their methodological individualism. Not all methodological individualists are RATs but all RATs are methodological individualists. RAT, to reiterate, has been the dominant version of methodological individualism in recent sociology and for this reason deserves special attention in this chapter.

Beyond individualism and holism

As defined above, individualism and holism are different and incompatible principles of reduction. If we accept one then we cannot accept the other without contradicting ourselves. Either the parts are reducible to the whole or the whole is reducible to the parts. My argument, in what follows, is that both are wrong and that relationalism affords a third and preferable alternative.

My argument is centred upon the notion that 'the whole is greater than the sum of its parts'. Holism, as I have characterized it, interprets this to mean that social structures constitute a higher order of being than individual human actors and involve laws of development and/or functional prerequisites which determine, teleologically, what happens within them. What happens in the social world happens because it serves the whole, on this account, a position which precludes individual agency.

I agree with the various objections, reviewed above, that individualists make against this approach. I will not reiterate them here but they can be regarded as elements in my own, relational critique of holism. Furthermore, I contend that holism generates a problem of what historians and philosophers of science, noting its disappearance in other sciences, have termed 'substantialism' (Bachelard 2002; Cassirer 1923). The holist envisages society as a given, a pre-constituted entity or 'substance' with an underlying and determinate essence which can be invoked to explain what happens within it. They treat 'society', 'capitalism' or whatever as something which somehow lies beyond or behind the relations and interactions which instantiate it and which explains those relations and interactions. Historically contingent social arrangements are imputed an ahistorical essence and force such that their durability, where they do endure, is assumed rather than analysed. The holist fails to see that society is constantly in the making, always becoming, that it is wholly dependent upon what happens 'within' it for its identity, form and existence. Relational sociology challenges this substantialism, refusing to treat society as a solid object with fixed properties. It focuses upon the relational dynamics which make and remake societies continually. Society is not a 'thing' for the relationalist but rather a state of play within a vast web of ongoing interactions.

Individualism is problematic too, however. I do not accept the ontological individualist's empiricist contention that what exists necessarily exists for immediate sensory perception, such that human beings exist but relations, societies etc. do not. As I will argue throughout this book, we have many good reasons to believe in processes and structures which are not immediately given to our senses, reasons which can inform empirical research which, in turn, offers indirect but persuasive evidence of their existence. Invisible entities are invoked in other sciences and there is no reason why we should not allow ourselves this possibility, where appropriate, in sociology too. More importantly for present purposes, however, I contend that the whole is indeed greater than the sum of its parts in the social world, albeit in a different way to that suggested by the holist.

As a first step to establishing this I contend both that much human action is in fact interaction – this is true by definition of the 'social action', qua social, to which most social scientists limit their focus – and that interaction comprises an irreducible whole (see also Mead 1967; Elias 1978). When i and j interact, each responds to and affects the other such that they collectively generate a whole which is irreducible to them as individual entities: i's actions are influenced by j's and j's by i's (this point is elaborated in detail in Chapter 3).

This is not only a matter of dyads. Dyadic structures of interaction no more exist in splendid isolation than individuals. They too are embedded in the networks of multiple relations and interactions in which any actor is involved, and this embedding makes a difference. Simmel (1902), for example, famously demonstrates how the introduction of a third party transforms the dynamics of dyadic interaction, and the wider literature on social network analysis extends this point through a discussion of the impact of a variety of network figurations. Different patterns of connection generate different opportunities, constraints and dynamics for those connected in them, both generically and according to the actor's specific location in the pattern (see for example Burt 2005). Added to the literature on 'critical mass' (e.g. Schelling 1995; Oliver and Marwell 1993), which resonates with Simmel's (1902) related reflections upon the significance of 'numbers' for social behaviour, this work shows that both the (network) structure and size of interacting populations makes a big difference to what happens within them and how their members behave. Actors are not subsumed within the whole, as in holistic accounts of systems or historical laws, but we cannot disentangle their actions or understand them independently of the dynamics of the whole qua network.

This point has both ontological and methodological import and, as such, challenges individualism is both of its forms. Ontologically it points to the existence of structures (of interaction and also networks) which are both fundamental aspects of the social world and irreducible to individuals qua individuals. Note that this argument displaces the individual on two fronts; it both locates the actor within the context of an irreducible structure to which they belong and shifts the focus from 'the actor', as a supposedly underlying entity (or 'substance') to 'action' or rather 'interaction' as an unfolding *process*. Individualism, especially in its ontological form, is no less substantialist than holism, focused as it is upon 'the individual' as a supposed underlying bedrock of social life. Much of the relational critique of individualism will involve a challenge to this substantialism.

Methodologically, the irreducibility of interaction, the significance of networks and their centrality to sociology suggest that our basic unit of analysis is not or at least should not be individuals but rather structures of interaction, the relations which (I argue in Chapter 3) emerge from them, and networks of such interactions and relations. The individual is not the most basic unit of social life but rather a unit too basic to capture much that is most significant about the social world.

Some RATs, particularly those with an interest in 'game theory' (see Chapter 4) and 'exchange theory' (see Chapter 7) seem to recognize this. Their variants of RAT emphasize the importance of interaction and networks, acknowledging both their irreducibility and the necessity for special methods to deal with them (see especially Coleman 1990; Gintis 2009). Moreover, some game theorists, as I discuss in Chapter 4, have tried to make their accounts more plausible by introducing a notion of iterated interaction and thus 'relationships' (e.g. Axelrod 1985, 1997), whilst others have begun to explore issues of social influence (see Manski 2000). Indeed, social interaction, influence and networks are now accepted as fundamental amongst many authors who, in other respects, adopt an economic or rational action approach to social life, including some economists (Becker 1996; Becker and Murphy 2000; Coleman 1990; Ormerod 2005; Jackson 2008; Goyal 2007). This does not redeem methodological individualism, however, so much as raise the question as to what is supposed to be individualistic, methodological or otherwise, about it.

There is an important difference between relationalism and this more sophis-ticated, interaction-focused form of individualism, however. Individualists, both methodological and ontological, take 'the individual' as a stable bedrock underlying and explaining interaction. This, to reiterate an earlier point, is the individualist variant of the error of substantialism referred to with respect to holism above. Individualism abstracts the actor from their various networks of relations and interactions, and thus from both structure and process (time), or rather structure-in-process, to found sociology upon this abstraction. Moreover, it tends to attribute to individuals, qua individuals, properties which they only acquire and maintain in the context of interaction and collective life. The rela-tionalism that I am advocating, by contrast, posits that individuals, or rather actors, are formed and continually re-formed in and through interaction. In what follows in this chapter I will unpack the different aspects of this problem, as I see it. I begin with an argument from Marx.

Positions, structures, interests and actors

Arguing in a relational rather that a holistic or functionalist vein, Marx contends that:

> Society does not consist of individuals, but expresses the sum of inter-relations, the relations within which these individual stand. As if someone where to say: Seen from the perspective of society, there are no slaves and no citizens: both are human beings. Rather they are that outside of society. To be a slave, to be a citizen, are social characteristics: relations between between human beings A and B. Human being A as such is not a slave. He is a slave in and through society.
>
> (Marx, 1973: 265)

In other words, the actor in general, as conceived by the individualist, is an abstraction; indeed, an unhelpful abstraction. Actors or human beings never exist 'in general' but always in concrete and historically specific circumstances, which is to say in 'positions' within networks of relations to other human beings, with the various identities, interests, interdependencies and practical engagements that such positions entail. Actors always already exist in relation to others and who and what they are is shaped by these relations. They act but always and only ever as incumbents of these relational positions.

An adequate conception and analysis of social life, Marx is suggesting, demands that we keep these relations in play. Being a slave is not a property of an individual actor. There are no slaves without masters to whom they are enslaved. Likewise, there are no blacks without whites, no women without men and so on. This is partly a matter of identity and difference. To enjoy an identity as some-thing (e.g. 'black') one must be distinguished from others ('whites') who do not have that identity. Beyond this, however, Marx is suggesting that we cannot hope to understand the slave qua actor if we abstract them from their relation of slavery and their interdependence both with others slaves and with their masters. Whatever generic attributes of human nature the slave possesses, they are a slave not a generic and abstract human being, and sociological analysis must understand them as such.

This argument equally alerts us to the inability of individualism to distinguish between different types of society (see also Elias 1978). All societies, from the earliest hunter–gatherer formations to the most advanced forms of capitalism, comprise individuals, but for that very reason analytically reducing them to individuals is unhelpful. It ignores the properties that make them distinct. Feudal Japan was different, as a society, to contemporary Britain and we need a way of thinking about societies that allows us to capture these differences. Culture (including technology), as an emergent property (see below), is an important factor here but what Marx is pointing us to are relations. Social actors in Feudal Japan were connected to one another in a different way to that of actors in contemporary Britain. We are all human beings, all, at least in one sense (see below) 'individuals', but the way in which we are wired up to one another, forming a society, differs and this makes a difference. Populations of individuals, however large, do not in themselves constitute societies. Sixty million people living on an island like Great Britain is not, in itself, a society. We are a society by virtue of the fact that we interact and enjoy relations of interdependence. And the ways in which we are connected, the form and type of our relations, make a very important difference, configuring us as a specific type of society.

In part this is a matter of the qualities of relations. The relationship of the master to the slave is different to that of the relation between capitalist and worker, and this affects the way in which both can act. Relations are important because they enable and constrain action. And different relations do so in different ways. It is also a matter of broader networks of relations, however, which embed the individual relations within them, adding further opportunities and restraints. The way a society is 'wired up' affects what its members can do and thus what can happen within it.

Relations are 'more than' individuals who stand in relation, on this account. They have specific properties as, for example, relations of slavery or wage labour (or love, marriage, friendship, parenting etc.). And, to reiterate, they define the actors who are involved in them. Slave relations do not form when masters and slaves conjoin. Masters and slaves only exist as such in virtue of the slavery relationship. The identity of each is dependent both upon that of the other and the nature of the relation between them. We must analyse them as masters and slaves, rather than abstract human beings, always remembering that 'slave' is not the attribute or identity of an isolated actor but rather of an actor as they are defined by their relationship to another.

What this also suggests, as Rawls (1992) notes, is that interests derive from relational positions. RAT considers the 'preferences' which drive choice to be an individual property (although see my note on Becker (1996) below). What Marx suggests, by contrast, is that certain important preferences reflect interests which derive from relational positions: slaves, assumedly, would prefer either to be citizens or to live in societies where nobody is enslaved. Masters, one assumes, would prefer things to stay as they are. There are, of course, many problems with Marxist accounts of interests and we need to be cautious (Hindess 1982). We cannot simply impute interests to actors on the basis of the position(s) they occupy. We must acknowledge that actors occupy multiple positions and make sense of both those positions and their interests, discursively, in iterated conversations, both internalized and external. However, the slave example nicely illustrates one way in which an actor's expressed interests might emerge from their location in a network of relations.

The actor as an emergent property

These arguments suggest not only that the whole is greater than the sum of its parts but also that we cannot legitimately abstract actors from their location within such wholes. Abstract, atomic individuals are mythical beings. Individuals are always already located in networks of interaction and relations which make a difference and affect the way in which, as sociologists, we must deal with them. My claim against individualism is stronger still than this, however. My version of relationalism posits that individuals, or rather actors, are formed and continually re-formed in and through interaction. This operates on different levels.

On one level the actor is affected by the particularities of a given interaction at a given point in time. They assume different identities in different interactions, for example, for different purposes and in relation to different alters. How they act is shaped both by these identities and also by the stimulation of the interaction itself. Others provoke (sometimes new) thoughts and feelings within the actor, and shape their perceptions, all of which shapes their responses and further actions. Each is affected by the actions of the other, in various ways, and their own responses are shaped by these effects (this is explored further in Chapter 3).

Note that interaction remains purposive in this account. Actors respond and reply to one another. Their actions are not effects of antecedent causes. At the same time, however, they do stimulate, arouse, provoke and otherwise exert a causal influence upon one another. In effect, as Coleman (2006) notes, 'purpose' and 'cause' each capture an aspect of the reality of our collective life. Human beings are not simply passive receptacles of external forces which act upon them. We are purposive actors. But this does not make us immune to causal influence, and not only in the sense that some definitions of causality hinge upon purposive action or treat purposes and reasons as causes (see Goldthorpe 2000; Bhaskar 1979). We are affected by events in our environment and these effects impact upon the purposive responses we make to those events. More importantly, those 'events' often comprise the actions and interactions of others. Others affect us in both intended and unintended ways.

At another level we both acquire and maintain durable interaction dispositions by way of interaction. Before I expand upon this, a brief note on emergent properties is necessary.

Emergent properties

Collective life, which is the only life possible for human beings, has given rise to languages, moral codes and a range of further cultural structures which are properties of the collective qua collective and are strictly irreducible to individual actors. These emergent properties do not negate individual agency or subordinate actors as parts to a whole. But they do add to our list of the ways in which collective life is greater than the sum of the individual actors it involves.

Many emergent properties exist *between* individuals, in relations. The meaning of our verbal and written utterances, for example, necessarily presupposes both a speaker and a listener. Meaning, as I discuss in Chapter 5, arises between actors in communication (Mead 1967). Actors may learn to play both roles in relation to their selves, in 'internal conversations', and reflexively monitor and respond to their own utterances in external communication. Their capacity to do this arises only by means of interaction with others, however (see Chapter 5). Likewise, the exchange value, in economic transactions, presupposes two parties between whom objects are exchanged. It exists between actors as a relational property (see also Chapter 7).

Importantly, however, some emergent properties, such as language and moral systems, sediment as dispositions, transforming the biological organisms that we begin life as into social actors. Social actors are formed, maintained and transformed in interaction. Through interaction with others we acquire language and the ability to reason and think reflectively (Mead 1967; Vygotsky 1986); a sense of self, identity and the sense of 'the other' that underlies our moral sensibilities and our capacities for both strategic interaction and reflexivity (Mead 1967; Smith 2000); habits, morals, social (perhaps 'civilized') sensibilities and innumerable techniques and forms of competence which enable us to do so much of what we do in interaction (Elias 1984; Mauss 1979; Goffman 1971; Bourdieu 1984). Moreover, the durability of these dispositions is accounted for, in some part, by their iterative use in successive interactions. What we don't use we lose and use is occasioned by interaction. This point challenges methodological individualism head on because it denies social agents the primacy and foundational status that it claims for them.

Furthermore, somewhere between the effects of primary socialization and the fleeting influence of momentary interaction, is the influence of secondary socialization and reference groups, that is, influences which extend beyond the moment but not indefinitely. In a relatively early critique of RAT, which is predicated on the notion that individuals have fixed sets of (transitive[5]) preferences, for example, Heath (1976) draws upon various social psychological studies which indicate that preferences change across time, not least on account of the comparisons that individuals make between themselves and others. In making this claim he anticipates a flurry of more recent work which makes much the same claim (Kahneman 2003). Individuals, this work suggests, derive a sense of what they ought to be able to expect in life and what will satisfy them and make them happy by comparing themselves with others. Both satisfaction and preference are mediated by our relations with others.

Even the high priest of RAT, Gary Becker (1996; Becker and Murphy 2000), seems now to accept some version of this. RAT has traditionally bracketed out questions of why people desire or prefer the things that they do, he notes. It has done this because these aspects of the decision making process lie beyond rationality as RAT defines it. His own attempt to fill this gap in economic theory focuses upon relations with other people and their influence. We 'pick up' preferences, in the form of habits, on the basis of our experiences and, most importantly, our experiences of social interaction, according to Becker. Again then, the actor cannot be fully accounted for independently of their relations with others.

Drawing on Kojève (1969), we might add to this that objects often become desirable to us simply by virtue of being desirable to others. We desire them because we wish to be desired by others who desire them. The desired object symbolizes the desire of the other.

Interagency, individuality and the relational organism

It is important to emphasize here that I am not denying the importance of (purposive) agency or suggesting that actors are mere products of a process of acculturation. I have stressed throughout that actors are purposive beings and I believe that this property derives from our biological composition. Following Goldstein (2000), Merleau-Ponty (1965) and Mead (1967), I believe that the human organism, like many other organisms, is a purposive and intelligent system. This is one reason why we are able to enter into the interactions and relationships which 'socialize' us and, importantly, to play an active role therein. Socialization, in this conception, is not imprinting. It is a learning process in which we play an active part, something that we do, interactively, with others. We are actors in the processes which 'form' us, both in infancy and – as we are always, as actors, in-process – throughout our lives. As actors we are in a constant process of becoming by virtue of the interactions and engagements that comprise our lives.

More importantly, whatever 'scripts', 'norms' and 'values' might be imparted in the process, socialization is as much a matter of acquiring agentic capabilities, including some which allow us to subject our scripts, norms etc. to critical scrutiny and to move beyond them. Socialization is a process which enhances our autonomy, enabling us to take charge of ourselves to a degree, to make decisions and act upon them (see also Crossley 2006a: 88–101).

This is always, necessarily, an embedded autonomy, however. It is an autonomy which emerges within our social relations and is bounded by them, both in the respect that our relations and interdependencies affect the opportunities and constraints within which we must operate and in the respect that our perspective upon the world is formed by our relational position and history. We achieve autonomy within social relations but never autonomy from them.

Furthermore, the organism itself is not an underlying 'substance'. It is a dynamic system of biochemical interaction, dependent (e.g. for oxygen and food) upon an environment, both social and physical (Levins and Lewontin

1985; Lewontin 1993), with which it is in constant engagement and interaction. The organism is constantly reproducing itself at various levels and processing energy and resources drawn from its environment (Smith 1986). Even the basic structure of the organism is, as evolutionary theory indicates, a 'temporary'[6] effect of ongoing environmental (again social[7] as well as physical (ibid.)) interactions. Life, in the biological sense, is a contingent process in which random genetic mutations either flourish or perish in accordance with the environment they engage with. Nothing is necessary and everything is subject to change. The substantialist will find no refuge in 'the organism'.

In a similar vein I am not denying the social reality of individuals, individuality or individualism. They are real but, like autonomy, they too emerge and are nurtured within social relations. On a historical level, for example, as noted by Durkheim (1915) in his account of the 'cult of the individual' and also by Marx (1970), individuality, individualism and the individual are contemporary and collective cultural forms, practised and upheld by individuals and embedded in institutions which facilitate them (see also Abercrombie *et al.* 1986). The rise of individualism has not involved a stripping away of social relations. As Marx argues, the epoch that has given rise to the individual is 'precisely the epoch of the (as yet) most highly developed social . . . relations' (1970: 125). Our individualism is sustained by our shared belief in and celebration of it, in the details of our interaction conventions and in our legal institutions. At another level our individuality is something that we strive to establish in our relations with others, in part by marking ourselves out from those others. 'Man [sic]', as Marx argues, is 'an animal that can only individualise himself within society' (1970: 125), that is, by way of interactions and relations with others.

We must be careful not to confuse 'individualism' and 'egoism', however. Individualism, as Durkheim (1964) observes, is a healthy historical invention which can be sustained within the context of strong social relations to the good of all. In an individualistic society, as envisaged by Durkheim, everybody respects the individuality of everybody else and individual rights are sustained by keenly felt collective expectations. If social relations are thinned out, however, and actors become more isolated, we are left with egoism rather than individualism, and egoism is damaging at both the individual level, where it results in a sense of meaninglessness and self-destruction, and the social level, where it precipitates anomie and disintegration (Durkheim 1952). Individuals, from the relational point of view, are sustained as physical, psychological and social beings by means of their relations to others in the wider social networks that constitute their society. They are not the solid, pre-existing and independent supports of this society that sociological varieties of individualism assume them to be.

Conclusion

In this chapter I have attempted to lay the foundations for a relational approach to sociology by way of a critique of a dichotomy within sociological thought which tends to obscure the relational option: the individualism/holism dichotomy. I have suggested that both individualism and holism are deeply problematic, and in many respects this is for the same reason: both are reductive and both base their reduction on a belief in a prime mover which somehow explains the goings on of the social world without itself being in need of explanation. The holist invokes 'society' as an entity whose needs or historical *telos* explains all that goes on with it, whilst the individualist reduces society back to the individuals who compose it and whose atomic properties and interactions are deemed sufficient to explain it. Both are unsatisfactory. The social world comprises networks of interaction between actors who cannot be abstracted from these networks and who take shape as actors within interaction.

The implications of this argument are not only theoretical. They are methodological too. Many of our methods in sociology, including interviews and questionnaires, have a tendency to individualize actors. Even apparently structural or relational properties, such as 'class position', are often treated as individual-level properties, attributes or identities. We treat an individual's class as a fact about them rather than a position they occupy relative to others. Moreover, this is compounded, in qualitative research, by the fact, touched upon in the next chapter, that individual narratives and accounts inevitably retrospectively individualize attitudes, experiences and events (see also Tilly 2002). Relational sociology must endeavour to tackle the problem of individualism (there is no comparable problem of holism) at this level too, exploring methodologies and tools which foreground interaction, relationships and networks.

Moreover, it must endeavour to capture the action in interaction and the process. In a very forceful critique which revisits key themes in Blumer (1986) and the early Chicago interactionists, Abbott (2001, see also 1997) identifies a gap between theory and research in contemporary sociology. Whilst theory focuses upon actors, their actions and (albeit insufficiently) their interactions, he argues, research focuses upon variables and their interactions. 'Variable analysis' obscures the workings of the social world because it shifts the focus of analysis away from interaction between actors, where the work really gets done and outcomes are genuinely decided, onto labels which we treat as properties of individuals. Variables don't do anything, Abbott insists; actors interactively 'do' the social world and collectively determine the fate of their peers. And social analysis should reflect this.

Abbott's point is focused primarily upon survey research and quantitative analysis but a complementary critique could be made of much qualitative, interview-based research, which abstracts actors from their context and elicits reflective accounts of their experiences. Of course all methods have 'cons' and all have 'pros'. We no doubt need all of the methods we have, and more. But relational sociology must endeavour to capture and analyse the social world in interaction, which is to say, as a *process* arising *between* social actors.

3   Mapping the territory

In the previous chapter I indicated that relational sociology seeks an alternative to both individualism and holism by way of a focus upon interaction, relations and networks. In this chapter I explore these key concepts in more detail, along with several others, namely, worlds, conventions, resources and actors. The chapter begins with a discussion of the concept of relations and more specifically of a number of critiques of it that have been posited in the philosophical literature. My primary aim, having identified these critiques, is to devise a way of thinking about relations which does not succumb to them but I also seek to demonstrate the relevance of these critiques to sociology. I show how one of the key criticisms maps onto the individualism/holism dichotomy and discuss at some length how a further critique might apply to Bourdieu's version of relational sociology.

The concept of relations that I suggest is centred upon interaction. This prompts a discussion of the dynamics of interaction and also the different but overlapping dimensions of interaction that can be identified in the sociological literature, chiefly the strategic, symbolic, affective, convention–improvisation and exchange–power dimensions. Having discussed these I then return to relations, indicating both how relations affect interactions and how they too have different dimensions, building for the most part upon these different dimensions of interaction.

The chapter then turns to the concept of networks, and to the concept of 'social worlds' constituted through networks, conventions and resources. Relations, I suggest, no more exist in isolation than individual actors. They are always embedded in networks of relations and this affects them. It is not just networks that are important, however. Networks form and are formed around 'social worlds' which centre upon specific shared or overlapping interests which bring actors together in collective action and also upon both conventions, which form and are formed in this context, and resources which are mobilized in collective actions and (unevenly) distributed through the network.

Having briefly discussed networks and worlds I turn finally to the question of what can become an actor. I noted in the last chapter that actors emerge (from biological organisms) in and through networks of interaction but just who and what can be transformed into an actor in this way? This question is motivated by two developments in recent sociology: the tendency, even amongst some method-ological individualists, to treat corporate entities, such as business organizations and governments, as actors (e.g. Hindess 1988; Coleman 1990), and the claims regarding non-human actors posited by actor–network theorists (e.g. Latour 2005). In response to these developments I argue that 'corporate actors' are indeed actors and should be treated as such but that actor–network arguments, which treat non-human and especially non-living objects as actors, are flawed. We should not ignore the material world and its objects in our analyses. They are important and actor–network theory, amongst other approaches in sociology, shows us why, but treating them as actors is not a very useful way of handling their significance.

The problem with relations

Relational sociology is focused upon 'social relations', but what are social relations? They assume different forms, of course, whose exact properties vary: friendship, hatred, economic exchange, slavery, sex, trust, political alliance etc. But what is it that, in spite of these variations, leads us to refer to them all as relationships? This is an interesting question which resonates with a deep controversy in the history of both science and philosophy (Kennedy 2003). In this section I will briefly review two key objections that have been made to the notion of relations, discussing their relevance in relation to sociology and, in particular, to both the individualism/holism dichotomy and Bourdieu's 'relational' sociology.

For much of the intellectual history of western societies it was believed that relations, as such, do not exist (ibid.). The dominant ontology did not include relations as a type of being. The ins and outs of this history are not relevant for us but one of the key objections to the concept of relations, the argument of 'the one and the many' (ibid.: 101), provides a useful way in to our own concerns. The argument claims that objects are either connected, in which case they fuse to form a single object (the one), rendering the notion of 'relations' redundant (as there is only one object and therefore nothing for it to be related to), or they remain distinct (the many), in which case, again, the notion of 'relations' has no place because we have only a set of discrete objects. Only perceptible 'objects' exist, according to this argument, and there can be nothing connecting them, therefore, that is not an object itself. If relations did exist they would be objects, akin perhaps to bridges, but as such their effect would be to merge 'the many' into 'the one'. There are no relations according to this argument, therefore, only objects.

For all of its problems, some of which I discuss below, this argument resonates with the individualism/holism dichotomy discussed in Chapter 2. The holist's tendency to subordinate actors to and dissolve them within the social whole effectively reduces the many to the one. Individuals (the many) are subsumed with society or the whole (the one). Society is treated as an entity in its own right, in the singular. Individualism, by contrast, reduces society to the many, to aggregates of individuals. Both approaches focus upon what they take to be an object (individual or society) effectively denying the reality of relations. My argument, by contrast, is that relations are real and that the social world comprises actors-in-relation – in networks.

Before I define 'relation', however, another common criticism, again premised upon the notion that objects alone can be said to exist, must be considered. Proponents of this argument claim that relations exist only 'in the eye of the beholder'. They are psychological constructs rather than real or empirical entities (Kennedy 2003). From this point of view relations are akin to comparisons. If John is taller than Jane, for example, then he enjoys a 'taller than' relationship to her but a 'taller than' relation, so the argument goes, exists only in the mind of the person who makes the comparison. It isn't a real object in the world. John and Jane exist and each has a different height but height is an atomic property of each taken individually. For one to be taller than the other requires that somebody, perhaps a third party, compares them and that taller than relation exists only in the mind of that somebody.

The final part of this criticism does not apply in all cases. The fact that Jane is richer than John, for example, cannot be reduced to purely individualistic states of affairs because being rich requires money, which is a social institution and, as such, presupposes interaction between individuals (Simmel 1990; Searle 1995). Money, by definition, has an exchange value and therefore presupposes a community in which it is exchanged. Its value derives neither from the physical material of which it is composed nor the individual who possesses it but is rather an emergent property arising out of human interaction and more specifically the exchange of goods (value is discussed further in Chapter 7). Money has no value for Robinson Crusoe, for example, because he has nobody to buy things from (see also Elster 1985: 94). We are jumping ahead, however. For present purposes note that the critic may respond that a 'richer than' relation, like a 'taller than' relation, is a comparison drawn in the mind of an individual, not a real thing.

I respond to this shortly but first we should note that this criticism, like the argument of the one and the many, has some bite in relation to contemporary sociology. In particular Bourdieu's 'relational' position can be criticized on these grounds. Relations are central to Bourdieu's sociology but he adopts a very odd definition. He deems 'empirical' or 'actual' relations between concrete actors, instantiated in observable interactions, such as are studied by symbolic interactionists or Weberians, superfluous in relation to 'real' relations. His concern is with 'structural relations which operate in a permanent fashion' rather than empirical relations which are 'actualised in and by a particular exchange' (Bourdieu and Wacquant 1992: 113). Structural relations, as he defines them, derive from positions in 'social space' which, in turn, he defines by reference to distributions of economic and cultural capital. He visualizes this space, using the techniques of multiple correspondence analysis, in the form of a two-dimensional[1] scatter-plot whose vertical axis represents the overall volume of capital possessed by an actor and whose horizontal axis represents the ratio of economic to cultural capital in their 'portfolio' (see Figure 3.1). Every actor (as well as practices, occupational categories and other social elements too, potentially[2]) occupies a position in this space in virtue of their overall volume of capital and the ratio of economic to cultural capital within this volume. More important, for our purposes, each enjoys 'relations' of proximity and distance to others in virtue of their location in this

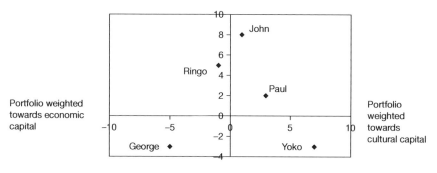

Figure 3.1 A hypothetical illustration of Bourdieu's 'social space' and 'structural relations'

Note: An actor's position on this graph represents their position in social space, and their spatial proximity/distance from one another represents their social proximity/distance. 'Relations' are relations of proximity or distance in this respect. Actors are relatively close to or distant from one another.

space. Their direct relations are to the forms of capital which they possess but this gives them an indirect relation to other actors. They are closer to or more distant from others by virtue of their portfolio of capital. This is what Bourdieu means by 'structural relations'. Moreover, he claims that actors manifest different sets of dispositions (e.g. tastes or preferences, manners, competence), different habitus, in accordance with their location in this social space. This, of course, is the celebrated argument of *Distinction* (Bourdieu 1984).

Exactly how much significance 'actualized relations' are afforded in this schema is unclear but it is not great and is secondary to 'structural relations'. Arguing against social network analysis, which I will argue is central to relational sociology, for example, Bourdieu claims that:

> The task of science is to uncover the structure of the distribution of species of capital which tends to determine the structure of individual of collective stances taken, through the dispositions and interests it conditions. In network analysis, the study of these underlying structures has been sacrificed to the analysis of particular linkages (between agents or institutions) and flows (of information, resources, services etc.) through which they become visible.
> (Bourdieu in Bourdieu and Wacquant 1992: 113–14)

Furthermore, he suggests that, through the mediation of the habitus, 'structural relations', shape actual relations:

> As social positions embodied in bodily dispositions, habitus contribute to determining whether (biological) bodies come together or stay apart

by inscribing between two bodies the attractions and repulsions that correspond to the relationship between the positions of which they are the embodiment.

(Bourdieu 1996: 360)

In other words, structural relations shape habitus, which then affect the types of concrete relations that actors form both by influencing what they do (and thus who they will meet) and determining how attractive they find others upon meeting them (because people like others similar to themselves).

I will take issue with Bourdieu at a number of points in this book. For now, however, my main criticism centres upon his notion of 'relations'. What Bourdieu calls 'structural relations' are simply comparisons of the amounts of two types of capital that social actors possess in varying amounts and ratios. As such, following the line of argument regarding comparison outlined above, they are not 'real' relations at all and, in some respects, exist as relations only in Bourdieu's 'head' (or 'discourse'). At best his approach identifies structural positions. There are no relations, real or otherwise, involved here, except perhaps the relations of possession which actors have to different forms of capital. 'Relation' has largely metaphorical meaning at best.

At certain points Bourdieu seems to acknowledge this. In his work on social class, for example, he notes that the groups he identifies (within social space) are only groups 'on paper' and will only become real groups to the extent that they identify and associate as such, a process which he believes is often mediated by way of third parties, such as political parties and trades unions (Bourdieu 1987, 1993; Crossley 2008f). This acknowledgment only compounds the problem, however, because we must now ask why, if classes exist only 'on paper', the 'structural relations' of which classes are composed are deemed more real than and determinate of actual relations? Furthermore, if classes have to be actualized through identification and association on the behalf of their members, why is this not true of the relations that comprise them? Aren't relations only real when actualized through interaction?

Even if we allow that Bourdieu is analysing relations, however, he falls foul of the errors of intellectualist abstraction that he condemns in others in his treatment of 'actual relations'. Structural positions do not pre-exist actual relations in reality. We occupy a structural position in virtue of the family that we are born into, the schools that we go to, the jobs we take etc. In each of these cases we are involved in actual relations which, importantly, are the key sources of the capital and forms of social (dis)advantage which determine our structural position as Bourdieu defines it, as so much of his own work suggests (e.g. Bourdieu 1996; Bourdieu and Passeron 1996). Structural positions (or relations) are not prior to actual relations. They are derived by abstracting from actual relations, and as such, if anything, are therefore secondary to and derivative from actual relations. To suppose otherwise is to give one's model of social reality ontological priority over the reality it is supposed to be modeling – an intellectualist error of abstraction that Bourdieu is fond of criticizing in others.

Furthermore, we do not develop or acquire habitus before we enter into actual relations, partly because there is no time in our lives that comes before our embedding in actual relations (parents anticipate their children before they are born) but also because there is no way of explaining 'group specific' habitus other than by way of processes of mutual interaction and influence within groups. Bourdieu's account lacks any plausible mechanism to explain either the formation of habitus or the concentration of particular habitus within specific regions of 'social space'. How, for example, can the possession of certain resources (e.g. money and qualifications), in and of itself, dispose an actor to prefer one sport (e.g. rugby) over another (e.g. football)? Would a rise in my income make me more likely to follow rugby? And if so, why? The claim is absurd. We can only explain the preference for a particular sport or whatever within a given class by reference to processes of mutual influence between members of that class, not least because, as Bourdieu (1998) is often at pains to point out, practices have no necessary relation to particular positions in social space and tend to shift position over time. What was once a middle class sport can become working class and vice versa such that what ties the sport to the position is not an essential connection between the two but rather a derived and perhaps temporary 'consensus' (in practice if not opinion[3]) between occupants of that position that the sport is good, a consensus necessarily arrived at by means of interaction. I do not mean to imply an explicit process of preference formation here. Obviously much of this is implicit, unintended and perhaps not noticed by those involved. The point, however, is that it works by means of interaction and thus what Bourdieu dismisses as 'actual relations'.

Of course these preferences will then shape further processes of relationship formation. Having grown up amongst members of one social group and acquired certain dispositions on this basis, I am more or less likely to meet and more or less likely to hit it off with certain alters rather than others (though there is considerable leeway for 'deviation' from the path my background sets me upon). But this is because dispositions and interactions/relations are mutually influencing. The former are in no way prior to or determinate of the latter.

Three more brief critical notes on Bourdieu and relations are necessary. First, the social network analysis (SNA) which Bourdieu criticizes is capable of the levels of abstraction that he calls for and affords various possibilities for 'positional analysis', as I show in Chapters 8 and 9 (see also Bottero and Crossley 2010). As such his criticism is misplaced. Moreover, though it is capable of such abstraction, SNA always begins with a focus upon actual relations and, as such, maintains a genuine relational foundation that is missing in Bourdieu.

Second, Bourdieu's conception of 'positions' rests upon his concept of 'capital' which, like 'money', necessarily presupposes exchange value and thus exchange: that is, actual, concrete interaction and relations in which goods are exchanged. This is just one more reason why Bourdieu's efforts to denigrate actual in favour of structural relations is doomed to failure.

Third, Bourdieu's rather dismissive attitude towards actual relations and the failure of his concept of structural relations to engage with connections between actors in any serious or meaningful way (i.e. the fact that structural relations aren't really relations at all) leaves him with a relatively atomized view of the social world and an individualistic position. His vision of the social world is a world of differently positioned but discrete actors being propelled through social space by force of their portfolios of capital. Indeed, the statisticians who worked with Bourdieu in his later work suggest an apt metaphor when they talk about and visualize (in their correspondence analyses) social space as a 'cloud of individuals' – something like Figure 3.1 but with thousands of disconnected dots blacking out a cloud in the graph space.

Interaction

This critique of Bourdieu suggests a way in which we might begin to think more constructively about relations, namely, in opposition to his own inclination; that is, in terms of concrete interaction between actors. Social relations, I want to suggest, are *lived trajectories of iterated interaction*.

Note that this circumvents the criticisms of the concept of relations discussed above, i.e. the argument of 'the one and the many' and the claim that relations are comparisons in the eye of the beholder. Both of these arguments rest on the assumption that only objects exist and conceptualize existence in purely one-dimensional, spatial terms. But one can never argue a reasonable case for the existence of 'relations' if one makes these assumptions, especially if one also assumes that relations are not objects. The argument assumes its conclusions in its premises and is therefore circular. More importantly, the premises are wrong. Reality has a temporal dimension and our ontology must accommodate this by admitting of processes and other temporal phenomena. A social relation is not an object, akin to a bridge, but rather a shifting state of play within a process of social interaction. *To say that two actors are related is to say that they have a history of past and an expectation of future interaction and that this shapes their current interactions.*

In the section which follows this I elaborate upon this definition. As a necessary prelude, however, I want in this section to explore 'interaction' in more detail. I begin with a general reflection on the dynamics of interaction and its mechanisms before shifting focus to five key dimensions of interaction: the (1) symbolic, (2) affective, (3) convention–improvisation, (4) strategic and (5) exchange–power dimensions.

Interaction dynamics

When we interact we mutually modify one another's conduct, forming an irreducible and dynamic whole: John's actions influence Jane's and Jane's influence John's. In such cases it is impossible to understand or explain the actions of either party without reference to both. This is one good reason why, as sociologists, we need to focus upon interaction, because little that we do can be properly understood or explained without reference to the relays of interaction in which it is embedded and which give it context and meaning. We might call this *the interaction frame of reference.*

The temporal unfolding of interaction is important. Interactions take shape across time. They simultaneously generate and follow a path. What happens early on in an interaction may both facilitate and constrain what can happen later. And, as Gadamer observes, the parties to an interaction (in this case a conversation) are not necessarily in control of this trajectory:

> The way one word follows another, with the conversation taking its own twists and reaching its own conclusion, may well be conducted in some way, but the partners conversing are far less the leaders of it than the led. No one knows in advance what will 'come out' of a conversation.
>
> (Gadamer 1989: 383)

Interaction is dynamic and sometimes unpredictable. Actors remain distinct loci of action, but as the action of each is a response to the action of the other, both (or however many) can find themselves doing and/or saying things that they might not have imagined in advance and might not have done or said had they not been drawn along that particular path of interaction. The path does not exist independently of them. They co-create it. But it is not reducible to them as independent actors. Merleau-Ponty, again referring to conversation, puts this point nicely:

> In the experience of dialogue, there is constituted between the other person and myself a common ground; my thought and his are interwoven into a single fabric, my words and those of my interlocutor are called forth by the state of the discussion, and they are inserted into a shared operation of which neither of us is the creator. We have here a dual being . . .
>
> (Merleau-Ponty 1962: 354)

The common ground Merleau-Ponty refers to is, in part, what interactionists call a shared but perhaps tacit 'definition of the situation'. Interlocutors either tacitly agree about or negotiate their subject matter, the way they will frame and conduct their debate and the parameters of acceptability they will observe. They perhaps agree what roles or identities they will respectively assume in the debate. Beyond this, their 'common ground' consists in a shared rhythm. They, 'mutually tune in' to one another, as Schutz (1964) puts it, like musicians or dancers, each having 'a feel' for when to move and a sense of what the other will do and when. In some cases, moreover, they work upon and towards a shared product, e.g. a common decision or view of the resolution of a conflict.

Even if they don't agree, their individual views on the matter are still shaped by the process of disagreement and discussion. I may find myself arguing for a position that I do not usually embrace because the other has assumed my usual position and has managed (if only playfully) to provoke me. Indeed, Billig (1991) argues that opinions and attitudes are precisely positions which we take up vis-à-vis one another in ongoing debates, and may vary according to whom we position ourselves relative to. Opinions and attitudes, in other words, aren't monadic properties of individuals but rather relational stances (see also Blumer 1986; Habermas 1989; Bourdieu 1995). It is for this reason that some sociologists are critical of attitude and public opinion research which surveys random samples of individuals on a 'cold call' basis. This research mistakes opinions for invariant individual properties, failing to capture their necessarily contextual and dialogical or interaction-dependent character (ibid.). Opinions form and lodge between actors not within them.

The above examples concern verbal exchanges. The same applies to other types of interaction, however. Fighting and posturing between armies in a war or boxers in a ring, for example, generate a path which draws the parties in and along, shaping the stances they adopt and the strategies they pursue. The escalation of the arms race between the East and the West in the latter part of the twentieth century is an obvious example (Schelling 1981). Nobody can anticipate how they will respond because nobody knows in advance what direction the interaction will take and what effect it will have upon then. A process of mutual response and mutual adaptation shifts the 'ground' that actors stand upon, sometimes making the previously inconceivable not only conceivable but obvious, necessary and even automatic. Immersion in an interaction context which acquires an unusual dynamic and trajectory draws the actors involved into ways of behaving that they would not previously have countenanced.

It is only a small step to recognize that, were such unusual patterns ever to become usual, so too would the individual patterns of behaviour involved. Actors are shaped by the interactions in which they are involved. Trajectories of interaction can transform the way in which they act, feel and think.

Elias's (1984) account of the civilizing process demonstrates this on a grand historical scale. 'Civilization' and 'civilized' conduct and sentiments are not inevitable or given, for Elias. They are outcomes of a long historical process of interaction, held in place by interactions and the control mechanisms (external and internal) these have given rise to. If the web of interactions (what Elias calls the 'figuration') comprising society were to take a different direction, they would take civilization and 'the civilized individual' with them. We could all become 'barbarians', acting, feeling and thinking as 'barbarians', if the balances and control mechanisms institutionalized within our patterns of interaction were to collapse and subsequent interaction dynamics carried us in that direction.

What and who we are is shaped, on different levels, by the network of interactions in which we are located. It is our interactions which shape these networks and institutionalize the abovementioned mechanisms but, as just noted and as the sociological preoccupation with 'unintended consequences' suggests, the direction in which our interactions move and take us is often beyond both our individual control and even our full knowledge and comprehension.

This entails that actors do not simply 'do' interaction. They are affected by it. And what they do in it is shaped by how they are affected by it. The actions of the other 'call out a response' from me, to borrow Mead's (1967) phrase. They provoke, stimulate or arouse, drawing responses from me that I may find surprising myself. Thus, to continue Merleau-Ponty's above cited quotation:

> the objection which my interlocutor raises to what I say draws from me thoughts which I had no idea I possessed, so that at the same time that I lend him thoughts, he reciprocates by making me think too.
>
> (Merleau-Ponty 1962: 354)

There is creativity here. Merleau-Ponty had no idea that he possessed the idea that he expressed because, technically, he did not 'possess' it at all prior to expressing it. He only arrives at it via his discussion with the other, perhaps because it is a critique of the other's idea or a refinement of it or simply because the other's actions offered refreshing stimulation. This is why the idea surprises and excites him, because it might as well have been suggested by someone else for all he knew of it before this point. Indeed, as he later notes, it may be impossible to say whose idea it is because the process by which it was arrived at involved multiple stages of generation and refinement, each party contributing and stimulating further contributions from the others. Perhaps a number of speakers spoke the idea simultaneously, having worked through the logic of their preceding discussion at the same time and arrived at the same conclusion. The conclusion does not belong to any one of them but to the argument they have co-constructed. Merleau-Ponty concludes his train of thought with an interesting reflection, however:

> It is only retrospectively, when I have withdrawn from the dialogue and am recalling it that I am able to reintegrate it into my life and make of it an episode in my private history.
>
> (Merleau-Ponty, 1962: 354)

He at least hints here of a process, also discussed by Tilly (2002), whereby individual self-narratives tend to recast interaction in individual terms, ripping the intersubjective fabric into distinct pieces and ignoring the dynamics and contingencies of discourse by projecting its outcomes back into one or more of the actors involved. We tend to attribute properties and outcomes to self or other, as individuals, that only emerge in interaction between self and other. We may regard this as an 'epistemological obstacle' (Bachelard 2002) to a properly relational sociology; lay accounts, which of course we have to work with, sometimes edit out relationality in preference of an individualistic format.

Even Merleau-Ponty's account is problematic, however, if it is taken to imply that interaction is something that we sometimes do, something which has neat beginnings and ends. As Strauss (1993), following Dewey (1896, 1988), argues, human beings are constantly acting. We are always doing something. There is no time out from the constant flow of interaction. We never start from a stop position but are always already engaged in something. And action is always interaction. At the very least, for example, we must interact with our physical surrounds but much of our interaction involves engagement, both real and imagined, with other actors. Merleau-Ponty's attempt to make the results of his interaction an episode in his private history, for example, involves a conversation (interaction) with himself which, as he acknowledges elsewhere and Mead (1967) more famously suggests, he has acquired the competence to conduct by way of an internalization of the roles of others which allows him to become other to himself (see Chapters 5 and 6), and which will attend to the issues and concerns of others. Merleau-Ponty can anticipate what the other will say of their conversation and must therefore adjust and position his account in relation to what he anticipates. Moreover, as he reconstructs both the interaction and its outputs he will anticipate the reactions of others, both specific and generalized, and engage with them. Our lives are lived within networks of others. The inescapable flows of action which comprise our lives are entangled in and shaped by those networks.

This account of interaction suggests a path beyond the problem of the one and the many, and beyond the atomism/holism dichotomy that instantiates it within sociology. Interaction is irreducible to the actors involved in it because it entails interdependence between actions and properties which only emerge as it unfolds, as a function of that unfolding, properties which belong to the interaction between the actors rather than to any of them in isolation. Interaction is a whole greater than the sum of the separate individuals who constitute its parts. However, if 'the many' lose some of the independence and distinctness suggested by that term, they do not merge into the singular and unified object suggested by 'the one'. Interaction is driven from below, by inter-actors, and has no overarching *telos* (determinate or otherwise) distinct from the purposes of those involved in it, in the sense suggested by the more extreme 'historicist' (Popper 2002) and function-alist varieties of holism (see Chapter 2). Where interaction and history 'go', what happens, is contingent upon the interactions of those involved and upon the way in which their often competing, conflicting and evolving inclinations play out. Inter-actors constitute distinct poles within interaction and collectively drive it. Interaction is more than 1 + 1 actors. Actors are entangled within it to the point of inseparability. But it remains tied to and driven by the contributions of actors who establish distinct identities within it. It always comprises different and jostling perspectives and energies.

Note also that this conception makes *time* and more specifically *process* central. Interaction unfolds through time such that our subject matter is always 'in process'. This need not imply constant change but it suggests that durable patterns within the social world are durable because they are constantly reproduced and preserved within interactions (though not necessarily intentionally) across time.

Interaction mechanisms

The point of relational sociology is not merely to marvel at interaction and its unintended consequences, however, but rather to identify its mechanisms and effects. We can identify patterns in interaction, in terms of who interacts with whom (e.g. homophily), how interactions unfold (e.g. patterns of conflict escalation), how identities and outcomes are shaped for individuals (e.g. self-fulfilling prophecies) and so on. These are not 'laws' of social interaction and sometimes a mechanism may be only equally as likely to kick in as its opposite. As Jon Elster (2007) notes, 'birds of a feather flock together' (homophily) but 'opposites attract'. When they do kick in they are recognizable as mechanisms, however, and tend to have predictable outcomes. Furthermore, one of the tasks of relational sociology is to explore both the conditions under which they are more or less likely to kick in and any further mechanisms which may help us to understand and explain them.

Dimensions of interaction

In addition to mechanisms, we can further explore interaction by identifying its forms and elements. I suggest that interactions are characterized by five interrelated and overlapping dimensions which are always present to some extent but which may be more or less prominent in any given instance or phase: the (1) symbolic, (2) affective, (3) convention–innovation, (4) strategic, and (5) exchange–power dimensions. Interactions are 'symbolic' in the respect that actors (1) 'read' one another's actions; (2) 'typify' one another (Schutz 1972); (3) reflexively read and respond to their own actions; (4) establish shared or differentiated situational definitions and identities (individual and collective); and (5) (re)negotiate, in various tacit and explicit ways, a definition of their own relationship as, for example, friendship, collegial, romantic, comradely etc. Moreover, drawing upon Mead (1967), we might add (6) that actors 'internalize'[4] one another's 'roles' such that they enter into and influence one another's internal conversations, thereby shaping one another's 'private' thoughts and senses of self (see Chapters 5 and 6).

Interactions are affective in the respect that perceptions, thoughts, memories etc. of others are tinged with an emotional hue and manifest an emotional motivation (e.g. we seek out and think often of these we are fond of, sometimes in spite of ourselves). Of course we may have routine interactions, perhaps with shopkeepers or business associates, which seem affectively neutral but neutrality itself is an emotional hue. As Heidegger (1962) reminds us, emotion is not something that is turned on and off, such that we are sometimes emotional and other times not. It is a permanent dimension of our being-in-the-world and being-towards-others, albeit one that becomes more conspicuous on occasion when strong or inappropriate. Furthermore, to rejoin the above point about 'internal conversations', our feelings about and emotional relations with ourselves are shaped by the expressed feelings of those whose perspectives we internalize. Children deprived of love and respect may find it difficult in later life to love and respect themselves, for example, because they have no suitable role within their 'internal network'[5] to draw upon.

Conventions enter into interaction insofar as inter-actors (1) draw upon them in order to communicate meaningfully (see Chapter 5) or establish a footing for interaction; (2) develop their own shared conventions and rituals of engagement;

and/or (3) engage within institutionalized contexts. Different aspects of interaction can be conventional (e.g. where, when, how, why etc.) but we must be careful to specify what this means. As a number of writers have argued, conventions (or whatever cognate term they use[6]) are better conceived as flexible and meaningful patterns of interaction which admit of purpose and intelligence rather than mechanical templates. They do not preclude improvisation and innovation (Merleau-Ponty 1962, 1965; Becker 1982; Dewey 1988; Bourdieu 1977, 1992; Crossley 2001). Strauss (1993) makes this point nicely. On one hand, he argues, innovation and improvisation arise when interaction becomes problematic and conventions either break down or cease to work. However, conventions (and institutions) are simply sedimented innovations and improvisations of the past, and the innovations and improvisations that kick in to resolve a crisis will often themselves settle into new conventions. Conventions are, in Becker's terms: 'earlier agreements now become customary' (1982, 29).

On another level, Strauss adds, no interactions are purely conventional or purely creative. Improvisation and innovation are always evident but, by the same token, they always necessarily draw upon convention. No two interactions are absolutely identical. All require some degree of minor adjustment and improvisation. But actors never create *ex nihilo*. As Becker's (1982) important work *Art Worlds* demonstrates, even the most creative and innovative of interactions draws in various ways upon conventions. From the language we speak, through the body techniques mobilized in overt movement to the subtleties of style and the ingenuity of strategy, we draw upon the sedimented and shared lessons of past experience, from convention, in all of our actions, however innovative or creative.

Interactions are strategic to the extent that actors (1) reflexively manage their relations, (2) weighing one another up, albeit perhaps in a pre-reflective way; (3) projecting into the future; (4) anticipating possibilities, positive and negative, in relation to the other; and (5) orienting to those possibilities with a view (6) to seeking advantage. Moreover, interactions invariably entail, at some points, (7) conflicts of interest which partners to them will seek to resolve in ways which are, at the very least, not disadvantageous to them. This is not to say that actors approach all relations from an instrumental or strategic point of view, nor that they lack empathy or other moral sentiments (see Chapter 4). It simply suggests that actors' interests, which derive in large part from their positions in social networks, cannot be bracketed out of a consideration of interaction, nor indeed their capacity, acquired by way of interaction, to reflect and plan.

Finally, interactions often entail an exchange of goods and services, if only in the form of the pleasures of 'sociability', in Simmel's (1971) sense (see Chapter 7). Interactions can be chance occurrences which, from the point of view of the actor, are accidental, but repeated interactions between actors, which give rise to an interaction history and thus, by my definition, a social relationship, are better explained by reference to the fact that actors find engagement with one another rewarding or anticipate that they will in the longer run. This need not imply a cynical or mercenary attitude on behalf of actors. On the contrary, it entails that relations have value for actors. We do not attach ourselves randomly to others but rather because they bring us pleasure.

Exchange often generates interdependency (material, emotional or whatever) between actors and thereby a balance of power between them (Emerson 1962; Elias 1978). Actors grow to rely upon one another for required 'goods' and this reliance is a lever which each can use, however unwittingly, to steer the behaviour of the other, refusing the desired good if the other fails to comply with their wishes. This is never unidirectional. Parties are *interdependent*. Each gains something from their relationship and each therefore has a lever. But where one is more dependent upon the other the power relation is imbalanced and favours the less dependent party. From the baby whose cry mobilizes a doting parent into action, through the would-be lover who struggles to attract and please the object of their desire, to the hard-nosed negotiator who threatens to 'pull' a deal unless all of her demands are met, all social relations involve a balance of power rooted in interdependence.

Relations

A social relationship, to reiterate, is *the lived trajectory of iterated bouts of interaction between actors*. It comprises the sedimented past and projected future of a stream of interaction. I use the term 'lived' in the phenomenological sense here, to convey that past experiences shape and frame present experiences, such that interaction in the present is affected by what has happened between actors in the past. If John and Jane argued last time they met then their current meeting begins there. They must negotiate a resolution to the conflict which marred their last contact. If they have 'been through a lot together' this may be relatively easy because they have learned to give and take and know one another too well to hold one another in contempt. Note, however, that they can never undo what has happened. Relations might change such that a friend becomes an enemy. And relations can become latent in the sense that we no longer interact with another on the basis that we once did. But relations can never be undone. If John and Jane part ways and do not meet for 25 years, they will still meet as two people who knew one another 25 years previously. Time is irreversible and though they go through ups and downs and may change radically, so too, therefore, are relationships. We cannot return to a point where the other is unknown to us.

In this way, relations, which are generated by way of interaction, act back upon those interactions or, rather, 'relation' is the name we give to the way in which the history and projected future of a stream of interaction affect its present. A relationship is the state of play in a trajectory of interaction that may ultimately extend across decades (although it may only extend across hours in some cases).

In what follows in this section I will unpack this notion further. I begin by exploring the idea of relations as temporary states of play within a temporal trajectory of interaction. I then reconsider the internalization of the role of the other, as described by Mead (1967), and presentation and disclosure of selves, following Goffman (1959) and Simmel (1906, 1955), before considering the role of expectations, strategy and exchange-power in social relations.

Sedimented interaction

The history that comprises a relationship may exist for those involved in it in a reflective mode. We can and do tell stories about our relationships, for example, relating how we met and what events we have been through together. Such story telling serves a purpose in the present but it draws upon a shared and (broadly) agreed past to do so. Moreover, stories may be jointly created and edited in the way suggested in my discussion of Merleau-Ponty above. We weave stories of 'we' together, in interaction, jointly constructing them. In this respect relationships are 'storied', built up by means of stories (see also White 1992, 2008).

No less important, however, is the pre-reflective embodiment of our relational histories in 'habit'.[7] Our ability to pick up a conversation, without forethought, after a lapse of weeks or even years; to steer conversations 'intuitively' around issues likely to be 'difficult' for a particular alter; and even our ability to recognize a familiar face, all point to the way in which our contact with others generates and sustains a habitual sediment, a disposition towards the other which affects our interaction with them. We experience them in the present through a lens or 'typification' (Schutz 1972) shaped by our experience of them in the past. We have a habitual sense of who and what they are, what they are about and how we can and should engage with them. We have a level of (dis)trust in them, sensing how they will respond in particular situations and under particular pressures, and treating them accordingly (see Chapter 4). This is not merely cognitive, moreover. It is affective. Through interaction over time we become disposed to feel in particular ways towards the other.

Though they take root in individuals, these embodied dispositions are relational in at least three respects. First, they are 'intentional' in the phenomenological sense. My typification of and trust in you is not a characteristic of me but rather of the way I relate to you. It only exists in my relation to you. Second, these dispositions are shaped by my interaction with you and may, like shared stories, be the joint product of our interactions. They are, to reiterate an earlier point, shared conventions. Perhaps we have developed a shared vocabulary and rituals that we deploy when together. Perhaps I have developed, through interaction with you, a distinct way of 'handling' you, a distinct identity or role for myself, fitted to your peculiarities, or, more accurately, perhaps we have developed that identity or role for me within interaction. We have 'decided', however tacitly, how each of us may engage with the other, even if neither of us behaves that way in other relations. Third, as this latter point suggests, these conventions are generally only triggered by my contact with you.

The habitual or conventional aspect of a relationship is only one aspect, however. Negotiation is a chronic feature of interaction and relationships. They have to be constantly 'done' and maintained. Both reflective memories and habitual orientations are tested in interaction and may be subject to correction, not least because every interaction is, in some respects, unique and thus not necessarily covered by whatever mutual understandings and agreements have been achieved in the past. Agents reflexively manage their relations with others, deploying varying degrees of conscious awareness in doing so.

Incorporating the other, presenting the self

Another important aspect of this, which has both reflective and pre-reflective aspects, is the internalization of the perspective of the other as discussed by Mead (1967). By interacting with others, Mead notes, we acquire a sense of them, a feel for how they will respond to particular situations. We (often involuntarily) imagine what they would say to us or think or do in particular circumstances. This internalized sense plays an important role in our thought processes and sense of self (see Chapters 5 and 6) but is clearly also an important aspect of relationship formation. To form a relationship with another is, on one level, to empathically incorporate a sense of their role or perspective such that they enter into the processes constitutive of our thought, self-hood and ultimately thereby our reflexive agency.

As with relational dispositions more generally this has affective as well as cognitive aspects. Invoking the perspective of others might both be triggered by and generative of specific emotional responses. We might draw upon the comforting role of a parent at a time of disappointment, for example, consoled by an internalized sense of the love they have for us. Conversely, we might feel guilt if we invoke an anticipation or imagined sense of their disappointment at something we have done. Furthermore, our internalization of their perspective and feeling for them makes us more sensitive to or at least aware of that perspective in our interactions with them.

Of course relations are not just about 'taking others into our selves'. They also entail presenting ourselves to others and, no less importantly, managing the information flow in which selves are constructed. One of the most fascinating aspects of Goffman's sociology centres upon the notion that individuals strive to control the flow of information regarding themselves which circulates within the networks in which they are involved (Goffman 1959; see also Simmel 1906, 1955). One reason that life in total institutions is so difficult according to Goffman (1961), for example, is that they reduce the scope for controlling the flow of information between one's different relationships and contexts of interaction. In a total institution one works, sleeps, eats and relaxes with the same people, or at least with people who belong to the same network, and who therefore tend to share gossip. Everything that happens within an inmate's life happens within the same connected network and, as such, is likely to become known to everyone else in that network, denying the actor the opportunity to manage their identity. This contrasts with the usual situation where, as Simmel (1955) notes, we move between different social circles, enjoying the opportunity to control at least some of the flow of information between them. Information about embarrassing incidents at home may be kept at home, for example, and not allowed to flow into the workplace or friendship circles. To control information, for Goffman, is to control one's self, an individual's self being the manner in which they are regarded and known (perhaps differently) across various contexts.

Building relationships, according to this model, might involve successive increases in personal disclosure. As we get to know someone we 'let them in', revealing aspects of our history that they might not otherwise know about. Doing this is often a trust building exercise, in consequence if not intention, because it makes us vulnerable and dependent upon the other to keep our secrets and thus our identity safe. In giving them information we afford them the power to discredit us, to ruin our reputation or perhaps blackmail us. We entrust them with our identity, insofar as our public 'face' now depends upon them exercising the same discretion with respect to information about us that we exercise ourselves.

As Simmel (1906) notes, however, secrecy is important in even the most intimate relations, not least because it generates a sense of mystery and interest, a tension and excitement. In practice we cannot know everything about the other nor would much of it be of interest. Information is not disclosed for its own sake but always for a reason, whether that relates to the building of the relationship or to the practical context in which an interaction is taking place. Even if it were possible, however, total disclosure would not be a good thing from Simmel's point of view because the dynamics of secrecy, of withholding, teasing and releasing the tension through disclosure are important to intimate relations.

This relates to a more general and equally important observation of Simmel's, to the effect that relations always involve elements of both attraction and repulsion. To form a relationship with someone is to move closer to them, to permit intrusions and interaction that would not otherwise happen and to disclose information to them. But it is equally always to set limits on that process and to resist complete absorption and fusion. To be related to another is to hold them at a distance. How far and in what ways is, for Simmel, one of the key ways in which we can distinguish different types of relationships.

Note that this latter point bears in an interesting way upon the problem of the one and the many. Simmel is arguing that though we move closer to others as we form relations we never merge into one. A relationship involves two relatively, but only relatively, autonomous poles. We retain distinct identities, and relations are marked by the tension of attraction and repulsion.

Institutionalized conventions

A further layer is added to this by way of institutionalized conventions and identities which we may orient to, mobilizing norms of interaction. Although the concept of roles has been rightfully criticized for painting an overly culturally deterministic picture of certain relations and interactions and for failing to recognize both the possibility and the necessity for active co-construction of relations and interactions (Giddens 1984; Wrong 1961), it would be foolish to ignore the role of institutionalized definitions and expectations in all relations and interactions.

Parsons' (1951) analysis of 'the sick role' may be woefully inadequate to account for the range of contemporary medical interactions, for example, and may be premised upon a highly problematic form of functional explanation, but we cannot deny that there is a public discourse about 'doctors', 'nurses' and various kinds of 'invalid', nor that these discourses give rise to 'typifications' and other conventions towards which we orient in our interaction. When I visit the doctor I do not expect her to tap dance on the table or tell me what is wrong with her. Likewise, when I declare myself ill I expect a bit of sympathy and leeway in relation to my obligations. Of course the discourse covering these matters is ambiguous in places, complex and often contested. It is subject to differential interpretation and uneven use. That is why we have to negotiate, so that we can find a common ground on which to interact. But we draw upon these conventions in interaction. And in many domains or social worlds (on 'worlds' see Chapter 8), including medicine, education, employment and even the family, we may have recourse to the law and other authorities in doing so.

This is not to say that such expectations and conventions are only operative in formal organizations, however. Though there may be no legal definition of 'friendship', 'acquaintance', 'romance' etc., we have (varied) expectations about these types of relationship which we bring to bear within them. Perhaps we do not expect to become too intimate with an acquaintance, for example, and may feel the need to reassert boundaries if they barge into intimate areas of our lives uninvited. Likewise, we may expect a level and type of loyalty from our friends because, according to institutionalized definitions of friendship, that is 'what friends are for' (for an illuminating discussion of friendship see Pahl (2000)).

Strategy, exchange and power

Much of the above relates to the symbolic, conventional and affective aspects of interaction. However, relations are equally rooted in the strategic and exchange dimensions of interaction. I will discuss in Chapter 4, for example, how iterated 'tit for tat' strategic interactions can give rise to relations of cooperation and how relations may be rooted in conflict. Furthermore, as already noted, interactions are more likely to be repeated, becoming relationships, when parties to them find the exchange involved beneficial, a situation which leads to interdependence and a balance of power within the emerging relationship. All relations involve some level of interdependence and thus of power, and this derives from the exchange dimension inherent in all interaction.

It is evident, I hope, that each of the above elements of relations is or at least points us towards mechanisms which steer interaction towards certain outcomes. Power dynamics, for example, make certain outcomes (e.g. compliance of the disadvantaged party) more likely than others. Internalization of the other and the empathy that it involves lessen the likelihood of actions which might be damaging towards the other etc. Relations matter because they make a difference and relational sociology seeks to explore them in order to determine just how they do this.

Networks and worlds

My discussion hitherto has focused primarily, if only tacitly, on dyadic relations. The reality of the social world, however, is that we are all involved in multiple relations across a variety of 'social worlds'. As Simmel (1955) suggests, we are each a point of intersection between multiple worlds. I am a link between my family, my university, the world of sociology, my gym etc. and the various networks which have taken shape in each of those contexts. I link those networks, making them, in some respects, into one big network.

Networks make a difference. We can no more understand a relationship in isolation than understand an individual in isolation. How relations are configured in wider networks affects them. Friends who share mutual friends, as Simmel's (1902) reflections on triads suggest, for example, are subject to different dynamics and pressures than those who do not. More importantly, differently configured networks and different positions within such networks generate a range of opportunities and constraints for their occupants (see Chapter 8). As such, networks are replete with a variety of mechanisms which shape interaction and its outcomes and are a primary focus of relational sociology. Interaction and individual dyadic relations are important but we need to be able to look beyond such dyads to the structure, indeed the 'social structure' (see Chapter 8) in which they are embedded and which shape their possibilities. For analytic purposes at least, networks are composed of dyads, but in combination the network whole is greater than the sum of these dyads and mediates their likely effects.

But networks are not just patterns of connection. They are also patterns of non-connection. Networks involve both ties and absences of ties and both are important. Lack of connection might be a cause of conflict, relative inequality and/or, as both Marx (1959) and Durkheim (1952) recognized in different ways, alienation and psychological distress. A focus upon networks can be precisely intended to identify and explore such fault lines. It can highlight and investigate the effects of isolation and exclusion. Furthermore, gaps can generate what Burt (1992) calls a 'structural hole', a network position which can prove highly rewarding and advantageous to an actor who occupies it. Structural holes are mechanisms which tend to produce advantage for some within networks.

There is a need for relational sociology to be able to transcend (without losing its purchase upon) the dyadic level, therefore, and to focus upon networks. We need a purchase upon individual 'ego-nets' (i.e. the networks formed around particular individual actors, which embed those actors); upon 'complete' networks within specified populations of actors; upon various 'two-mode' networks, in which actors link and are simultaneously linked by various intermediary entities or events; and upon links between various clusters or groups or actors, however they might be defined. Furthermore, combining all of this, we need at least to be able to imagine the global social world as a vast web of relations and interactions, on multiple scales and involving a multitude of types of both relationships and actors.

I discuss the concept of networks and various ways of mapping and measuring them in more detail in Chapter 8. For present purposes, however, note that my own conception draws upon a long-established and strong methodological tradition of social network analysis within social science (see Scott 2000; Wasserman and Faust 1994; Carrington *et al.* 2005). Networks, from this point of view, consist of a set of nodes and a set or sets of relations between them which can be mapped either within a matrix (Figure 3.2) or a graph (Figure 3.3).

There are many variations in the type of information that can be recorded in these matrices and graphs, and the techniques of network analysis are equally varied (ibid.). What really matters for our purposes here, however, is that network analysis (1) identifies structural properties at the level of the whole network, subgroups within it and individual nodes; (2) identifies interesting and important structural configurations within networks; and (3) offers good empirical evidence to suggest that these properties and figurations generate opportunities and constraints for interaction. As such network analysis is an invaluable tool or perhaps rather methodology and set of tools for relational sociology (see Chapter 9).

	John	Paul	George	Ringo	Yoko
John	–	1	1	1	1
Paul		–	1	1	0
George			–	1	0
Ringo				–	0
Yoko					–

Figure 3.2 Mapping relations in a matrix

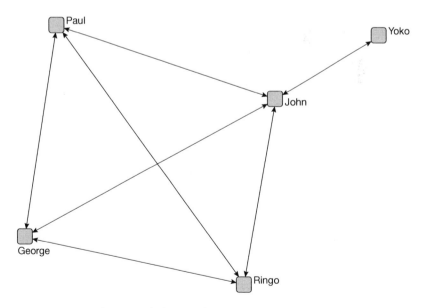

Figure 3.3 Mapping networks in a graph

Networks, conventions and resources in social worlds

Patterns of connection are only one aspect of what must be a wider conception of networks for sociological purposes, however (Edwards and Crossley 2009; Edwards 2009), or rather we must recognize that social networks, narrowly defined, are one amongst a number of key elements in what interactionist sociologists call 'social worlds' (Crossley 2010a,b). I discuss the social world concept in greater detail in Chapter 8. For present purposes, however, note that, in addition to networks, the concept of worlds implies a population of interacting actors mobilized around shared or overlapping interests, and mobilizing both resources and social conventions in their interactions. The concept of social worlds adds further sociological substance to the notion of social networks by factoring in a consideration of the *purposes* underlying specific interactions, the *resources* exchanged in those interactions and their distribution through the population in questions, as well as the *conventions* which typically structure the different types of interaction involved. Examples might be the worlds of academic sociology, punk music, pigeon fancying, drug dealing, Islamic militancy and competitive gymnastics.

Worlds 'cut' networks, in the respect that actors limit the transmission of certain goods (and perhaps bads) to only those of their alters who belong to a specific world. I do not update my family or gym buddies on the latest trends in social network analysis, for example. I only circulate that information to fellow academics and, even then, to fellow academics with an interest in networks. However, at the same time networks sometimes cut across worlds and connect them. The money I get from working finds its way into my home and gym, for example, and the claims which each makes upon me compete for my time to some extent, such that what I give to work I take from my family and vice versa. Whilst worlds to some degree differentiate the social world, therefore, this is only ever to some degree and all social worlds are, in the final analysis, connected in a vast network. These issues are taken up in Chapters 8, 9 and 10.

What can become an actor?

I suggested in Chapter 2 that actors are not prime movers in relational sociology. There are no interactions, relations or networks without actors but actors take shape within those interactions etc. in a constant process of formation or becoming. This raises a key question, namely, what can become an actor? I have referred almost exclusively to human actors so far. Are they the only actors we can or should admit? This is not an idle question. On one side numerous writers have made a claim for what some call 'corporate actors'; that is, it has been argued that certain forms of human collective, such as trades unions, business organizations and national governments, can be regarded as actors (Hindess 1988; Coleman 1990). On the other, 'actor-network' theorists seek to open the door to a whole range of non-human actors, including other animals and pieces of technology, indeed anything that can be perceived to generate effects within the context of a network (Latour 2005).

Corporate actors can and should be included as actors within relational sociology. Businesses, for example, interact, form relations, occupy networks and can be analysed in much the same way as human actors can. Moreover, as I argue in Chapter 10, if we want to focus on the 'big picture' in sociology, that is, upon the macro-cosm, it is sometimes necessary to focus upon the big players; that is, upon corporate actors and the networks formed by their interrelations. The worry about corporate actors is that they are reducible to the human actors who staff them. It might be argued that a political party is not an actor, for example, but rather a set or network of actors. This may apply in some cases and, of course, it is always possible to analyse a corporate actor as a network of human actors. As I discuss in Chapter 10, however, there are instances and respects in which some collectives of human actors become capable of making and acting upon decisions which are strictly irreducible to the actors involved in them, qua individuals, such that it is both legitimate and important to treat corporate actors as actors in their own right, interacting with other such actors in their own networks. Different theorists have suggested different reasons for this (Axelrod 1997; Coleman 1990; Hindess 1988) and collectively they constitute a strong case.

Corporate actors do not share the same properties as human actors. Much of my focus in this book will be upon human actors because inter-human interaction is capable of a richness and complexity not possible when other forms of actor are involved. Corporate actors don't have emotional or intersubjective relations, for example, even if the human actors involved in them do. They are important actors all the same, however, and we need to incorporate them.

The claims of actor–network theory (ANT) are more murky and difficult to address. Actor–network theory raises many important issues, poses an interesting challenge to the current academic division of labour and is certainly right to stress the significance of the materiality and the technological infrastructure of the social world. However, it glosses over important difficulties and contradictions in its conception of non-human actors which dissuade me from following its example. These points need unpacking.

On the positive side, ANT reminds us that human relations are invariably embedded in and mediated by a material environment which impacts significantly upon them. In some respects the Marxist notion of 'relations of production', wherein social classes are defined by their relations both to the means of production and to one another by way of the means of production, constitutes an early recognition of this point. But ANT has generalized the point and opened it up. Many of our (inter-human) networks presuppose the physical network of the telephone system and internet, for example, or road, rail and airport networks. I agree with this point and believe that it is important. As we know to our cost, failures in the technological infrastructure of our world can have drastic effects.

Furthermore, many contemporary world problems pay no regard to the academic division of labour, such that they require interdisciplinary research and perhaps a mixed or hybrid approach to networks, similar to what is proposed in ANT. In relation to health and environmental issues, for example, it is clear that we need analyses which cross-cut many of the traditional divisions that organize intellectual life, not least the distinction between the social and the biological sciences. The way in which we compartmentalize knowledge is sometimes a burden. Sociologists should join with specialists in other domains where appropriate, and perhaps trace networks comprising and constituting multiple types of 'actors'.

Finally, ANT's signalling of the non-neutrality of objects, the way in which particular technologies shape action in historically contingent ways, is important. Again we can look outside ANT for antecedents of this view. Becker's (1982) analysis of musical and other instruments in *Art Worlds*, for example, which explores how arbitrary (Western) musical conventions are embodied in the design of instruments, a process which tends to perpetuate those conventions as players acquire their competence in relation to and thus rely upon such instruments, at least hints at what the ANTs are suggesting (I incorporate this in my discussion of conventions and their *materialization* in Chapter 8).

Our conception of human (including corporate) networks should never lose sight of their embeddedness in and embedding of material and technological environments and networks. Indeed we may wish, on occasion, to explore such technical embeddings and networks in detail. There are good reasons not to treat non-human entities as actors, however.

First, sociologists generally the lack the competence to understand and explain the behaviour of non-human entities. How, for example, is the sociologist to include a household pet as an actor in her analysis without having the knowledge of the animal behaviourist? And if the pet is infected by ('has connections with') a particular virus, and this too is part of the story, then the sociologist must be a virologist too. Of course this doesn't matter if what we are interested in is the significance that these entities assume within human networks, for human actors, but in this case we are not affording them the parity that calling them 'actors' suggests.

If all ANT asks is that we look at how human beings make sense of and respond to non-human entities which impact upon them, then I agree this is sometimes necessary and important, but I don't believe that we are granting those non-human entities the status of actors if that is all that we are doing. To treat non-human entities as actors requires analysing them on their own terms, as we analyse human actors on their own terms, and I do not believe that sociologists have the competence to do that.

Following on from this, second, even ANT sociologists do not seem interested in the 'point of view' of the non-human actors they deal with. Latour (e.g. 2005) is often at pains to emphasize the significance of the actor's point of view but in practice this means the point of view of human actors. When (in the guise of Jim Johnson (1988)) he analyses doors and the various mechanisms for controlling their opening and closing, for example, his discussion is framed entirely in terms of human concerns (e.g. keeping in the heat). There is no suggestion that a door has a point of view or brings relevant interests into the situation which it seeks to advance. Of course he can't say that because doors don't have subjective interests or points of view and even if they did we couldn't know what they are. But therein lies the problem. To call something an actor, for sociological purposes, is to say that it has a point of view and that this point of view matters and should be taken into account. It implies that the actor has a stake in the world under investigation, that it is meaningful for and matters to them. ANTs do not seem to depart significantly from this conception when dealing with human actors – Latour (2005) insists upon it – but they appear to forget it when dealing with non-human actors. Their accounts are human-centric, which is a good thing and would not be a problem if they did not pretend to be doing otherwise.

Third, non-human actors can't enter into interaction with human actors in the way that human actors enter into interactions and relations with one another and, for this reason, aren't typically regarded as actors by human actors. Of course we rant at technologies which break down as if it were their fault but only on the spur of the moment. We do not seriously believe that they intend to thwart our plans and activities. And as such we do not treat them as actors. This is a problem because, to reiterate, ANTs claim to want to remain faithful to the points of view of actors.

To reiterate, I am not suggesting that we exclude non-human entities from our analyses. Of course we should recognize the impact of technologies, viruses, the built environment, the weather etc. upon what we do. But we have to recognize that these objects are not 'actors' in the way that sociologists usually use that term, aren't susceptible to the usual assumptions and practices of sociological research (which assume that actors understand what they are doing, have a researchable point of view etc.) and, unless we are working with experts in other areas, can only be approached from the point of view of their impact upon human actors and the significance which human actors attach to them.

4 From strategy to empathy

In Chapter 3 I suggested that social interaction and relationships have a number of distinct but overlapping dimensions. They have symbolic, affective and strategic dimensions, and also convention–innovation and exchange–power dimensions. In this chapter and the three that follow I unpack this claim and offer a more detailed account of these various dimensions. I begin, in this chapter, with a discussion of the strategic dimension, specifically as developed in game theory – a mathematically based spin-off of rational action theory (RAT) which simulates strategic interaction and its outcomes in the context of various hypothetical scenarios or 'games'.

Game theory is discussed, in part, because it can be a useful and insightful approach to the analysis of social interaction, particularly in the hands of its more sophisticated and sociologically attuned advocates (e.g. Axelrod 1985, 1997; Coleman 1990; Gintis 2009; Hardin 1993). We have much to learn from it. For all of the mathematical complexity of its more advanced forms, however, game theory operates with an idealized and oversimplified conception of interaction and social relations. As such it provides a useful foil against which to consider what a more adequate conception might look like. We can learn both from what game theory gets right and what it gets wrong, moving towards a more sophisticated understanding of both interaction and relations.

Some writers treat 'strategic interaction' as a distinct type of interaction which can be contrasted with other types. Habermas (1991, 1987), for example, distinguishes strategic and communicative forms of interaction. As indicated above, I prefer to think in terms of a strategic dimension which enters into interaction, with a greater or lesser weighting relative to other dimensions, when triggered by certain conditions. Many instances of interaction manifest a strategic dimension or at least potential but this is generally mixed with other dimensions and may be more or less central depending upon circumstances. I will sometimes refer to 'strategic interaction' in the course of the chapter and the book but this is just for the sake of convenience and brevity. I am not suggesting a typology of interaction.

The chapter makes a number of arguments. First, following the above point, I argue that strategic interaction both presupposes and generates other dimensions of interaction. In particular it often presupposes symbolic and conventional dimensions. In a related move the chapter also draws from Simmel's (1955) reflections upon conflict to show that this mode of interaction, closely related to strategic interaction in many accounts, has important social and symbolic dimensions and can be socially generative as well as destructive because of this.

Second, building upon this, I argue that strategic interaction is not the primordial 'state of nature' that some RATs and game theorists claim (e.g. Laver 1997). It is not the manifestation of a basic and unmediated human nature and we cannot, as they suggest, adequately explain the rest of the social world by reference to its emergent effects. Strategic dynamics in interaction can have interesting emergent properties, including some which are far removed from the Machiavellian scenarios that game theory likes to assume as a universal starting position. Axelrod's (1985, 1997) analysis of the strategic basis of cooperation, which I will discuss, is a good example. But strategic interaction cannot be assumed as a pure and asocial origin from which the social world has sprung. I suggest, by contrast, that it (1) is a response to specific – albeit quite common – conditions; (2) draws upon forms of competence and dispositions which are acquired in other, earlier interactions; and (3), to reiterate, generally presupposes other dimensions of interaction and thus the very social world that more radical game theorists purport to explain by way of it. Even if strategic interaction draws upon invariant and hard-wired human tendencies it is equally always socially conditioned.

Continuing this point, my third argument is that social conditions can channel strategic interaction in cooperative and pro-social directions not ordinarily associated with it. It can be strategically wise to be 'nice'. Specifically this is so in the context of *relationships* (as opposed to fleeting, so-called 'one shot' interactions) and *networks* (as opposed to relatively isolated dyadic encounters and relations). It pays to be 'nice' towards those with whom one is in a relationship and with whom one therefore expects to be interacting again. Likewise it pays to be 'nice' towards those with whom one shares mutual contacts with whom one expects to interact in the future. Even if we were purely and primordially strategic beings we would have reason to be nice to those with whom we have relations and share common ties. Given that most of our significant interactions are with alters who belong to our wider networks and with whom we have durable relations, this is an important point. Many of the games dreamed up by game theorists are either unrealistic or trivial because they abstract actors from networks and relations.

Relations and networks do not only make cooperative and pro-social behaviour strategically advantageous for us, however. My final argument is that they also tend to generate and inculcate non-strategic influences on behaviour. Specifically, they generate (1) *norms*, which can be oriented to in a strategic fashion but which might also be oriented to by way of a socially derived sense of (2) *duty*. And they generate both (3) *trust* and (4) *empathy*.

The point of the chapter, to reiterate, is not to suggest that, in modelling the social world, we must choose between strategy and any of these alternatives but rather that interactions are steered, to varying degrees, by a combination of these (sometimes competing) factors. In some interactions one factor predominates to the almost complete exclusion of the others, on account of the circumstances of the action, but in most interactions several of these relational elements come into play together. Strategic concerns might compete with the call of duty, for example, and duty might conflict with empathy.

The chapter begins with a reflection on strategic interaction and game theory's best known game, the Prisoner's Dilemma. Having identified certain sociological limitations to the game theoretic approach I turn to the work, referred to above, which explores the emergence of cooperation within strategic 'games'. This leads to a reflection upon norms and duty, followed by a discussion of trust and then empathy.

Strategic interaction and game theory

Strategic interaction can be defined as interaction involving parties who (1) have a conflict of interest, either partial or total; (2) (inter)act rationally (in the RAT sense) and, thus, (3) seek selfishly to maximize their own gains; and (4) anticipate that the other will do likewise. When deciding how to act in a particular situation, each actor anticipates the other's likely course of action, considering that the other will be doing the same, and acts accordingly. This type of interaction has been a central focus of much work in rational action and game theory.

Game theorists typically explore strategic interaction by constructing and modelling hypothetical situations ('games') in which two or more actors have a number of courses of action open to them, each of which has a number of possible payoffs attached to it, depending upon the way in which the others (who are doing likewise) act. The aim of game theory is to identify the likely course any game will take and the most profitable strategy to adopt. The value of this exercise, for those who advocate it, is that the outcomes of games are often surprising and depart significantly from the intentions imputed to individual players (Schelling 1981, 1995). This is important from the point of view of relational sociology because it offers a strong example of the irreducibility of social interaction. Interaction outcomes are shown to be 'more than' a simple aggregation of the intended outcomes of individual actors.

For some, game theory is an analytic pursuit. They purport to explain social life by way of their games. Other game theorists adopt a normative stance. They claim to be able to advise actors (e.g. governments and other organizations) on strategy. These are really two sides of a coin, however. Game theoretical advice is of little value unless we assume that games plausibly simulate real-world situations and strategies. In this chapter I treat game theory as an analytic attempt to model and explain the real-life interactions that are of interest to relational sociology. More specifically, I consider that some of its games might be considered 'mechanisms' in the sense introduced in previous chapters; that is, that they might capture relational/interaction conditions and dynamics that recur in social life, with relatively predictable outcomes.

The Prisoner's Dilemma

To illustrate the approach and its conception of strategic interaction we can consider its best known game, the Prisoner's Dilemma. In this game two crooks have been arrested by police and locked in separate cells where they cannot communicate. The interrogating police officer asks each to give her information which will convict the other of a serious charge in return for a reduced sentence for themselves: the so-called 'defect' option. If one prisoner defects and the other doesn't, opting to stay silent (the 'cooperate' option[1]), then the defector goes free and the cooperating crook gets ten years. If both defect then both will be convicted but their defection will be taken into account and they will get five years each. If neither defects the police only have sufficient evidence to convict them of a minor offence and each gets one year. Their dilemma is represented in the grid in Figure 4.1.

Observe that the reward for mutual cooperation (a sentence of one year) in the above example is better than the mean average of the best and worst payoffs (no and ten years respectively). This reflects a fixed order of payoffs in the Prisoner's Dilemma. The highest payout is for those who defect whilst the other cooperates, followed by cooperating when they cooperate, followed by defecting when they defect, followed by cooperating when they defect (the so-called 'sucker's payout'). This is significant in relation to a scenario I consider later. It suggests that actors who elected to alternate their strategies across successive 'turns' would still be worse off than if they managed to mutually cooperate.

Defection is what is called a *dominant strategy* in this particular game. It is dominant because it achieves the best result for any given actor whatever the other does. If A defects and B doesn't, then A goes free, compared with getting one year if neither defects. If both defect then A gets five years compared to the ten years she would get if B defected and she didn't. From the individual point of view, A should clearly choose to defect. Exactly the same is true for B, however, such that defect/defect is the inevitable outcome if both actors behave rationally.

		Prisoner B	
		Stay silent ('cooperate')	Give evidence ('defect')
Prisoner A	Stay silent ('cooperate')	A = 1 yrs in prison B = 1 yrs in prison	A = 10 yrs in prison B = 0 yrs in prison
	Give evidence ('defect')	A = 0 yrs in prison B = 10 yrs in prison	A = 5 yrs in prison B = 5 yrs in prison

Figure 4.1 A simple 'one-shot'* Prisoner's Dilemma

Note: *The 'one-shot' Prisoner's Dilemma is a Prisoner's Dilemma where actors make their decision to either defect or cooperate on one occasion only. It contrasts to what I discuss later in the chapter under the rubric of the Iterated Prisoner's Dilemma. In the iterated form, as one might guess, prisoners repeatedly choose whether or not to cooperate with one another or to defect.

Defect/defect is what is known as an *equilibrium point* here because if actors put themselves in this situation then neither can improve upon her individual outcome by means of a unilateral change of strategy. If either actor unilaterally changed her mind and withdrew her statement she would only increase her sentence. This generates an incentive for actors to stick with their strategy, hence the 'equilibrium' label. All things being equal neither actor will change her strategy and the situation will remain as it is.

The rub is that actors could do better for themselves if they were to cooperate. What is individually most rational is arguably not so if the perspective and likely action of the other is taken into account. Interaction complicates the calculation of benefits. The best case scenario for A is that she defects and B cooperates, taking the rap for both of them, but since B thinks and feels in the same way as A, that is not going to happen and their next best option is to each make a small sacrifice, by refusing to defect, thereby securing their second best outcome. The most rational option for the actors, assuming that both are prioritizing their own welfare and assuming that it were genuinely an option, would be to mutually cooperate.

There is a parable for social life here. For all of its hawkish celebration of competition, conflict and Machievellian actors, game theory very often indicates that life would be better for individual actors if they could cooperate with one another; what appears to be most rational when we focus upon the individual in isolation (e.g. the dominant strategy in the Prisoner's Dilemma) is not necessarily the most rational, for that same individual when we consider the impact of the actions of others upon their outcome. The selfish pursuit of individual self-advancement can be less profitable to the actor than a more cooperative strategy.

We will see later how game theorists believe that cooperation might come about in a Prisoner's Dilemma. For now, however, note that their prediction for its basic, one-shot format, as described above, is that it won't. This is telling. It suggests that game theory's actors are either (1) incapable of recognizing that mutual cooperation is their best 'real-world' option, which would make their 'rationality' somewhat limited and egocentric in the Piagetian[2] sense (i.e. not very rational as we usually understand rationality[3]), (2) extremely distrustful of others, such that they imagine they will be suckered if they opt to cooperate and/or (3) extremely untrustworthy and known to one another as such. Whichever it is – and different developments in game theory suggest different possibilities – these actors are somewhat asocial and not particularly good strategists. This is not to say that actors who always opted to cooperate would be more rational or more realistic as representatives of 'real life' actors. The problem is that game theory identifies defection as the dominant strategy and the strategy that the actor will therefore necessarily follow, not allowing them to rise above this obviously self-defeating option where that might be a profitable possibility.

Looking at this another way round and anticipating arguments later in the chapter, this very basic form of game theory, whilst on one level elevating actors by making them capable of complex calculations and privy to clear information on outcomes and options that is often not available in real-life situations, at the same time deprives them of resources that actors very often would have in real life, e.g. the possibility to cooperate, relations of trust with their alter etc. Game theory constrains its actors in ways which leave them little option but to behave in an adversarial manner.

Another way yet of looking at this would be to argue that *modelling interaction on a presumption of atomized and egoistic actors falls well short of adequacy*. Game theory brackets out important dimensions of real-world interaction. That, in many respects, is the key argument of this chapter.

Strategic constraints

I return to the Prisoner's Dilemma later. Before I do, however, I want to reflect further upon the constraints that game theory builds into its models. Some game theorists believe that strategic interaction, as represented in these games, is a primordial state, rooted in human nature, from which the social world has emerged and through which it can be explained (e.g. Laver 1997). The social world and its 'furniture' can only be explained, they maintain, by recourse to an asocial state which pre-exists it, and strategic games capture this point of origin (ibid.). I disagree. The games of game theory both constrain actors in ways that are often highly contrived, such that they represent an unlikely 'state of nature', and also presuppose conventions, 'framing' (Goffman 1996) and thereby previous symbolic interaction, such that they cannot be deemed primordial in the way these accounts suggest. These points need to be unpacked.

Goffman (1969: 89) calls game theory's games 'miniature scenarios of a very far-fetched kind'. I agree that they are far-fetched but, like Goffman, feel that they can also be useful if handled with caution. They allow us to abstract conditions of interaction which encourage specific dynamics and outcomes. In this respect, though they deal in pure forms, unlikely to be replicated exactly in real life, they can provide a rich source of the relational mechanisms referred to in earlier chapters. It is not beyond the pale, for example, that situations with a formal similarity to the Prisoner's Dilemma might emerge in various contexts of the social world, and that this game might therefore serve as a useful device for predicting and explaining what happens in those situations – although empirical experiments in game theory suggest that actual behaviour often departs from what is predicted, such that the theoretical models stand in need of refinement (Green and Shapiro 1994).

Contrary to the reductive assumptions regarding human nature posited by some game theorists, however, I suggest that the theory indicates that actors are induced to act strategically by the (sometimes 'far-fetched') circumstances they find themselves in. Strategic interaction is not a default position for social actors, on this reading. It is triggered by particular circumstances, such that it might be deemed a function of those circumstances rather than of 'human nature', and such that concepts of strategic interaction are more or less applicable depending upon conditions. It is noteworthy, for example, that many classic game theory scenarios are constructed in such a way that actors cannot communicate with one another. Prisoners in the Prisoner's Dilemma, for example, are locked in separate rooms and cannot talk. Likewise in what Elster (2007: 323) calls the 'Telephone Game', an actor's 'phone breaks down' leaving ego and alter to second guess one another's actions. And in 'Chicken', where actors drive their cars directly at one another to see who will lose their nerve first, actors seem only to communicate by visibly constraining themselves in such a way that it is obvious to all that they cannot alter the course of their action (Elster 2007: 321–22). By disallowing communication in many of their best-known games, game theorists deny players the most obvious means of arriving at a mutually cooperative solution. Actors are forced to act strategically because no other options are open to them. Indeed, by some definitions they do not interact at all. They are prevented from interacting whilst finding themselves in a situation where they affect one another through their actions. If they could interact (e.g. communicate), the dilemma might dissolve.

Goffman (1969) muddies the water slightly here when he notes that we can use language to mislead and deceive as easily as to cooperate. Prisoners who agree verbally to cooperate, he notes, can still defect when the time comes. I will be suggesting later that communication does make a difference, but for the moment, note that Goffman himself explores cooperation by reference to conditions which constrain actors to cooperate. There are mechanisms which encourage cooperation as well as mechanisms which encourage strategic defection for Goffman.

The most important of such mechanisms, for Goffman, are social norms. Actors are constrained not only by physical factors (e.g. being locked in a soundproof prison cell), he observes, but also by norms of the social world. The behaviour of prisoners in the Prisoner's Dilemma might be different if there was a norm prohibiting 'grassing' in the criminal community to which they belong, for example. A norm of this kind might alter the prisoner's behaviour either because norm-violation would attract punishments which make defection more costly and therefore less desirable, or because some norms are deeply internalized (in the form of conscience) and guide action irrespective of projected payoffs or simply because some norms act as rules of thumb which we draw upon without deliberation and which relieve us of the burden of calculation. Defection simply might not occur to a prisoner as an option.

The existence of norms in game situations raises a number of complex issues. I defer my discussion of them until later. Note for present purposes, however, both that the game theorist's tendency to bracket norms out of games puts a highly artificial constraint upon the actors involved and that, by their own admission, game theorists and RATs struggle to explain norms despite acknowledging their existence and importance (Elster 1990; Coleman 1990).

A further circumstance which tends to induce strategic interaction in game theoretical scenarios is the presence of a conflict of interest between actors. Schelling (1981), a pioneer of game theory, explicitly defined strategic interaction, as I have above, as interaction between parties who have a conflict of interest. This leaves open the possibility of multiple situations in which actors do not have a conflict of interest and therefore interact in other, non-strategic ways. Again, strategic interaction is a function of a context of interaction (i.e. interaction where there is a conflict of interests) and not of an invariant tendency of actors towards competition or conflict.

It is not quite as simple as that. 'Conflicts of interest' are more or less common in the social world depending upon how one defines actors and their perceived interests. If we assume actors to be petty, egoistic and calculative, then they will experience a great many conflicts of interest on a daily basis. Actors can potentially bring a strategic orientation to the most mundane situations, as many parodies of the materialistic neo-liberal ethos of the 1980s, including Brett Easton Ellis's (1991) *American Psycho*, demonstrate. That such representations are parodies is instructive, however. Most people, thankfully, are not like Ellis's psycho.

Furthermore, even when mundane situations do provoke strategic interaction, such interaction presupposes socially acquired forms of competence and inclination. Actors learn to be strategic and their tendency (or not) to bring strategic orientations into particular situations is at least partially affected by their interaction history. Insofar as strategic interaction presupposes that actors reflect upon the likely actions of alters, putting themselves into alters' shoes, for example, the theory presupposes intersubjectivity. It presupposes actors capable of and disposed to put themselves into the shoes of the other. I will suggest in Chapters 5 and 6 that such intersubjective dispositions are cultivated in early childhood relationships and interactions. Small infants lack an awareness of the perspectives of others and only learn of those perspectives, acquiring the capacity to imaginatively project themselves into them, by interacting with and imitating others (Mead 1967; Piaget 1961).

Moreover, their capacity and disposition to utilize this capacity for strategic purposes derives from further learning experiences, such as playing real games (e.g. chess, cards or football) where it is required (Mead 1967). Part of learning to play games in childhood is learning to anticipate the likely response of the other and pre-empt it, learning to thinking several moves ahead, learning to maintain a 'poker face' and so on. This does not seem to come naturally to children.

It is only a small step to consider that this ability and disposition is more likely to be generalized amongst actors for whom strategic interaction is the norm in the main contexts of their lives. That, of course, was the point of the parodies of the 1980s referred to above. When 'markets' and 'games' are the guiding metaphors of actors' working lives, reinforced at various levels, it is not surprising that thinking in such terms becomes a habit which is transferred to other situations. It is perhaps also not surprising, for this same reason, that economics students are more likely than other students to behave as predicted by game theory in empirical experiments![4]

My discussion of trust later in the chapter will add to this argument. An actor's level of trust, I will argue, is determined in large part by their relational experiences, especially in childhood. This is significant in relation to the strategic dimension of interaction because the tendency to orient strategically towards others is a function of distrust. At the extreme a strategic orientation is a paranoid orientation.

To briefly summarize my argument so far: without denying that interaction can manifest a highly strategic aspect, I have sought to challenge the idea that this strategic aspect is primordial and can be invoked to explain other aspects and the wider social world. Whatever part 'human nature' might play in strategic interaction, it is (1) triggered by circumstances, (2) presupposes other dimensions of interaction and (3) draws upon socially acquired forms of competence and possibly inclination. Furthermore, the games of game theory, though useful, are extremely artificial and constrain actors in peculiar ways. This further undermines any claim game theorists might have to capturing a 'state of nature' underlying the social world.

Social games

Pushing these arguments one step further, many 'games' presuppose that all parties to them adopt a strategic orientation. One party cannot play the game, adopting a strategic orientation, if the other(s) do not do likewise. The game must be collusively constructed and maintained by its players. In many cases this presupposes that players collectively define and agree upon their game. It requires that they have a mutual understanding of the game they are playing and orient to its conventions. In other words, strategic interaction presupposes prior symbolic interaction.

The pattern of interaction that game theorists call Chicken, for example, presupposes certain conventions. It entails that two players simultaneously pursue lines of action which, if both continue long enough, will lead to their mutual destruction (or at least to significant damage to their interests). The first to pull out of the game is the loser (the chicken) and the point is to hold one's nerve and win. The game can only be played if both recognize it as a game and actively play, however. Under most circumstances driving one's car very fast in the direction of another on-coming vehicle would be regarded idiotic. And unless it is interpreted as a challenge, that is, unless it is interpreted in light of the conventions of Chicken and attributed the meaning, 'Chicken', any rational alter would simply get out of the way. Furthermore, since the payoff in Chicken is kudos, it presupposes an audience who will reward the winner with praise and admiration. It is only praiseworthy when all relevant parties understand that a game of Chicken is in play and lend the game their support and recognition by treating it as such. Chicken has to be 'framed' (Goffman 1996), for all involved, as 'Chicken' in order to work. It presupposes a 'definition of the situation' and thus symbolic interaction.

Likewise, prisoners in the Prisoner's Dilemma, though they do not communicate directly with one another, communicate with the police officer who makes the offer to them. And they understand what she says. They know what 'ten years in prison' and 'reduced to one year' mean. If they don't the game cannot be played. This may sound trivial but it suggests that strategic interaction is preceded by symbolic interactions which define its parameters and frame it. Of course the Prisoner's Dilemma is supposed to stand for a multitude of situations which have a similar strategic structure but have nothing to do with prison. The point would apply in all of these cases, however. Games have to be understood and oriented to by their players. They only merit the term 'game' insofar as they do.

White's (1992, 2008) reflections on 'control' in interaction and his claim that 'identities' (I prefer 'actors'[5]) 'seek control', touch upon this same point. White maintains that interaction can only occur where actors establish a footing or common definition of their situation of interaction, a definition which extends to the identities and ties they are activating as well as the nature of the interaction. Any two actors might simultaneously be colleagues, neighbours and friends, for example, and might need to establish the capacity in which they are speaking, as well as the type of speech act they are making (a complaint, a joke, a point of information etc.) if their interaction is to succeed. To 'seek control', in White's terminology, is to seek to establish these grounds. My point is that these 'symbolic' and 'conventional' dimensions are necessary to many strategic games. If actors do not share a definition of the situation then they cannot compete.

The celebrated seventeenth-century English philosopher, Thomas Hobbes (1971), whose classic work *Leviathan* anticipates and informs important themes in game theory, also anticipates this concern with convention and symbolic control. Hobbes is best known for his claim that the human 'state of nature' is a 'war of each against all' in which actors, using both force and cunning, seek advantage over one another – a situation which he deems unstable and, more famously, 'nasty, brutish and short'. We are only lifted out of this state, Hobbes argues, by the emergence of a powerful state which enforces peace and cooperation. Strategic actors effectively agree to defer and delegate some of their own autonomy to a central actor (the state), who will punish them for legal transgression, in return for protection from others, who are likewise constrained. The situation is akin to a Prisoner's Dilemma in which each prisoner realizes that mutual cooperation is their best bet and agrees to stay silent but does not trust that the other will stick to the agreement and so engages a third party to enforce its terms by punishing defection; Goffman (1969) too reflects upon the significance of third parties in this respect.

As Rawls (1992) notes, however, Hobbes spends seven chapters of *Leviathan* discussing issues of speech and discourse before he even introduces the idea of strategic actors and their conflicts. He imagines the chaos of a situation in which every individual formed their own 'language', ideas and meanings on the basis of individual experiences, concluding that not even the conflict-ridden situation he envisages at the origin of political life would be possible in the absence of a common language, shared meanings and communication. Moreover, for Hobbes, individual rationality presupposes mastery of language and communicative competence. Conflict and strategic interaction, in other words, rest upon a foundation of symbolic interaction and social-symbolic convention.

The social properties of conflict

We can advance this line of argument by briefly considering the various ways, outlined by Simmel (1955), in which conflict can be regarded as a social form. Strategic interaction is not necessarily conflictual but Simmel's points are sufficiently general in scope to be relevant to our discussion and are, in any case, interesting and important.

In the first instance Simmel notes that, in conflict, actors manifest an interest in one another and mutually modify one another's actions. They interact and enjoy a relationship to one another, albeit an antagonistic relationship. Conflict is therefore social. It is a form of social interaction not an absence of social interaction.

Second, developing this, he claims that most relations, including relations of conflict, involve a combination of positive and negative values and emotions. Conflict need not preclude positive ties. It can be our love for another, for example, which brings us into conflict with them or generates tension. Certainly what they do must matter to us if it is to bring us into conflict. We must agree that something is worth disagreeing over. Conversely, we can come to respect another, even if only as an adversary, through conflict. Their capacity to outwit us in specific instances may incline us to respect them even as it frustrates us. Indeed, strategic interaction precisely presupposes a certain respect for the other. We credit them with the wit to prove a worthy adversary. What they do matters to us and we know that they are not stupid and will act so as to best advance their interests as we do.

Developing this point, Simmel argues that conflict is part of most relationships at some point in time. As noted in Chapter 3, relationships are constituted through interactions and, as such, are always in process. Conflict, for Simmel, is a common feature of this process. Relationships often alternate between harmonious and more conflictual, tense phases.

Third, Simmel notes that combatants in conflict often appear to agree on strategies of self-limitation (see also Huizinga 1950). Each party could act in ways which would be more damaging to the other side but they don't. They limit the damage, assumedly in the hope that the other will see and respect this, and will follow suit. They cooperate even as they conflict. Axelrod (1985), whose work I discuss below, offers a good example of this. He discusses historical work on trench battles during the First World War which points to the evolution of a moral code and communication system between ordinary soldiers on the two sides which allowed them to minimize the damage each inflicted upon the other. Each would, for example, signal before mounting certain types of attack, thus allowing the other side to take refuge. And each would allow the others to engage in activities which made them vulnerable, without exploiting that vulnerability through attacks. Simmel's argument here is that mutual understanding can develop within the context of conflict and that conflict, as such, can lead to more sociable relations. Conflict is, in some cases, generative of more cooperative social relations and of mutual recognition between parties (Hegel's (1979) 'struggle for recognition' is, of course, the classic statement of this view).

Framing, symbolic interaction and again 'control', in White's (1992, 2008) sense, are important in relation to this idea because damage limitation agreements must be communicated and achieved. In a discussion which informs Goffman's (1996) account of framing, for example, Bateson (1972) observes how play fighting amongst animals involves 'meta-communication'. On one level, he notes, animals might snarl and appear very aggressive. By means of small touches and the style in which they execute their attacks, however, they also communicate that 'this is just a game', and these communications are made intermittently throughout the fight in what can be understood as an effort to preserve the meaning of the interaction (as play, not real fighting). Animals strive to control the interaction by maintaining a definition of it as 'playful'. The same applies to other forms of conflict, combat and strategic competition.

Finally, Simmel notes that conflict shapes those who are party to it. Specifically, he believes that conflict focuses, centralizes and unifies actors. Much of what he says about this focuses upon collectives. He is interested in the way in which groups come together and adversaries join forces when under attack from a third party. A common enemy affords them a common identity and purpose otherwise lacking. They join forces, forming a single combat unit. Conversely, escalation of conflict and an increase in its stakes can whittle down a group to its most dedicated members, as the less dedicated make an exit. Similar factors can be observed at an individual level too, however, as conflict induces actors to think and act strategically, adopting a hard-line position and attitude, and perhaps aligning themselves more closely with an identity or discourse that was previously much less important to them. This is a particular example of the more general point, made in earlier chapters, that interaction transforms the actors involved and cannot therefore be reduced to them. Conflict qua social interaction shapes combatants.

Cooperation, relationships and networks

Strategic interaction doesn't necessarily give rise to conflict, however. It may equally give rise to cooperation, as Axelrod's (1985) important work suggests. Axelrod is a game theorist who has worked upon what is called the Iterated Prisoner's Dilemma, that is, a Prisoner's Dilemma in which the same actors play repeatedly against one another for an indefinite number of times. Imagine criminals who are repeatedly caught together and offered a chance to cooperate or defect. Or if that seems unrealistic imagine any scenario where two actors have repeated opportunities to cooperate or not with one another, where the payouts for doing so are equivalent to those of the Prisoner's Dilemma.

Axelrod suggests that, insofar as the number of iterations remains indefinite and/or unknown to the actors involved, the incentive structure of this game is different to that of the simple, one-shot Prisoner's Dilemma. Although actors do not communicate linguistically they have an opportunity to 'reply' to the other's action in any given iteration of the game by way of their own action in the next. Each can punish the other for failing to cooperate. As such it is possible for them, over time, to build up a pattern of cooperation from which they would both benefit and which would be to their mutual advantage.

This is only possible if the number of iterations is indeterminate or unknown to the players. If players know which iteration of the game will be the last then each has an incentive to defect on that turn and each knows that the other has this incentive. The consequence of this is that the last iteration is effectively lost to both – they will each defect – but this means that there is no effective sanction against defection in the second-to-last iteration, so both should seek to defect in that iteration too, which removes the sanction from defection in the third-to-last iteration and so on. The only way to pre-empt this is by making the number of iterations indefinite. When this condition holds, players approach each iteration in the knowledge that there may be another and thus that alter will have an opportunity to punish defection on their part. This, Axelrod notes, provides an incentive to cooperate.

It is not obvious that a player should cooperate, however, because there is no dominant strategy in an Iterated Prisoner's Dilemma. There is no single response which produces the best outcome for a prison irrespective of the actions of the other. Notwithstanding this, however, Axelrod conducted a series of empirical experiments designed to identify the best strategy and this work suggested that a form of cooperation is, indeed, the most profitable approach under most circumstances. This empirical work deserves brief discussion.

Experimental cooperation

Axelrod organized a tournament of game theorists and interested others. Each had to submit a strategy, in the form of decision rules which a computer could simulate, and each was then pitted against every other over a series of iterations whose number was unknown to players in advance. Strategies could be asocial in the respect that actors followed a pattern irrespective of whatever the other did. They might be social, however, in the respect that, following a first, 'blind' turn, responses were conditional upon the action of the other. The winner was the strategy with the highest score when the scores from each of their games, with each of their partners, were added together at the end.

Different strategies were more or less advantageous depending upon the strategies they were pitted against. Overall, however, Axelrod found that the most effective strategy was what he calls a 'tit for tat' strategy. This entails that the actor gives the other the benefit of the doubt on the first turn, and elects to cooperate, but from that point onwards emulates the last move of their partner. If the partner cooperates on this turn, they cooperate on the next. If the partner defects, they defect and so on. In Axelrod's terms this strategy is (1) 'nice' (it never defects first), (2) 'provocable' (it always punishes defection), (3) 'forgiving' (it reverts to cooperation if the other does) and (4) both 'clear' and 'consistent' such that others know where they stand and can orient to it. This doesn't work against every adversary but those who do well against it tend to score poorly against other adversaries and, overall, tit for tat does best.

Having established this point Axelrod fed this information back both to the original players and to others who had become interested subsequently, inviting them all to have another go and effectively to take on his 'tit for tat' champion. Many did but tit for tat emerged victorious once more.

Pushing this experiment one step further, Axelrod (1997) next tested 'tit for tat' in an evolutionary context. He translated success in the various rounds of his tournament into reproductive success. All strategies were represented by an equal number of players at the beginning of the game but these numbers were revised at the start of each round in accordance with their relative success in the preceding round. Unsuccessful strategies eventually died out whilst the most successful strategies became more numerous. Axelrod was thus able to explore the evolutionary 'fitness' of different strategies. Furthermore, manipulating the starting conditions of these evolutionary games allowed him to explore 'stability'. For example, could any strategy which began in a minority thrive and grow into a majority? Were particular strategies vulnerable to take over by minorities even if they started in a majority?

The results from this later research are complex but there are two headline conclusions. First, tit for tat again proves stable and robust. Second, it can survive and flourish in populations dominated by much more aggressive (defection oriented) strategies providing that a big enough minority (critical mass) adopts it in the first place. The size of this critical mass varies in accordance with the reward structure of the game but can be quite small.

This second point indicates the effect of networks as well as critical mass. Those who use tit for tat cooperate with others who cooperate with them. If there are enough of them and they interact, they flourish, but only if they find one another and interact. Connection was guaranteed in Axelrod's tournament – since every actor interacted with every other – but in real life it is contingent upon dynamics and contingencies of network formation. Actors do not connect with all alters in their population, at least not necessarily, and cooperation may only or at least best flourish, therefore, in instances where co-operators find and connect with one another in a cohesive network cluster. Isolated co-operators who find themselves in a population of competitive individualists will perish.

Although we must be extremely careful in extrapolating from these experiments it is difficult to resist the observation that this sheds light upon Hobbes' (1971) aforementioned account of the evolution of social order and suggests an alternative path out of it. Where Hobbes suggests that the only way out of the 'state of nature' is for selfish and strategic actors to hand over a portion of their liberty to an all-powerful state which will enforce fairness in their dealings with one another, Axelrod suggests that strategic actors, mindful that conflict breeds conflict which is damaging to all, might elect to cooperate. Moreover, his work suggests that networked cooperation, that is, a situation in which actors who wish to cooperate find and connect to one another, will be more successful than populations of competitive individualists in the long run. Perhaps stable societies have emerged, where they have, out of small networks of mutually cooperative actors which have grown and flourished at the expense of utilitarian populations of the type imagined by Hobbes.

Note also here, however, that, as Axelrod concedes, the strategy of cooperation may be as much based on a rule of thumb as on anything else; it may be a facet of a bounded rationality. As noted above, the strategy is not dominant in game theoretical terms and, as such, actors could not really know that it was the best strategy, even if they knew the potential payoffs attaching to their interactions (and were mutually restricted in the options available to them). Before Axelrod conducted his experiments nobody would have a solid basis upon which to know that cooperation is superior, and in many respects the claim is counter-intuitive.

My own belief is that where tit for tat is practiced, and I believe that it is quite widely practiced, it has been learned through (perhaps sometimes painful) experience and then also passed on. We learn very quickly in social interaction that it pays to cooperate and our culture is full of proverbs informing of us of the dangers of adopting an adversarial position, e.g. 'what goes around comes around', 'live by the sword, die by the sword', 'there will always be someone bigger than you', 'don't shit on your own doorstep' etc. As such, tit for tat is very much a social and cultural strategy. It belongs to the popular wisdom of our collective life.

Social relations and networks

Axelrod's work is important because it points to the effect of *relationships* on interaction and, in particular, their 'taming' effect upon the mutually destructive tendency towards defection that game theory predicts in the one-shot Prisoner's Dilemma (and, by extension, in the wider social world). Axelrod frames his discussion in terms of iteration but iteration is a facet of relationships. I defined relationships, in Chapter 3, as lived histories of interaction with tacitly projected probabilities of future interaction. Relationships involve, amongst other things, an expectation of indefinite future interactions. In this sense Axelrod is pointing us to the effect of relationships upon interaction. Actors interact differently in relationships than in so-called 'one-shot' interactions because relationships involve the prospect of further, future interactions.

This has enormous implications because much of our interaction in everyday life and much of our interaction in situations involving conflicts of interest is interaction with others with whom we are likely to interact on an indefinite number of occasions in the future, that is, *others with whom we have relationships*. Indeed, interactions which we know to be one-shot are relatively infrequent and usually trivial, e.g. strangers talking on a train journey. The vast majority of our meaningful interaction is with neighbours, family members, colleagues, friends and associates. 'Defecting' in these interactions, whatever that might entail, would invite retaliation and possibly escalatory cycles of tit for tat attacks. I am not suggesting that this doesn't happen in everyday life but a 'strategic' actor would seek to avoid the damage this involves, under many conditions, and opt to 'cooperate'.

This dynamic is further reinforced within certain network structures, specifically structures in which parties to an interaction have mutual contacts within a network. If A defects on B, their mutual contacts may be inclined to punish her. And even if they do not they will hear about what has happened and may refuse to trust A in the future. A will have damaged her reputation and, in doing so, will have damaged her ties with many others upon whom she depends, jeopardizing her access to the resources that those ties provide, not least of which is trust. As Coleman (1990) and Burt (2005) both argue, this is particularly evident in the case of 'closed networks', that is, networks (or sub-networks) in which most people know one another (high density) and there are few connections to others outside of this dense grouping. In such networks news about ego spreads quickly and, assuming that ego is relatively dependent on her alters, reputation tends to be important. Each of ego's ties is effectively policed and enforced by the others. Damage to one tie risks damage to them all.

Again this is very important because most of our interaction takes place within established networks where any given alter has ties to some of the others. Our friends have ties to one another, so do our neighbours and our colleagues. Isolated dyadic relations are the exception rather than the norm. This observation complements Axelrod's observation on the survival advantages of networks of cooperation. Cooperation is both more likely in networks and, for different reasons, more advantageous for those involved.

Norms and duty

Insofar as tit for tat or the cooperation that it can generate are repeated through numerous iterations and across numerous relations between actors in a network they can become institutionalized as norms; that is, parties to a relationship will come to expect cooperation from others and to anticipate that they are expected to cooperate by others. Many game and rational action theorists accept that norms play a role in social interaction (Coleman 1990; Elster 1989, 1990, 2007). They tend to problematize them, however, by recourse to their utilitarian assumptions.

Norms, by this account, are agreed rules or conventions to which actors conform, to the extent that they do, in anticipation of either reaping rewards or avoiding punishments. Like Durkheim (1964), game theorists conceive of norms as rules backed by sanctions. This, however, presupposes that others take responsibility for enforcing norms (i.e. administering sanctions) and, in some cases, in engaging in the deliberative processes necessary to their establishment, both of which raise the 'free rider' or 'collective action' problem that informs much RAT and game theoretical work on 'collective action' (see Olson 1971; Hardin 1982; Oliver and Marwell 1993). That is to say, because actors benefit equally from the establishment and policing of norms irrespective of whether they are directly involved in those activities, the rational actor would do better to sit back and let others pay the costs. In cost–benefit terms it pays to 'free ride' on the efforts of others. Rational actors are motivated to sit back and let others formulate and police norms. However, as this applies equally to all (rational) actors nobody should ever be motivated to make the effort.

The 'collective action problem' is badly framed in many formulations and collective action is less anomalous, in terms of RAT, than this exposition suggests (Oliver and Marwell 1993). There is an interesting kernel of a problem here, however, which merits brief discussion. As a first step we should observe that, as the above example suggests, norms do not always emerge out of deliberative processes. They may, for example, when governments negotiate over new norms of trade or carbon emission. But they may equally emerge, organically, from conventional patterns that emerge within interaction over time. Durkheim (1964), for example, suggests that norms evolve from conventions and traditions which, in turn, evolve out of regularities in (repeated) interactions by way of processes of habituation and institutionalization. What we feel that we and others *ought to do* emerges from *what we have always done*.

Second, where custom and practice do not suffice and deliberation is necessary, the problem of free riding may not be as great as RATs predict because, as much social movement theory suggests, social problems generate a demand for change which, in turn, creates incentives for moral and political entrepreneurs who will service that demand in return for the material and symbolic rewards that attach to such accomplishments. Taking the initiative to solve the problems of one's community is a course of action which the community are often prepared to reward, thus providing the incentive for someone to do it. Politicians and legal professionals who haggle over laws on behalf of 'the people' in return for a good salary and public recognition represent one highly institutionalized form of this mechanism. Protestors who gain status within their political networks and 'worlds' (see Chapter 8) for their sacrifices represent another.

We should also note here, however, that actors may observe, co-devise and enforce norms out of a sense of duty. 'Duty' is antithetic to the utilitarian world-view of the game theorist but this says more about the shortcomings of game theory than duty. The classic position on duty is Kant's (1993), which explains it as a facet of individual rationality – albeit in a rather different sense of 'rationality' to RATs' strategic sense (see below). We find a more relational, sociological spin on the idea in the work of both Mead (1967) and Durkheim (1973, 2002), however. Our sense of duty arises within social interaction, as an emergent product of it, they argue. It is an internalization of the shared views of the group(s) to which we belong, what Mead (1967) calls the generalized other (see Chapter 5).

A sense of duty arises when we judge our own actions, plans and options from the point of view of the community to which we belong. It elevates the actor from the particularity of their individual viewpoint, entailing that they adopt the more universal perspective of their community (or one of the communities to which they belong). For this reason, however, actors only have a sense of duty to the extent that they interact with others in networks and derive a sense of this generalized perspective. Actors are not forced to agree with the view of the generalized other or follow its prescriptions, as they represent them to themselves, but qua social actors they are aware of and affected by the moral call of these representations in their decision making processes (see Chapters 5 and 6 for more detail).

The rational is relational

Duty involves affect. It may, for example, entail guilt or a projected anticipation of guilt. Both duty and norms also entail rationality, however, and, importantly, call for a more expansive sense of rationality than is granted in game theory. Rationality is not only a matter of devising efficient means of securing desired ends but equally of transcending the particularity of one's own viewpoint and subjecting it to the test constituted by others' views. As such, rationality is irreducibly intersubjective (Husserl 1990; Merleau-Ponty 1962; see also Crossley 1996: 1–7).

This may have a strategic manifestation. The prisoner in the Prisoner's Dilemma who knows that defection is the dominant strategy for both herself and the other, and who therefore seeks to achieve mutual cooperation, is being rational in this sense. They recognize the other is no sucker and that compromise will get them both a better outcome.

Beyond this, however, behaving rationally entails behaving in ways which 'make sense' to others and remaining open to their claims and views. We need not necessarily agree with others but where we disagree, to be rational, we must move towards a resolution through the exchange of arguments (Habermas 1991). Rationality is a social process in which individual views engage to form a higher view. And both norms and duty may be rational in just this social or relational sense.

We are constrained to be rational, from this point of view, by living amongst others who expect us to account for our actions and recognize their viewpoints. Rationality is a socially imposed constraint:

> [T]he very process of controversial discussion forces a certain amount of rational consideration and . . . the resulting collective opinion has a rational character. The fact that contentions have to be defended and justified and opposing contentions criticised and shown to be untenable, involves evaluation, weighing and judgement.
>
> (Blumer 1969: 93)

And we become rational, in this sense, to the extent that we internalize these demands (e.g. for views and actions to be defended) and incorporate them within our own, individual decision making processes. The rational actor is one who incorporates the other within their own thoughts and actions. Moreover, norms may be rational to the extent that they are thrashed out in communicative processes of the sort alluded to by Blumer in the above quotation.

None of this detracts from the fact that, on some occasions, actors orient to their duties (either to obey norms or enforce them) in utilitarian terms and 'free ride' in expectation that others will do the work of creating a stable society for them. My point is only that, as social beings, which is to say, as actors who are born into, live and take shape within networks of interaction, we are no more pure utilitarians than we are pure deontologists. Where our wants and our duties come into conflict we experience this as an internal tension and, insofar as we are rational, talk it through either with ourselves or with others. As Axelrod hints and Mead and Durkheim more fully articulate, living within a flow of networked interactions has a transformative impact upon actors and their interests which, in turn, impacts back upon interaction such that it is always multi-dimensional and more complex than reductive and simplified models can hope to capture.

Trusting relations

Social relations affect interaction in Axelrod's work by way of their projected future. Prisoners don't defect in the Iterated Prisoner's Dilemma because they anticipate reprisals in future interaction. Or again, defection is less likely between members of a closed network because each anticipates damage to their standing in their network, which will disadvantage them in the future. Relations affect inter-action by way of their past too, however. Actors may know one another well enough to trust that cooperation will be reciprocated. Trust, as a feature of their relationship, makes alternative lines of interaction possible. In particular it may increase the likelihood that an actor will 'cooperate' or perform their duty in advance of reciprocation by others – because they trust that others will reciprocate.

Note that trust has an intersubjective structure in this case. It is not enough that A trusts B. She must trust that B trusts her because if B thinks that A will defect then B will defect too. Each must trust the other and trust that the other trusts them. But what is trust?

Trust has been a key topic of social scientific writing in recent years and a great deal has been written about it, from a variety of perspectives. I do not have the space to review even the major contributions here. I will base my discussion around one particularly persuasive contribution which has emerged from within the game theoretic literature: that of Coleman (1990).

Coleman asks two questions: (1) is it ever rational (in the RAT sense) for us to do what we have been trusted to do? And (2) is it ever rational for us to trust others? Apart from a brief allusion to 'internalized moral restraint' which he does not elaborate upon (but which suggests a recognition of the role of duty), Coleman's answer to the first question is that if we have something to gain by breaking trust, then it is only rational to honour it if we have other, stronger incentives not to, such as those discussed above. It is rational when we are likely to interact with the same person again or when we share mutual alters who we may want to trust us and thus have a reputation to maintain.

The decision whether to trust, he continues, fits the basic criteria of what RATs call 'decision under risk' and can be addressed in the same way. Three values are involved: the probability that the trustee will prove trustworthy (p); the potential gain if they do (G); and the potential loss if they don't (L). It is rational to trust, he argues, if $p/(1-p) > L/G$. If $p/(1-p) < L/G$ then it is not rational. If the two scores are equal then it is a matter of indifference. Coleman is not suggesting that actors actually perform such a calculation. The claim is that his model incorporates the factors that affect trust and produces outcomes akin to those that we find empirically.

This probability-based definition of trust is common amongst RATs and game theorists. Many conceptualize it as a subjective probability estimate. Gambetta, for example, defines trust as:

> A particular level of subjective probability with which agents assess that another agent or group of agents will perform a particular action, both *before* he can monitor such action (or independently of his capacity ever to be able to monitor it) and in a context in which it affects *his own* action.
>
> (Gambetta 1988: 217, his emphasis)

Likewise Hardin describes trust as an 'instinctive Bayesianism' (1993: 507). It entails a probability value that is modified over time in accordance with experiences that either confirm or disconfirm it, experiences which are, in some part, a function of the level of the trust that the actor has before exposing herself to them (see below). Hardin insists, however, that this is 'instinctive'. It is not something we consciously calculate. It manifests itself to us only in our willingness to trust. We do not decide to trust. Rather we find either that we do or do not.

Coleman's model is interesting because it is dynamic and potentially explains a range of peculiar features of trust. On one side, for example, he suggests that it explains those situations in which we are inclined to say that an actor trusts because they 'need to trust'. Trusting because one needs to, he argues, is being in a situation where potential gains are high and potential losses are low. In this situation, he notes, even a low probability value will be greater than the ratio of gains to losses, making the risk rational and the actor more likely, therefore, to trust. It is for this same reason, moreover, that even careful people are sometimes caught out by conmen. Conmen manipulate perceptions of the probability of outcomes but they also manipulate perceptions of the magnitude and ratio of gains to losses such that probabilities need not be so high to persuade a rational actor to trust.

On the other side, Coleman suggests that we can often be slow to trust new friends because, if that means sharing confidences and making ourselves vulnerable, potential losses are high whilst gains might be relatively low, at least if we have other friends with whom we share confidences and gain is measured as an improvement upon what we already have. Unless my current confidant is proving unhelpful I have little incentive to take on an additional one because that increases my vulnerability without giving me anything I haven't already got.

The relational origins of trust

The obvious question that Coleman's account begs is where the value p comes from? He offers a number of suggestions. First, he suggests that we can consider what the other has to lose by defecting. If they have a good reputation which would be threatened by evidence of dishonesty, for example, then we may be inclined to trust them. They have too much to lose by cheating on us. Second, we seek information about others, again considering reputation, and we check out their claims. Such research might be costly but we deem it worthwhile, in Coleman's view, if the stakes are high.

More interesting for our purposes, however, is his third suggestion, that p is based upon our previous experience. This has both a general and more specific manifestations. Some alters whom we know well will have their own p value (for us). We all have a sense of how reliable and trustworthy our friends are, for example, based upon how reliable and trustworthy they have been in the past. In addition, however, Coleman refers to a standard estimate of trustworthiness which we derive from our experiences in general and which we may apply to all strangers (he calls this p*). If we have found strangers to be trustworthy in the past then we reckon on any new stranger being trustworthy too (to a level p*).

This account echoes many others from outside of the RAT and game theoretical traditions. Even Giddens' (1984, 1990, 1991) psychoanalytically infused model of trust boils down to a claim that our capacity to trust is based upon our prior experience of trusting relations. If we have enjoyed good trusting relations in our early life then we will tend to be more trusting as we grow up. Indeed, Hardin (1993) draws upon the same key psychoanalytic source of reference as Giddens in his game theoretical account of trust (i.e. Erikson 1963) and arrives at a similar conclusion about the importance of early childhood experiences which effectively shape our earliest p values (what Giddens calls our 'basic trust'). Early experiences have particular importance if only because they determine the extent to which we will expose ourselves to 'trust situations' in the future, which, in turn, determines the possibility that we will revise our initial estimates. If we learn distrust early on then we are unlikely to trust others and thus unlikely to learn that it pays in many cases to trust.

Similar processes, Hardin adds, can occur on a more collective level. Newcomers to a community enjoy less trust from others, for example, which can disadvantage them and perhaps thereby make them more likely to pursue dishonest means of achieving their goals, which will reduce the trust attributed to them further (if they are caught). Moreover, trust levels within a community will often be self-reinforcing. In low-trust communities actors will seldom trust one another and the basis for an increase in trust will be absent. In high-trust communities (assuming trust is respected), by contrast, actors will often trust and will thereby learn that it pays to do so, reinforcing their disposition to trust in the future.

This experiential model could be elaborated. We might introduce contextual considerations, for example, such that we judge certain friends or strangers more trustworthy in some contexts than others. Likewise, we may introduce Schutz's (1972) 'typifications', such that some types of stranger (e.g. women) are deemed more trustworthy than others (men). And finally we could include Hardin's contention that both the p values attached to specific others and our generic p* are subject to constant revision in accordance with new experiences. As such, trust might be conceived as a process (see also Khodyakov 2007). I am more concerned here, however, to explore the significance of these reflections for the 'rational' and 'strategic' model of interactions and relations which frames this chapter. Two points are central.

First, note that Coleman and Hardin take a more relational approach to the actor than RATs are generally inclined to do. Action is influenced by the actor's p and p* values and these, in turn, are functions of the actor's interaction history. Actors are not atomized decision makers but rather products of a relational past. Their outlook and inclinations are shaped by a sedimented history of relations and interactions. Furthermore, that history and therefore the 'capacity for trust' that it engenders are as much products of the activities of others as of self:

> [An individual's capacity for trust] is very much the by-product of experiences over which the individual may have had little control, experiences which the individual did not even undertake. For example, you may have a great capacity for trust because you grew up in a wonderfully supportive family and because your later life has been in a society in which optimistic trust pays off handsomely. You are accountable for little or none of your capacity, you are merely its beneficiary.
>
> (Hardin 1993: 525)

Second, Coleman's p introduces an inductive element into human action. This is significant because induction, as Hume (1984) famously demonstrated, is non-rational. The fact that something has happened repeatedly in the past provides no rational justification to believe that it will happen in the present or future. Hume is not suggesting that we abandon induction. He acknowledges both that life would be impossible without it and that we are inclined by nature to rely upon it. Recourse to induction, via trust, marks a (further) departure from a purely rational model of the actor, however, even if, as Coleman suggests, it is brought into play alongside a reflection on projected gains and losses in strategic reflection.

As discussed here, trust further advances our understanding of interaction and relationality. Trust does not preclude strategic interaction. Indeed, the goal of maintaining one's reputation as 'trustworthy' might enter into strategic deliberations. However, trust cannot be reduced to strategic considerations because it is inductive. Furthermore, it may offset a tendency towards 'strategy'. Actors who trust one another are less likely to resort to strategic manoeuvres because they trust that the other won't either. Trust, in this sense, is an intersubjective property of relations. And I have suggested that trust might characterize whole communities, not least because it derives from interaction and will tend therefore to cluster in networks; actors will only learn to trust in environments where others practise trust and prove trustworthy. I have also, on this same basis, discussed the tendency of individual actors to trust (e.g. Coleman's p and p*), however, explaining this in terms of an actor's history of relations. This is a further way in which the actor who instigates interaction is also shaped by it.

Empathy

Trust affects the means available to actors in interaction. If they trust one another, then options that would not otherwise be available are open to them. Other factors influence both means and ends of action. One important example is empathy. If we empathize with the other then we are inclined to take their interests into account in our interaction, perhaps refraining from certain courses of action and/or including their well-being in the ends we pursue.

Empathy has a rather interesting champion in Adam Smith (2000). Smith is best known for his claim, in the *Wealth of Nations*, that the collective good is best served if each individual is allowed to selfishly and strategically pursue their own interests because the 'invisible hand' of the market will translate these selfish efforts into gains for all (Smith 1991). This is only one amongst a number of claims in that book, however, many of which qualify this grand claim, giving him a more sophisticated and nuanced position overall. And the position is more nuanced and sophisticated yet if we take into account the arguments of his earlier *Theory of Moral Sentiments*. The books opens:

> How selfish soever man may be supposed, there are evidently some principles in his nature, which interest him in the fortune of others, and render their happiness necessary to him, though he derives nothing from it, except the pleasure of seeing it.
>
> (Smith 2000: 3)

This might assume a relatively abstract form, as when we feel concern for others we do not directly know, but Smith equally elaborates his case by reference to immediate and embodied examples of empathy. He refers to the way in which we wince when seeing another being hit, for example, and how we 'writhe and twist' when watching a tightrope walker, as if we were wobbling on the high wire ourselves. Such empathy requires imagination:

> By the imagination we place ourselves in his situation, we conceive ourselves enduring all the same torments, we enter as it were into his body, and become in some measure the same person with him. . . .
>
> (Smith 2000: 4)

What is important here is not what the other feels, as such, but what we would feel in their shoes. Smith illustrates this by reference to our sympathy for the dead. They do not experience the coldness and darkness of burial, the isolation and loss of all that they might have achieved. They are dead and experience nothing. But we sometimes experience it in their place. Much of our distress at the death of a loved one is based in such empathy. We put our self into their cold, dark and lonely place, cut off from friends, family and the future they might otherwise have enjoyed. Though they experience none of this, we experience it for them. Likewise with those (e.g. children) who are incapable of understanding a terrible situation they might be in. We feel distress for them (or joy if their situation is positive) despite the fact that they do not understand the situation sufficiently to be affected by it.

Because empathy requires that we imaginatively put ourselves into the shoes of others, Smith continues, it also requires that we have an awareness and understanding of the other's situation and whatever has provoked them to act as they are. If we see a large rock drop onto another's toe we empathize instantly with their pain and may give off our own 'ouch!' reaction. If we can't see the cause of the pain, for whatever reason, however, identification is less likely and more difficult. We perceive the response but not the situation to which it is a response and that makes it difficult for us to respond empathically. We can't put our self into their position because it is a position that is inaccessible to us.

What Smith is moving towards here, to anticipate the argument of Chapters 5 and 6, is what I call a narrative conception of intersubjectivity. We empathize with others by imaginatively enacting their role in a story that we – usually with their help – have woven around them, but to do that we must be able to insert their action into a narrative structure in which one event follows another. The slapstick example of heavy objects falling onto toes is very simplistic but it makes the point. To empathize with the other we need to locate them within a story which we can, in some part, imaginatively re-enact with ourselves in the lead role. Empathy requires a plot, an intelligible sequence of events that we can both follow and put ourselves into as protagonists.

This process might operate on different levels. Rocks on toes are at one extreme but there is considerably more 'character development' in long-term friendships, where the other's history is gradually pieced together from various sources and their 'role' becomes ever more complex and nuanced. By talking with and about them we build a story around them, creating a character with which we can empathize. Of course much of this story comes directly from them. Their self-presentations and disclosures assume the form of a story that we are invited to empathize with and borrow from. But we fill in gaps by reference to what they unintentionally 'give away' and what we find out by other means, synthesizing these snippets into a whole.

There are limitations to this process. It may be difficult to put ourselves into situations which are very different to any we have experienced and we may be more or less adept, more or less practiced, at playing a role as the other would play it. Unfamiliarity with another or perhaps lack of personal insight may incline us to overestimate the extent to which the other would respond to a situation as we would. A cynic who lacked self-insight might always 'play' others as if they were cynics too, for example, thereby perhaps justifying further cynicism on their own part. The more experience we have of them and the greater the similarity of their situation to our own, however, the closer we get.

This discussion of empathy raises interesting questions of intersubjectivity which I will take up in the next two chapters, not least how we acquire the ability and tendency to put ourselves into the shoes of others. In these chapters I will argue that our capacity for empathy, like our capacity for trust, evolves out of a relational history. For the moment, however, what is important is, first, that empathy, as Smith discusses it, suggests an alternative source of action to the self-interest and strategy suggested in game theory, and second, that this source resides within the actor's relations with others.

Conclusion

Interaction often manifests a strategic dimension or at least a strategic potential. Whether that potential is realized may depend upon other factors, such as the level of trust between the actors involved, the presence (or not) of norms to which actors orient through a sense of duty and any sense of empathy they might have towards one another. These factors are not mutually exclusive. An actor can pursue their own self-gain, strategically, within the parameters allowed by norms or their conscience. And they may seek out the best strategic option for self and other together etc. Moreover, even where they do act strategically they will tend to orient to conventions, interact symbolically with the other, to establish the footing of their interaction, and draw upon socially acquired skills and dispositions. There is a strategic dimension to much interaction but 'strategic interaction' as a pure form is pure fiction.

Game theory is a useful way of abstracting this dimension and subjecting it to detailed analysis but we must not fall victim to its abstractions. It constructs situations which are often extremely artificial and which deprive actors of the resources and options that are often open to them in the real world. Moreover, it abstracts the actor from the networks of social relations which provide the context for most interactions, networks which foster both our strategic disposition and the various other (e.g. empathic or dutiful) dispositions which might counter-act it; networks which configure our conditions of interaction such that even the most strategic and self-serving of actors might opt to be cooperative and such that most actors, endowed with a sense of trust in their others, might not feel the need to consider 'defection'. That is to say, networks in which cooperation and consideration become rules of thumb.

Of course trust can break down and actors can resort to relatively brutal ways of engaging but this is not a return to a 'state of nature'. It reflects the fact that interaction can render actors distrustful, untrustworthy and uncooperative as surely as it can render them trusting, trustworthy and cooperative. There is no state of nature and there never was, or rather our state of nature is a state of living together in interdependence and how we behave can never be understood in separation from the relational dynamics and processes that this entails.

5 Mind, meaning and intersubjectivity

Individualism is often bolstered, both in academic circles and more widely, by a conception of the human mind or subjectivity as a private realm. The alleged privacy and singularity of our subjective lives evokes a sense of the individual as an isolated atom. Much of what I discussed in the last chapter chips away at this notion. I suggested that strategic interaction entails actors putting themselves into one another's shoes, for example, and presupposes shared meanings, understandings and situational definitions. Even when they compete, I argued, actors act together and often collude.

In this chapter I offer a more direct critique of the privatized conception of our subjective life and take the first steps towards a more intersubjective conception. The result, I hope, is a refinement and enrichment of both our conception of social interaction and relations, especially their symbolic dimension, and our conception of the social actor as emergent from networks of interaction. The chapter both explores the primordial bonds that tie actors to the world, and thereby to one another, and the process whereby interaction, and especially symbolically mediated interaction, gives rise to reflective thought and thus a thinking subject.

The wider ambitions of the book require that I keep my discussion of these complex and contentious philosophical issues relatively brief. I hope that I say enough to at least make the case interesting and plausible, however. I refer the interested but unconvinced reader to my earlier work on these issues (especially Crossley 1996, 2001) and to the key sources that I draw upon (Mead 1967; Merleau-Ponty 1962, 1965; Wittgenstein 1953; Ryle 1949).

The chapter begins with a classic statement of the privatized conception of subjectivity, in the work of Descartes (1969). Written at the dawn of the Modern era, Descartes' reflections on mind and body (or matter) still appear to inform much thinking about these topics, in spite of their considerable problems. A reflection upon some of these problems provides a useful way into formulating an alternative, more intersubjective conception of human life. Specifically, I argue that Descartes' argument is based upon (1) a flawed conception of mind and body as separate substances (his position is unequivocally substantialist); (2) highly problematic claims regarding introspection and its indubitability; and (3) a misunderstanding of the meaning of concepts used to render mental life. In the second part of the chapter I seek to develop an alternative to his conception, building particularly upon the work of G. H. Mead (1967). This account begins with a discussion of gesture, meaning and language, before turning to 'mind' and the process of thought. The chapter concludes by way of a brief reflection upon human self-hood and its relation to the other, which effectively paves the way for the chapter which follows.

Descartes and the problem of intersubjectivity

One of the key obstacles to a proper understanding of intersubjectivity is a popular conception of mind which dates back to Descartes (1969). Descartes equates mind with consciousness and defines it as a *substance*, distinct from the *substance* of the body. Where the body can and indeed must be known from the outside, he argues, the mind can only be known from within; that is, to itself. The body is matter and, as such, is defined in large part by its sense-perceptible properties. We can see, touch, feel, smell and taste bodies. They occupy space, are divisible and obey the mechanical laws of the physical world as known to science (Descartes' main works predate those of Isaac Newton by only a few decades). Mind, which is defined chiefly by the property of thinking, manifests none of these properties and in particular is imperceptible except by means of introspection.

Others can only ever perceive my body, according to this position. They cannot perceive my mind and as such they can never directly experience the real me. At best they can deduce that my body houses a mind. Only I know my mind and, according to Descartes, I know it with certainty because I am in immediate contact with it. My knowledge of my own mind is not like my knowledge of the external world, which is mediated by my senses and thereby subject to error and limitations. Consciousness is consciousness of itself and introspection is not fallible in the way that external perception often proves to be.

If a social world is conceivable at all upon this basis then it is a radically individualistic and atomized one. Societies must comprise aggregations of psychic monads, each 'in their own world'. Gilbert Ryle, an important of critic Descartes, spells this out:

> Mental happenings occur in insulated fields known as 'minds' and there is, apart maybe from telepathy, no direct causal connection between what happens in one mind and what happens in another. . . . The mind is its own place and in his inner life each of us lives the life of a ghostly Robinson Crusoe. People can see, hear and jolt one another's bodies, but they are irremediably blind and deaf to the workings of one another's minds and inoperative upon them.
>
> (Ryle 1949: 15)

As Ryle suggests, the connection between social actors qua sentient, intelligent beings who are oriented to purposes and meanings seems impossible from this position, or at least must be extremely indirect. In itself this should make us suspicious of the position. It is at odds with what, as sociologists, we know to be the case. I have offered a detailed critique of Descartes' position elsewhere and do not want to repeat myself at length here (Crossley 2001, 1996). However, a few critical remarks are necessary.

Against Cartesian substantialism

First, we need to challenge the notion that mind (or consciousness) is a substance. One way to challenge this notion is by reference to the many criticisms of mind/ body dualism that exist in the philosophical literature. Very few philosophers today hold that mind or consciousness is a 'thing' (substance) distinct from the body. I do not have the space to rehearse the many different arguments against dualism in the literature. Suffice it to say that there are many and that some are, in my view, conclusive (namely, Ryle 1949; Merleau-Ponty 1962, 1965; and for my contribution, Crossley 2001).

The consequence of this rejection of dualism is that 'consciousness' is no longer defined as a disembodied substance. I will outline my alternative definition in two stages. First, *consciousness is an emergent property arising out of inter- actions both within the neurobiological network comprising the organism and between the organism and its physical environment.* It involves *sensations* which take shape within and *are felt by* the organism as a consequence of its permanent but always changing conditions of *contact* with its environment. Consciousness is irreducibly embodied and, qua perceptual consciousness, which is its primordial form (Merleau-Ponty 1962, 1965), arises from contact and interaction between a sensuous organism which probes and explores an environment to which it both belongs and is, in some part,[1] sensitive, and the 'resistance' which that surround offers to this 'interrogation'.

This is not just a matter of brute sensations, however. It involves patterns of sensation which, qua patterns, have meaning. The organism interrogates its environment, focusing in and out in search of patterns which it has learned to recognize and which it uses to organize its inter-activities, from the faces of others, through the mundane objects of everyday life to the complexities of written or spoken language. Meaning, at this level and in this context, arises between the perceiving organism, which apprehends objects in the form of patterns of felt sensation, and those objects themselves. It is a collaborative outcome of the sense-making efforts of the organism and the resistance it encounters from its environment.

This view challenges Descartes' conceptions of both mind and body. Mind, qua consciousness, is not a distinct, disembodied 'substance' but rather an emergent property arising from interaction between a physical organism and its physical environment. Equally, however, 'the body' qua organism is not a 'substance' or mere assemblage of physical parts, reducible to their perceptible qualities. It is a living system, irreducibly interwoven with an external environment upon which it depends (e.g. for oxygen and food), to which it belongs qua physical being and which it perceives. 'The body' is not merely a combination of the sense-perceptible properties identified by Descartes but equally a sensuous, perceiving subject. It is, as Merleau-Ponty (1968) puts it, a 'reversible' being; both sensuous and sensible, perceiving and perceptible. The body has, or more correctly is, a point of view upon its environment.

Consciousness as relation: intentionality

Second, consciousness is 'intentional' in the phenomenological sense of the word. It is, as Husserl (1990) demonstrates, always *consciousness of* something and, as such, has two poles: the intended object and the intending subject. Again this challenges the notion that consciousness is a substance, suggesting rather, as both Mead (1967) and Merleau-Ponty (1965) note, that it is a structured relationship. I do not have a consciousness; rather I have a conscious connection to the world. I am connected to the world by way of my consciousness of it. Moreover, the 'I' referred to here, the *perceiving subject*, does not pre-exist its connection to the world any more than it is preceded by the *perceived world*. The perceiving subject and perceived object are necessarily coterminous products of the aforementioned engagement of an organism and its surround. The two poles of consciousness, the two sides of this relationship, are mutually constitutive.

This does not mean that there is no 'reality' independent of our consciousness of it, nor that we should be agnostic about its existence or bracket it out (as Husserl (1990) does). The intransigence of the world, the resistance that it puts up to our various attempts to understand it and our capacity to be mistaken about what we perceive and imagine, all point to a reality beyond our empirical experience, as Mead (1967) and Merleau-Ponty (1962) both note. However, it implies that our perhaps most salient tie to the real is mediated through consciousness and that, as such, sociologists must always take into account the lifeworld of those whom they study, that is, the world as lived and experienced. Much (but not all) of the impact that the world has upon the actor is mediated by their sensuous experience of it, which is, in turn, a function of their active engagement with it and not merely a reflection of 'what is there'. *The* world and *my* world are not the same and social science must attend to both.

This is not only a matter of embodied, perceptual sensations but also, as Merleau-Ponty observes, of bodily perspective and our embodied grasp upon the world. Whenever we perceive something we do so from a particular perspective provided by our bodily relation to it. We see things from above, for example, or from afar, from close up or behind. And our perception of them, as such, always entails a tacit reference to our own bodily relation to them.

At another level, the meaning of objects is defined for the embodied actor by their habitual use (Mead 1967; Merleau-Ponty 1962). This affects perception in the respect that we see objects in accordance with their potential for use – what Gibson (1979) calls their 'affordances'. Doors are perceived as an opportunity for entrance or exit, for example. Intelligent use of objects enters into the very definition of intentionality for Merleau-Ponty. Intentionality is not only a matter of the way in which I perceive and think about objects in the world but also the meaningful and knowledgeable way in which I handle and use them. My feet intend the pedals of my car when I drive, for example. The pedals exist for me by way of my use of them. Intentionality entails practical involvement in the world.

We are not only, contra Descartes, connected to the world, in Merleau-Ponty's view. We are practically connected. Practical involvement is our primary mode of being-in-the-world. Where Descartes identifies our essence as thought and, insofar as he acknowledges our relation to the world, theorizes it in terms of reflective contemplation, Merleau-Ponty suggests that we are fundamentally practical beings, always already in amongst the hurly-burly of the world and engaged with it. This is not to deny that we think, reflect or indeed reflexively contemplate ourselves. Any philosopher would have a hard time denying that. But it suggests that these are secondary structures which emerge out of a more primordial, practical entanglement with the world from which we can never extract ourselves except through death – and even then, of course, we dissolve back into the world that spawned us.

Later in the chapter I observe that the environment in and with which we are practically engaged and entangled is one peopled by others, such that we are always already interacting with and thereby connected to others. Interaction between organisms and, in particular, between human organisms is especially interesting because it generates symbolic communicative systems which, in turn, have a transformative effect upon the organisms involved. Indeed, communication and the tools of communication (i.e. language), forged through our long history, facilitate reflective thought and thereby allow us to take on some of the properties that Descartes (wrongly) deems primordial. The thinker is first a speaker and the speaker first an organism actively engaged with and attached to a world populated by others. Before we get to this, however, there are further criticisms of the Cartesian position to consider.

Intentionality and introspection

The concept of intentionality also challenges Descartes' claim that we have immediate knowledge of our own minds. Only I have my conscious experiences but this does not entail that I enjoy direct access to my own mental life, as Descartes implies. In the first instance, consciousness of objects outside myself does not imply consciousness of self. As I discuss in more detail in the next chapter, self-consciousness is a secondary structure of consciousness arising out of social experience. More importantly for present purposes, however, because consciousness is always *consciousness of* something, an inspection of the contents of consciousness is necessarily an inspection of that something. Right now I am conscious of the computer in front of me and a description of the contents of my consciousness would be a description of the computer as I perceive it.

This may be psychologically revealing but only in an indirect way and, as such, in a way equally or even more apparent to others. The fact that clouds always look like judgemental faces to me may say something psychological about me but it does not do so directly. What I perceive directly are judgemental faces. What that says about my mind is a matter of interpretation and whether it says anything at all depends upon how it compares to the experiences of others. If everybody sees judgemental faces then we might surmise that clouds just look like that.

From the phenomenological point of view all of our so-called 'mental states' have this intentional character. They are structures of consciousness, directed towards alterity, rather than objects of consciousness. An angry person does not perceive their anger, for example. They perceive the world angrily, through an angry lens. Likewise a happy person or someone who is in love does not directly experience their love. Rather, they perceive and act towards the other with whom they are in love in a loving way. I am not denying that we can recognize that we are happy or angry or in love. Through social experience we become reflexive beings who are perfectly capable of doing so (see Chapter 6). However, I am questioning the fact that we know these things about ourselves, as Descartes (1969) suggests, through an immediate acquaintance that we enjoy with ourselves through a special mode of perception (introspection). Furthermore, aligning myself with what I take to be a fairly common aspect of everyday experience, I am suggesting, first, that an actor may fail to notice their mental state and second, that they may be mistaken about it. Actors may fail to notice that they are becoming angry until others point it out to them or may insist, in good faith, that they are not jealous of another when it is plain to others that they are. The reason is that 'mental states' are not objects of consciousness but rather aspects of its structure. They are our connections to the world and illuminate the world in particular ways for us but, as such, they belong to the tacit background of our experience (Leder 1990). We do not experience them so much as experience by way of them.

Continuing this line of argument and rejoining Merleau-Ponty's abovementioned 'practical' emphasis, this is not only a matter of perceiving but also of acting. Love, anger, happiness etc. are not only ways of perceiving the world but of engaging with it and handling it:

> We must reject the prejudice which makes inner realities out of love, hate or anger, leaving them accessible to one single witness; the person who feels them. Anger, shame, hate and love are not psychic facts hidden at the bottom of another's consciousness: they are types of conduct or styles of conduct which are visible from the outside. They exist on this face or in those gestures, not hidden behind them.
>
> (Merleau-Ponty 1971: 52)

The point here is not that 'anger' or whatever corresponds to particular mechanical actions, gestures or even styles of action. Being angry takes many different forms, depending upon context. The point, rather, is that it is an embodied mode of being rather than an inner reality known only to the person who 'has' it. Furthermore, as Ryle (1949) also insists, the activity which embodies 'the state' is 'the state'. It is not merely an outward expression or effect of it. 'Mental states' are embodied ways of being and, to return to our central argument, of relating to objects in the world (including other human actors). Anger is an embodied, practical connection to the world.

This does not preclude the fact that we may 'have sensations' when in a particular 'state' – that is to say, sensations which we become aware of in their own right rather than perceptual sensations which intend and give us a world[2] – but it suggests that 'mental states' are not felt sensations. For present purposes consider three objections to the notion that 'mental states' are sensations. First, the same sensation may signal many different 'states' depending upon what the actor is doing and in what context. A slightly sickly feeling in the pit of one's stomach may indicate anxiety or fear about an action one is about to perform, guilt about an act one has performed or mild food poisoning. Second, different sensations may signal the same state. Love might manifest as agitation (beating heart, 'nervous' stomach, tense muscles) or its opposite (complete relaxation). It might mean laughing till you cry or just crying and crying. And there are 'states within states': e.g. *love* might entail *happiness* upon seeing the other, *sadness* upon leaving her, *nervousness* and *excitement* upon anticipating a further meeting, *jealousy* when she is with others etc. Love is the pattern of all of these responses when read together and in context. Finally, many states are deemed to persist over periods where sensations surely could not. To say that a couple have been in love for over twenty years is not to imply, for example, that each has had an on-going sensation for that period of time. These points apply, in different combinations, to all emotions.

Likewise, they apply to cognitive processes and states. What is it, for example, to understand? The Cartesian will say that it is an inner event and may point to such experiences as a 'click of comprehension' to reinforce their point. I know that I understand, they will say, when a feeling of comprehension comes over me. This account is deeply flawed, however. As Wittgenstein (1953) and Ryle (1949) both point out, we would be quick to retract our claim to understand something and to disregard any feeling that prompted this claim if, upon trying whatever it is, we find that we cannot do whatever is required. Understanding calculus, for example, entails being able to do it. Whether one feels or has a sense that one can do it is beside the point and not necessarily even indicative of understanding. One may feel that one can do it, only to find that one cannot, as indeed one may discover that one does understand it without ever having a 'feeling' of understanding – I understood the last sentence when reading back over it but can't say I felt anything. Understanding is, to paraphrase Wittgenstein (1953), being able to 'go on' and do something. It is practical and embodied, a matter of competent, embodied activity.

The looking-glass self

Note also here both that self-attribution presupposes the agreement of others – to know that I understand calculus, in the final instance, requires that my use of it agrees with others' uses – and that we find out whether we understand things by way of action. I do not come to know that I understand calculus by looking within myself. I arrive at this self-knowledge by acting in a context where others, whose expertise is vouched for, can confirm or deny my success.

The same applies to all 'mental states'. I learn about myself by reflecting both upon my actions (including my plans and dreams) and upon the reactions of others to those actions. Self-knowledge, contra Descartes, takes shape in an intersubjective world of practical and embodied activity. And, again contrary to the Cartesian position, our subjective states are available to others. They are not hidden. Others can see that I am angry or in love, that I don't understand calculus, that I am confused or distracted.

Cooley's (1902) reflections on 'the looking-glass self' are interesting in this respect. We build a conception of ourselves, he argues, on the basis of the information about ourselves that others 'reflect back' to us in our interactions with them. Such ideas, which are also discussed in psychoanalysis under the rubric of 'projective identification', have acquired a bad name in sociology, at least in the context of labelling theories which, in their cruder variants, seem to explain all manner of social deviance in terms of the deviant having been labelled as such; if others call me a criminal and I believe them, so the story goes, then I might see myself as a criminal and start acting criminally. The obvious problems with such vulgar accounts should not dissuade us from recognizing the importance of labelling and other 'looking-glass' effects, however. Moreover, Cooley's idea is important because, in a persuasive reversal of Descartes' position, which I discuss further in Chapter 6, it argues that actors, rather than enjoying privileged access to their own 'mental lives', are often their own 'blind spot' and need information from others to form a coherent and realistic conception of their self. This is partly a matter of the intersubjective basis of meaning and judgement; to assess whether or not I understand calculus I must compare my efforts against those of others who claim to understand it. However, it is also entails that actors do not have a very good vantage point upon themselves and depend upon the views of others.

Of course actors can hide 'feelings' and 'manage' the impressions they give off. I discuss this in the next chapter. Likewise, others can be mistaken about them if they (the alters) don't know 'the whole story', which, given that none of us are joined at the hip, is always true to some extent. This does not alter the basic fact, however, that others are an important source of actors' senses of self. I will show in the next chapter that this looking-glass dynamic presupposes an earlier relational dynamic in which actors learn to see themselves through the eyes of others. We have pushed this point far enough for present purposes, however.

The language of mind

I have advanced this argument, hitherto, by largely phenomenological means. The argument can equally well be advanced on a more linguistic front, however. As Wittgenstein (1953) observes, the language that we use to attribute mental states to ourselves is a public language that we have learned from others, will teach to others and that we use to communicate with others. As such its use and thus meaning cannot hinge upon reference to private mental states which are, in principle, inaccessible to all but the one person who experiences them (irrespective of whether such states exist). How, for example, could we ever have learned the meaning of 'understand' or 'jealousy' if their meanings entailed reference to private mental states? We have learned to use the terms 'understand' and 'jealous' by observing their use and grasping their meaning in concrete interaction situations. This entails that their meaning resides in the functions they serve, as concepts, within such situations (Wittgenstein 1953; Dewey 1988). In some cases their meaning may not be strictly referential. To say 'you're jealous' is in some cases a way of undermining another's claims or perhaps warning them against inappropriate behaviour rather than literally describing what we take to be their state of being. But insofar as they do refer to anything, psychological concepts necessarily refer to practical and embodied inter-activities in concrete contexts. Being jealous is a way of interacting and connecting with others, not an inner state.

A final addition to this point is that it is by no means obvious how we should interpret our experiences and that, insofar as we do so, we are generally reliant upon theories and 'vocabularies of motive' (Mills 1967) which are available to us within our culture. Only I have my dreams but I need to compare them with others' to work out whether they are odd and thus revealing in relation to me. Moreover, I have no immediate sense of their meaning and will therefore have to rely upon the various interpretive schemas available in my culture. Perhaps I will read Freud or a New Age guru. This applies to all experiences, not just dreams. As Merleau-Ponty puts it:

> The adult himself will discover in his own life what his culture, education, books and tradition have taught him to find there. The contact I make with myself is always mediated by a particular culture, or at least by a language that we have received from without and which guides us in our self-knowledge.
>
> (Merleau-Ponty 2004: 86–87)

I do not, to reiterate, experience my 'mind' or consciousness directly. My experiences are experiences of objects which transcend me. These may be psychologically revealing but only indirectly and only as interpreted by way of psychological theories which I encounter in my wider culture.

Towards intersubjectivity

This debunking of the Cartesian myth of subjectivity as a private, inner realm is important for a theory of intersubjectivity. It suggests that our subjective lives are available to others and are subject to public definition and negotiation. In what follows in both this chapter and the next I want to build upon this by offering a more positive alternative to the Cartesian model, an alternative which puts intersubjectivity at the centre of our model of both interaction and the actor. My main point of reference is the work of G. H. Mead (1967).

The conversation of gestures

Mead's starting point is the observation, noted above, that organisms respond to and act upon their environment, forming a system with it. The environment impacts upon the organism by means of perception; the organism impacts upon the environment by way of action; action shapes perception, which shapes the impact of the environment on the organism and so on in an unbroken circuit (see also Merleau-Ponty 1962, 1965). To understand animal behaviour, including human behaviour, Mead maintains, we have to engage with this interaction. Organism and environment are always already interlocked and must be analysed as such.

As animals belong to one another's environments this interaction is often social. The action of one organism triggers a response in the other, which triggers a response from the first and so on – although note that all parties are likely to respond to one another simultaneously in the first instance such that, technically, no one (or everyone) makes the first move. Mead famously illustrates this by reference to two dogs squaring up aggressively: one moves forward; the other moves back; the first bares it teeth; the second growls; and so on. Mead refers to this as a 'conversation of gestures' and, again, deems it important in the human case. Humans too respond to one another's actions and gestures.

The link of action and reaction is, for Mead, the basis of meaning. The meaning of an action or gesture is the response that it elicits, or rather, meaning lies in the relation of action and reaction. This meaning need not be conscious or intended. Indeed, Mead claims that in its most basic form it is not. In the most basic conversations of gesture actors mutually influence one another without conscious awareness of doing so. They 'give off signals' without realizing that they are doing so and they respond to the signals given off by the other without necessarily reflecting consciously upon those signals or indeed upon their own response. The gesture of the other has the meaning 'aggressive' in virtue of its raising my hackles but I need not be reflectively aware of this meaning. Indeed, in a fast moving combative situation I will respond without thinking.

This definition of meaning resonates with certain recent literary theories, which suggest that the meaning of a text does not lie within the text itself but in the response of the reader, or rather, between the text and the reader as embodied in the reader's response to the text (Fish 1980). The meaning of an action lies not within the action, Mead argues, but in the interplay of action and response. Note here, however, that Mead is referring to action not text. This is fundamental to his approach. His theory of meaning progresses to issues of language and aesthetics but always remains anchored in interaction between embodied actors.

Significant symbols

There is an asymmetry in conversations of gesture. Ego is not aware of the signals she gives off to alter or of their meaning. Certainly she does not affect herself by way of her gesture as she affects the other. When this asymmetry is removed, that is, when our own gestures are accessible to us, such that we too respond to them, we have what Mead calls 'significant symbols'. A significant symbol is *a gesture which has a standardised use and thus meaning and also a gesture which is available to the sender in much the same way as to the receiver such that the sender, in effect, communicates with and to their self as they communicate with the other.* Communication with significant symbols is therefore reflexive. Significant symbols make the communicator aware of what they are communicating and thereby bring them into interaction with their self.

The most obvious example of this, for Mead, is language. When I speak, to take verbal language for the moment, I hear what I say, as the other does, at the very same moment that the other does. And what I hear is meaningful for me as it is for the other. Furthermore, the relatively conventional and standardized nature of linguistic symbols ensures that, for most practical purposes, the meaning is the same for both of us. The key point here is the mutual accessibility of the vocal gesture for self and other but the same point applies to the written word. I read what I write, as I write it, and it provokes a response from me that amounts, according to Mead's approach, to meaning. The process of editing what we say or write, whether before communicating with the other or during our communication with them, is illustrative of this point and, indeed, suggestive of its import. When editing we become aware of how certain communicative formulations sound, what might be understood or misunderstood by them, and we play with formulations until we find out what it is that we really want to say.

Of course editing does not guarantee effective communication. What ego says may have a personal resonance for alter which ego does not hear, either because she does not know alter very well or because she has not sufficiently put herself in alter's shoes (see below and Chapter 6). Significant symbols may always be tinged with a personal significance that is not shared between parties to a conversation. Furthermore, as conversation analysts remind us, discourse has to be organized, and this organization can break down, leading interlocuters to talk at cross-purposes. None of this detracts from Mead's basic point, however.

Meaning and convention

Significant symbols are conventional and work, to the extent that they do, because of this. Mead doesn't elaborate upon this conventional aspect. We can briefly and usefully do so by reference to Wittgenstein (1953). Like Mead, Wittgenstein locates language and meaning, in the first instance, within the context of human interactivity, what he calls 'language games'. And like Mead he argues that shared meanings are dependent upon shared conventions, which he glosses as 'forms of life' and explores by way of the concept of 'rules' (see Chapter 8). Shared meanings are possible, he maintains, because and to the extent that actors share 'forms of life' and more particularly orient tacitly to shared rules of linguistic usage which they understand and which allow them to 'go on' in situations. If I shout 'here' in the midst of a football game, for example, both I and the person with the ball know that I am asking for the ball to be passed to me. Understanding what I say is being able to respond to that request appropriately.

Even dictionary meanings rest ultimately upon convention according to this approach. Dictionaries define words by reference to more words, displacing rather than resolving the question of what a word means. The *prima facie* solution to this problem is ostensive definition; that is, we can point to an object and say its name, forging a link between the two. Wittgenstein critiques the foundation of ostensive definition, however. I will use an example from Winch (1958) to illustrate his point.

Winch imagines someone trying to explain the meaning of the word 'Mount Everest' by pointing to it and saying its name as they fly over in a plane. The problem, he notes, is that it isn't clear from the act of pointing what is being referred to. We would point in exactly the same way to exactly the same thing if we were trying define 'Mount Everest', 'a mountain', 'rock', 'snow' (on top of the mountain), the colour 'white' (of the snow), the shape of a particular constellation of rocks etc. Moreover, it is not self-evident that pointing is an act of naming. I might be pointing to the mountain in the course of indicating my desire to climb it. Anybody who has tried to grasp a foreign language in action will recognize this problem. Unless we know that something is being named and what, specifically, it is (a colour, shape, object, category of objects etc.), the act of pointing whilst repeating certain words can be more confusing than enlightening. Needless to say, the process is even more complex when an infant is learning their first language and hasn't learned to make the distinction between, for example, objects, their colour, their shape etc. Even the act of pointing is ambiguous and presupposes convention according to Wittgenstein. He notes that dogs, for example, often stare at the finger when having something pointed out them. They do not get that they are supposed to 'follow' the finger to whatever it is pointing towards.

So how do words become meaningful? The bottom line, for Wittgenstein, is a pattern of consistent use, a convention, which can be formulated in the manner of a rule. To understand the word 'Everest' is not to associate it with a particular mountain in Nepal but to be able to use it in ways consistent with its pattern of use within a community of language users, to follow a shared rule (on rule following see Chapter 8).

Language is Mead's key example of significant symbols but he also suggests that natural responses, such as crying in pain, may acquire this status, insofar as they are universally recognized and acquire a function within a language game. Likewise hand signals, the signing system of the deaf community, flags and even clothing. All can function as 'moves' in a language game, thereby acquiring a symbolic significance.

Winch (1958) extends this paradigm to meaningful behaviour as a whole. Actions are meaningful, with or without language, he maintains, by virtue of the function they serve within a 'game'. Kicking a ball between two posts only gets the meaning 'scoring a goal', for example, by virtue of the game of football. And the same is true of writing a cheque, celebrating a birthday, giving an order and playing the fool. Each, qua meaningful action, presupposes a game and 'constitutive rules' or conventions (see Chapter 8) of the game for its meaning. Note, however, following what I have said about meaning above, that this is at least as much a matter of how we read the actions of others as how we act ourselves. In reading the action of the other I necessarily frame it in terms of established conventions which give it meaning.

This observation contributes to our account of intersubjectivity because it suggests that understanding between actors is achieved through their orientation to shared rules or conventions. The actions of the other are intelligible to me, not because I get inside their head but because we orient to the same rules and conventions – rules and conventions which neither of us have invented (except in the limit case of some artists) and both have learned through involvement in our wider community.

Before closing this section we should briefly note that shared conventions presuppose relatively cohesive networks for their emergence and reproduction (Milroy 1987). That is, they are reinforced to the extent that actors both encounter them and find them effective in most of their communicative exchanges because most of the people they engage with adhere to them too. Conversely, conventions are threatened to the extent that actors begin to interact with others who do not adhere to them (ibid.). It is for this reason that we find, for example, geographical clusters of and variations in linguistic use (e.g. regional accents and dialects) and, indeed, different languages.

Thought as internal conversation

Use of significant symbols does not only transform interaction, making it 'symbolic interaction' in Blumer's (1986) sense of the world, it equally transforms the social actor, heightening whatever nascent self-consciousness they enjoy by making them aware of 'what they are saying' and also setting in motion a process whereby the actor, affected by and responding to their own utterances, begins to interact with their self in a manner constitutive of reflective thought. This occurs firstly in the context of interaction with others. Speakers hear and respond to their own utterances as they engage with others. Over time, however, they replay such conversations in private, effectively conversing with their self.

This is crucial for Mead. Internal conversations are integral to what he means by 'mind' and 'thought'. To 'have' a mind is to think and to think is to engage in a conversation with oneself, a process which is only possible by way of language and internalization of the conversational form. In internal conversations, as in external conversations, we can propose ideas then criticize them, refine them, approve them etc. This dialogical process is the essence of mental life for Mead.

There are four points to note here. First, reflective thought occurs in language. We think and become aware of what we think (which is an integral aspect of thinking) by speaking, either to ourselves or to others. This is not a matter of language determining thought or vice versa. Rather, speech and thought are two sides of the same coin.

Second, I respond to my own thoughts, thereby giving them meaning. One (verbalized or written) thought triggers another and so on. This is the 'conversational' element referred to by Mead and it is essential to thought. It brings different points of view (see below) into dialogue, which is the essence of (especially rational) reflection, and allows for the formulation of new, synthetic or hybrid points of view.

Third, a degree of self-consciousness is generated here and, indeed, self-control. In becoming aware of my thoughts I become aware of myself as a thinker. Moreover, I can edit and rehearse what I am going to say in private before blurting it out and, as such, can work upon it to control its effects.

Finally, what Mead is suggesting is that 'mind' is an emergent property of social interaction. To think is to communicate, whether with others or with one's self. Eventually we learn to do this silently, to ourselves and in private but what we are doing silently, to ourselves and in private is what we have first learned to do out loud, with others, in public. Moreover, as I note below, internal conversations involve the perspectives or roles of others, as incorporated by us.

It is also important to Mead, however, that interaction and communication are modified by the 'thought' that emerges within them when significant symbols come into play. 'Mind' emerges within interaction but then also transforms and shapes it. Specifically, interaction becomes reflexive in the respect that participants monitor their own responses as well as those of the other, bringing an awareness of self into their interaction with the other. *Society, as we know it, is only possible on the basis of 'mindful' interaction according to Mead.* The coordination involved in even relatively simple and minor human encounters would not be possible in the absence of mindful reflexivity.

This argument allows for no reductionism. Mind is not straightforwardly reducible to interaction and society since interaction and society are modified by the emergence of mind, but equally interaction and society are not reducible to mind since mind only emerges within them. *Mind and society form part of an irreducible structure.*

To summarize this section, the process of expression using significant symbols brings a self-conscious actor, a thinker who exists for herself qua thinker, into being. This is an intersubjective, relational conception of the actor. Language is an emergent property of collective life, generated by interaction, and linguistic utterances are, in the first instance, public. Languages are, before anything else, means of communication. They emerge historically out of the efforts of actors to influence one another's conduct. That they also give rise to the internal conversations constitutive of reflective thought is a happy coincidence. To the extent that we are thinking beings, this is a side effect of the fact that we are social beings who communicate.

Particular and generalized others

Linguistic competence is one factor in the emergence of reflective thought and thinking actors but it is not the only one. Equally important is the ability and inclination to assume the role or perspective of others in relation to ourselves. When replying to our own utterances in an internal conversation, Mead notes, we do not reply only as ourselves. We anticipate the likely responses of others and bring these into the conversation too. Perhaps we imagine that certain others in our circle will disagree with a plan we are contemplating and, anticipating their likely objections, we bring these objections into our dialogue. As we turn from claim to counter-claim we swap roles from advocate to critic and then back. We are not forced to concede to the imagined response of our various alters and, of course, we may well imagine a range of responses. We may concede, either to the force of a better argument or in anticipation of sanctions, but there is no necessity to this. The outcome is worked out within the internal dialogue, and dialogue, as we discussed in relation to Gadamer (1989) in Chapter 3, can be unpredictable. It follows its own path.

The point here is that thought itself, as a process, is inherently dialogical and social. Thought necessarily transcends the individual because it entails an interplay of points of view. This may be achieved by the individual, in a simulated dialogue which draws from perspectives with which they are familiar, but this not only presupposes the actor's familiarity with those specific viewpoints, it presupposes an actor who is aware of others and of other points of view; an actor who has become aware of their own particularity and to some extent therefore liberated from it or lifted out of it through their encounter with others. This theme is explored in more detail in the next chapter. For present purposes it must suffice to offer a few basic observations on the incorporation of others within internal conversations.

An internal conversation can be akin to a rehearsal for specific interactions, in the manner described by Goffman (1959). One purpose of conversing with ourselves is to prepare ourselves for an engagement with others. This is not necessary, however. Even in our more abstract reflections we borrow the thoughts and perspectives of others, sometimes purely for our own purposes. Sociological essays in which 'Mead would argue . . .' and 'Merleau-Ponty would reply . . .' are one example of this. The sociologist is under no illusions about meeting these long-deceased figures or having to persuade them of an idea. But if the perspective offered by such writers strikes a chord then it becomes a cultural–cognitive resource for the sociologist. When thinking through a problem they slip into the role of Mead, Merleau-Ponty or whoever as a means of working out a puzzle, utilizing that role as a way of thinking through and resolving it. Moreover, they bring such figures into dialogue with others who have very different views: 'Mead would say . . . but Durkheim would reply . . . etc.'

The various imagined alters who enter into our internal dialogues may be 'named'. We may be aware, for example, that we are anticipating the likely response of our spouse when we contemplate a night on the town. This is not necessary, however. We may have internalized the role or perspective of a significant other but ceased to attribute their thoughts specifically to them and perhaps lost (or repressed) the ability to do so. We engage with 'a point of view' or perhaps just 'have a feeling' without knowing where (or who) it comes from. In all cases, however, the other enters into thought.

Furthermore, Mead notes that, in addition to specific others, we can orient in our thoughts to the role or perspective of 'generalized others'. By this he means that we absorb and anticipate views and beliefs which are characteristic of whole communities or social circles that we belong to, rather than just specific individuals. The perspective of the generalized other may be enshrined in written texts (e.g. holy books) or codified systems (e.g. laws and rule books) or it may consist of the relatively inarticulate dispositions and prejudices that are shared within a community, that the individual has developed a sense of by living in that community. Again the actor is not forced to agree with or concede to the view of generalized others. The relationship is dialogical. But the actor is aware of the perspective of generalized others – again, either named or anonymous – and will take their perspective into account, even in private reflections.

Although there is some equivocation, it is generally agreed that generalized others are plural for Mead (Blumer 2004). Like Simmel (1955), he conceives of the individual as occupying multiple social 'circles', some of which are nested and concentric, others of which are distinct and intersect only through that one individual. Insofar as these communities make competing claims upon the actor, this 'web of group affiliations' (Simmel 1955) can generate the need for internal conversations. Competing claims and prescriptions generate a tension which the actor must seek to resolve for their self through discourse. This might be difficult but, as Simmel notes, it can also be liberating. The individual can bring the different perspectives into play, against one another, carving out a distinct perspective for their self in the process. Moreover, the existence of distinct and competing perspectives allows the individual to see through claims to naturalness or universality made by any one of them. The self, constituted through reflexivity, becomes more cosmopolitan. How we acquire the capacity and tendency to take the role of the other is the topic for the next chapter.

Conclusion

Many of the issues raised in this chapter are discussed further in the next. For this reason it is not appropriate to draw strong conclusions yet. In essence, however, the chapter began with an outline and critique of the Cartesian model of privatized subjectivity which informs individualism. Our subjective lives, I argued, are not centred upon themselves and resident 'within our heads'. Our subjective lives involve us in the world and thereby in the subjective lives of others. Moreover, we are not as transparent to ourselves as Descartes suggests nor are others so opaque. We come to self-awareness and self-knowledge in the context of our interactions and relations with others and, in many respects, this awareness and knowledge are coterminous with and akin to our awareness and knowledge of others (as I discuss further in the next chapter).

The point has not been to deny the capacity for the reflective thought that Descartes deems constitutive of our being, nor indeed the fact that our subjective lives can be privatized and rendered inaccessible to others. I have suggested that we do, through interaction, become capable of reflective thought and there is no question that we can learn to keep our thoughts to ourselves and strategically manage the information flow emanating from and around us. However, my contention is that these possibilities are secondary and derived rather than pri-mordial. We are, in the first instance, practical beings, engaged with others with all that we are, if not entirely comprehensible (to us or anybody else), at least on view. Our 'higher' cognitive functions are emergent from this more primordial relational nexus as is our sense of our individual subjective life and any desire that we may have to make and keep it private.

Descartes and many philosophers following in his wake have wondered how private subjectivities ever achieve awareness of one another so as to generate an intersubjective world. I am suggesting that they have the process the wrong way round. We do not move from the private world of self and mind to intersub-jectivity and the social world; rather, self and mind take shape in an intersubjective context which necessarily precedes them. I continue this argument in the next chapter.

6   I, me and the other

In the final section of Chapter 5 I introduced the idea that actors can imaginatively assume the role or perspective of both specific others whom they know and also what Mead (1967) calls the 'generalized other', that is, the collective view of a community, social circle or network to which they belong, where such a view exists and is known to them. Actors play the roles of others in their 'internal conversations', I argued, and this role play is essential to the dialogical process at the root of thought. This chapter begins with a further reflection upon such role playing, tracing it back to early childhood and exploring its role in the emergence of both self-consciousness (our sense of self) and our intersubjective aware-ness of the perspectives of others. The aim of the chapter is to advance our understanding of (especially symbolic) interaction and relationships by way of a sustained reflection upon the constitution of both 'self' and 'other' or rather their co-constitution.

I begin with a reflection upon the way in which children learn of and learn to take the perspectives or roles of others by means of play and games, exploring the role of this discovery in the origin of a sense of both self and other. This is then developed through a discussion of Mead's (1967) conception of I and me (a conception persuasively pre-figured in the work of Adam Smith (2000)). Building upon this I suggest that our senses of both self and other, as well as relations of self and other, are built in some part through stories or narratives which give them form. The latter part of the chapter then turns to consider the importance of recognition in social relations and also the ways in which actors manage the information flow regarding their self in relations with others.

Playing the role of the other

As we move through our life we are constantly encountering new alters, specific and generalized, whose perspectives we must incorporate if we are to survive socially. Successful interaction in any given social circle requires that we have a sense of or feel for the ways in which others think and typically react. We need to be able to anticipate their likely responses by putting ourselves in their shoes, whether for strategic reasons or in order to achieve the empathic bond that lies at the heart of most intimate relations. Mead (1967) famously explains our initial incorporation of the roles of others, however, in terms of childhood play and games. Very young children, he notes, typically play at being other people, especially those upon whom they are most dependent or who occupy authoritative positions in relation to them (e.g. parents, nursery teachers, police officers). Within a matter of seconds the infant might move through various roles, recruiting teddies and other props to sustain a complex and multi-vocal interaction. First they are 'daddy', then the mechanic who mends his car. Next they endeavour, as 'mummy', to keep the children quiet and so on. Such play, Mead argues, is the prototype of adult role taking and internal conversation. It is the learning process that allows the actor, in adult life, to take the role of others and anticipate their responses. Indeed, it is the process through which the child learns that others have perspectives of their own and thereby learns of the particularity of their own perspective, effectively becoming self-aware. In addition, it is the basis of both empathy and a sense of justice. Our sense of justice is shaped by the intersubjective recognition that others are beings who think, feel and have plans and interests as we do.

The infant who engages in such play is not trying to empathize with others. Nor, at first, do they have a developed sense of others as subjective beings. The infant is copying the typical behaviour patterns of those around them in an effort to master and make sense of their environment. Others have an impact upon them and playing at being others is their way of making sense of this in an effort to control it. Play is a way of 'thinking through' events and significant environmental factors (mainly other people) for an infant who lacks the cultural and cognitive resources available to the adult. It has the side effect, however, that the child learns to see the world from the point of view of others and thus learns that others have such views. Playing at being others gives them a sense of the perspectives of others and, indeed, of that fact that self and other enjoy distinct perspectives. By incorporating the role of the other they increasingly appreciate that there are different sides to a story and different ways of viewing the same event. Like a method actor, but without the foreknowledge or intention, the child forms an impression of what it is like to be 'dad' by playing at 'dad'.

Moreover, they better equip themselves for future interaction by developing a capacity to anticipate likely responses of typical actors to typical situations and thus to avoid undesirable consequences. They form a 'typification' of 'dad', in Schutz's (1972) sense, for example, and incorporate 'dad', qua typification, within their own internal conversations and imaginative life. 'Dad' becomes a resource that the infant can use to think things through and even to manage her thoughts and feelings. Insofar as her dad reassures her, for example, by telling her not to worry and that things will be OK, she can, by playing dad, assume this calming role for herself. Dissociating from her own role and assuming 'dad's' affords both distance from the immediacy of the problem and a methodology for tackling problems. She knows what 'dad' would say in this situation and she simulates his response. Equally, however, 'dad' might be an alarm bell that rings when the child is about to or has just misbehaved. She can anticipate his response and take this into account, either by catching and stopping herself from committing the misdemeanour, finding a way of disguising it or having a good excuse ready. Having been incorporated, 'dad' becomes a 'voice' in the emergent conversations that comprise the infant's mental life.

Play, as Mead conceives it, only affords the child a sense of the perspective of specific, significant others. It does not yet afford access to the more abstract perspective of generalized others. This skill, he suggests, is acquired in game playing – which the child is prepared for by way of ever more complex forms of play, which gradually build up its social competence and awareness. Games involve abstract and generalized rule structures, principles and purposes. And they involve sets of interacting roles (our team, their team, winger, forward, goalie) which players must orient to simultaneously. That is to say, they involve a 'generalized other'. As such they emulate the basic characteristics of the adult social world and prepare the child for life therein. Mastery of these practices, becoming a competent player, inculcates the dispositions and know-how necessary to interaction in adult worlds.

Through play and especially games the child learns to orient to rules and to their duties. They learn to play fairly, to respect rules and to work with others. Games are also competitive, however, and develop the child's capacity for strategic interaction. Learning to play a game such as cards or chess, for example, does not consist only in learning the rules but also in learning to anticipate the moves of one's opponent and perhaps also deduce what they have in their 'hand' and how they will play it. For all of the many limits of the game as a metaphor for social life, it does involve the blend of convention, norms, cooperation and strategic competition that children will face as mature social actors in the wider world. And for this reason games are an important relational form which shape actors and prepare them for this wider world.

Intersubjectivity and the self process

In discussing the way in which children 'take the role of the other' Mead is engaging with the issue of empathy introduced in Chapter 4. By learning to play the roles of others the child learns to appreciate their different perspectives. This empathy forms a bond between the actor and her other(s). To form a relationship with another, for Mead, is, amongst other things, to incorporate their perspective amongst the plurality of perspectives that constitute one's own. This has a cognitive dimension – others are interlocutors in our internal conversations – but it has affective dimensions too. Our relations to others always entail an emotional intention, in the phenomenological sense. We perceive them through an affectively tinged lens: with affection, fear, loathing or whatever. And our internalized representations of them carry this same tinge. To invoke the response of another whom we fear in an internalized conversation invokes fear. Of course we may maintain an attitude of relative emotional neutrality towards some individuals with whom we engage. Even emotional neutrality is an affective intention, however. As Heidegger (1962) notes, emotion is never absent from our connections to others and the world. It is not something that we turn on and off, such that we are sometimes emotional and other times not. Our perspective always maintains an affective dimension. What varies is the flavour of affect.

On another level, the empathic connection generated by our internalization of the perspective of others is itself an emotional bond. It entails that, at one level, we feel with and for them. Events that happen to them impact emotionally upon us. We are happy or upset 'for' them. Likewise, we anticipate their likely response in planning our own actions. Later in the chapter I will suggest that this process is enabled through the building of shared narratives. Before I do, however, it is important to consider other, important outcomes of the internalization of the perspectives of others.

I have described the outcomes hitherto in terms of a process of relationship formation between actors but this is also a process which transforms the actor herself. On one level, for example, she becomes an empathic actor. She is attuned to the perspectives of others in a way that she was not previously. Moreover, she is further modified by the specificities of the particular others whose roles she internalizes. The representations of specific and generalized others which she forms become an active part of her, making her capable of internal conversation and forming the basis of her conscience, sense of duty and perhaps also 'inner demons'.

At another level still the internalization of the perspectives of others, both specific and generalized, is integral to the ongoing processes constitutive of self-hood. To acquire a sense of self is to acquire a sense of one's own particularity, a sense that one's perspective on events is one perspective amongst many. It is Mead's (1967) contention that the child does not have this sense before they try out the roles of others but that they acquire it by doing so. By copying the roles of others they acquire a sense of the perspectives of others and come to experience the world as an object upon which multiple perspectives can be and are taken. They thereby decentre their own perspective, coming to see it as one amongst many. They shake off what is sometimes confusingly referred to as childish 'egocentrism' and begin to appreciate that others have different experiences of the world to their own. This generates a sense of self because it dissuades the child from conflating their perspective on the world with the world itself, and from generalizing their thoughts, experiences, feelings, desires etc. to everybody else. They learn to recognize their experience as both distinctive and specific to them.

Furthermore, self-hood is generated in the respect that the child, in taking the perspectives of others, learns to see their self as an object in the experience of those others. They constitute their self as an object within their own flow of experience. The child who comforts a doll as they have been comforted by a parent is, through the mediation of the doll and the role of the other, developing a reflexive relationship with their self. They are relating to their self, via the doll, as an object upon which a perspective can be taken. Likewise, the child who 'keeps the children quiet whilst mummy is on the phone', learns to take an external perspective upon their own 'noise' and more generally their actions and impacts. Again, they become an object to their self.

What Mead is describing here is precursor to and pre-requisite of Cooley's (1902) 'looking glass' process, discussed in Chapter 5. Learning that the other has a perspective and more specifically a perspective upon them makes the child receptive to that perspective. In acquiring from others the general disposition to view themselves as an other, the infant also sensitizes their self to a process in which the specific content of others' views of them enters into their own sense of self. As I noted in Chapter 5, however, we should not view the actor as a mere sponge, absorbing the views of others. Selves are constructed in inter-action, that is to say, in a two-way process. These points require further exploration.

I and me

We are not immediately transparent to ourselves, according to Mead, and do not, in the first instance, feature as objects in our own experience. Our experience, as noted in the previous chapter, is an experience of the world beyond us. We can only achieve a purchase upon ourselves by achieving some 'distance' from ourselves, a distance facilitated by assuming the role of the other. Adam Smith has a similar view:

> We can never survey our own sentiments and motives, we can never form any judgement concerning them, unless we remove ourselves, as it were, from our own natural station, and endeavour to view them as at a certain distance from us. But we can do this in no other way than by endeavouring to view them with the eyes of other people.
>
> (Smith 2000: 161)

Likewise Merleau-Ponty:

> For myself I am neither 'inquisitive', nor 'jealous', nor a hunchback, nor a civil servant. . . . Consciousness can never objectify itself . . . [actors] can only do so by comparing themselves with others, or seeing themselves through the eyes of others . . .
>
> (Merleau-Ponty 1962: 434)

The sociological import of this view is made clear by Smith in a later passage:

> Were it possible that a human creature could grow up to manhood [sic] in some solitary place, without any communication with his own species, he could no more think of his own character, of the propriety or demerit of his sentiments and conduct, of the beauty or deformity of his own mind, than of the beauty or deformity of his own face. All these are objects which he cannot easily see, which naturally he does not look at, and with regard to which he is provided with no mirror which can present them to his view. Bring him into society and he is immediately provided with the mirror which

he wanted before. It is placed in the countenance and behaviour of those he lives with.

(Smith 2000: 162)

Where Descartes believes that the individual knows their own mind and self immediately (see Chapter 5), Mead and Smith claim that we enjoy no immediate knowledge of self and only achieve such reflexivity by assuming the role of another (specific or generalized). This is not a direct reversal of the Cartesian position, however. The point is not that we know others before we know ourselves but rather that learning to assume the role of others and internalizing the roles of others (specific and generalized) affords us a perspective upon both self and other. Both 'self' and 'other' come into being for us at the same time and by the same process. Knowing of the existence of others reveals the particularity of the self and assuming the roles of others provides a vantage point from which one's 'self' can become an object of one's own experience.

Self-hood, as conceived here, emerges from and is sustained by a reflexive process. The actor assumes the role of another in order to 'turn back' upon their self and constitute their self as an object. For both Mead and Smith this entails the actor, in a manner of speaking, splitting herself into two. She becomes both a known object and the subject who knows that object:

> When I endeavour to examine my own conduct, when I endeavour to pass sentence upon it, and either to approve or condemn it, it is evident that, in all such cases, I divide myself, as it were, into two persons; and that I, the examiner and judge, represent a different character from that other I, the person whose conduct is examined into and judged of.

(Smith 2000: 164)

Mead refers to these two 'phases' of the self-process as 'the I' and 'the me' and he stresses that their separation is temporal. The actor doesn't literally split into two agencies. Rather, they alternate between roles; acting, then turning back upon their action to make sense of it before reverting to action and so on. Although Mead's usage slips somewhat, 'the I' is the actor in this process and 'the me' is a historical reconstruction of itself that the I forms in moments of self-reflection. It is an image of self.

Mead's conception of 'the I' and 'the me', as with many aspects of his theory, has a strong anti-Cartesian aspect. Descartes' 'mind' is self-transparent. It enjoys immediate knowledge of itself. Mead's 'I' isn't and doesn't. Not only does the I have to adopt the role of the other in order to reflexively turn back upon itself but it comes to know itself by means of re-construction, that is, by a reflection backwards upon what it has done, said, thought etc. The I can project itself imaginatively, qua me, into future situations but the image and knowledge that it has of itself is always derived from historical reconstruction. Indeed, there is always a temporal lag between the I and the me. The I can never catch itself in the act. The act of self-examination which constitutes the me necessarily remains itself unexamined, escaping scrutiny, unless captured by a further, later examination; but then this later examination will be unexamined and so on. Ryle captures this point nicely:

> [M]y commentary upon my performances must always be silent about one performance, namely itself, and this performance can be the target only of another performance. Self-commentary, self-ridicule and self-admonition are logically condemned to eternal penultimacy. Yet nothing that is left out of any commentary or admonition is privileged thereby to escape comment or admonition forever. On the contrary, it may be the target of the very next comment or rebuke.
>
> (Ryle 1949: 186)

In this respect the I, qua actor in the present tense, is always necessarily elusive for Mead:

> As given, [the self] is a 'me', but it is a me that was an 'I' at an earlier time. If you ask, then, where directly in your own experience the 'I' comes in, the answer is that it comes in as a historical figure [i.e. as a 'me'].
>
> (Mead 1967: 174)

This suggests that our sense of self is achieved within a narrative mode (see also Crossley 2000). Actors build a sense of 'me' through a historical reconstruction of scenes, dramas or sequences of events in which they have been involved, that is, by way of stories in which they are the central protagonist. The me is a character in a story told by the I.

Given that the purposes which occasion self-reflection are manifold so too are the stories told and the consequent constructions of the me. Certainly the actor will take on different identities in their interaction with others, as the demands of situations vary. We are children to our parents, parents to our children, friends to our friends, employees to our employers and so on. Each of these identities may involve a different 'story' and a different 'character'. Before we get too carried away, however, it is worth noting that one key function of self-narratives for the I who constructs them is to pull the various aspects of the individual's life, their diverse roles or identities, together, reconciling their competing commitments, identities and the demands made upon them. Moreover, as Simmel (1955) and White (2008) both suggest, switching between different situated identities may actually generate and reinforce a 'meta identity' which, though emergent from them, is experienced as underlying them. Switching relativizes situated identities for the actor and distances her from them, generating a higher-level story of a 'me' who pre-exists and performs them.

The boundaries of the me are not necessarily those of the individual's own body. Cooley (1902), for example, suggests that an individual's possessions may enter into their sense of self, as evidenced by the sense of violation that individuals sometimes experience when, for example, their house is burgled or their possessions stolen. Their house, their 'space' and their 'things' are extensions of their self, props which are integral to sustaining a particular narrative projection of 'me' – and sustaining it not only for the other but for their self too. Goffman (1961) makes a very similar point. The attack upon the self in a total institution is effected in some part by the removal of the individual's private property. Stripping them of their 'stuff' goes some way to stripping them of their self and identities, weakening their defences against externally imposed regimes of reform.

In a different vein, the me may extend beyond the individual to a dyad or group, becoming a 'we' or 'us'. Coleman (1975) makes a very interesting use of Mead in this respect. Coleman is a rational action theorist (RAT) and, as such, faces the usual problem of how to reconcile the selfishness ordinarily attributed to actors within RAT with the many empirical examples of apparent altruism that critics of the approach point to. In his case he is prepared to run with the counter-examples to extremes, considering considerable acts of self-sacrifice that actors are prepared to make on behalf of others or the groups to which they belong. One solution that he proposes focuses upon social networks and the incentives they offer for self-sacrifice (Coleman 1988). I discuss this briefly in Chapters 8 and 9. Another, however, draws upon Mead. The self whose interests selfish actors seek to maximize is the me, in Mead's sense, Coleman (1975) argues, and the me is a construct which may extend beyond the biological individual to incorporate others and even whole communities. The me may be collective, such that the 'selfish' pursuit of interests is, from another perspective, altruistic. The soldier who risks their life for their country is an obvious example of this. They act strategically in pursuit of the perceived interests of their national 'me' or 'we'. The implications and premises of this position are not fully worked out by Coleman and I do not have the space to examine them here. For our purposes, however, the argument illustrates an important way in which the me might extend beyond the physical boundaries of the biological individual with important sociological consequences. Mead's conception of the me, because of the emphasis it puts upon both imagination and re-construction, is particularly well suited to this development. Our sense of who we are takes shape within an imaginative discourse, a narrative, and from this point of view it is perfectly possible that the identity constructed is a we. Stories of 'we' abound in social movements for example (Tilly 2002).

Stories are the means by which we make sense of our self and past actions. They are equally a means, however, of projecting ourselves in the future. We can project our 'me' into the future by means of an imaginative, anticipatory construction of future dramas and events. Moreover, stories contribute to the shaping of our (future) actions. On one level, for example, we can rehearse our part in the dramas we imagine ourselves likely to face in the immediate future: an interview, a date, a significant event. Moreover, stories and storytelling, both individual and collective, furnish the 'definition of the situation' that many sociologists deem central both to the steering of social (inter)action and to academic attempts to understand it. Through stories the actor defines both the scenario in which they will act and the character they will play (hero, lover, sympathetic friend). Of course the scene may play out rather differently if others have 'plotted' it differently or simply because unexpected things happen. This will lead the actor to rethink the story retrospectively and perhaps re-narrate their role. Actions and stories each inform the other in a chronic process of renegotiation, a process which produces, in the narrative mode, a 'me'.

It is tempting to think of Mead's 'I' as somehow pre-given and unsocialized. It is neither. In the first instance, only the I acts and, as such, all of the acquired social competence involved in action belong to it. The I uses language to construct its 'me' narratives and, as such, is thoroughly socialized. Likewise, the desires and impulses embodied in the I often manifest a distinctly social character – the desire for consumer goods being an obvious example. The I is a socialized and competent actor. More importantly, however, Mead is careful to argue that the I takes on its identity (as I) only in relation to the me. The I, as he defines it, 'is the response of the individual to the attitude of the community as this appears in his own experience [via the me]' (Mead 1967: 196). In other words, it is always a partner in dialogue. It 'brings things to the table', so to speak, sometimes perhaps socially unacceptable 'things', but qua action or actor it always responds to the (internalized) attitudes of the community and, indeed, to stories of the me. The I is only I in relation me. Note here also that both I and me are constantly in process. They emerge and take shape in interaction (with one another). And they evolve by means of this interaction.

Empathic narratives

Stories are also important in relation to our understanding of others. Indeed it is my contention that our sense of both self and other are embedded in stories. I touched upon this point in Chapter 4 when I considered Adam Smith's (2000) reflections upon empathy. Smith, I noted, claims that it is easier to put ourselves into the shoes of others when we can set their conduct within a context. If we see an individual drop a hammer on their foot we will wince with imagined pain before we have even registered their own response. However, if they appear to be in pain but we cannot work out why, it is much more difficult to empathize, even if the pain is evidently much greater. We can't 'get' the pain, empathically, because we don't know its 'story'.

Empathy, from this point of view, is not so much a matter of projecting ourselves into the 'head' of the other, as some early theories of intersubjectivity suggest (e.g. Husserl 1990). Rather, it is a matter of putting ourselves into the situation or rather 'the story' of the other. Our empathy for and identification with literary protagonists illustrate this. Literary protagonists exist entirely within a story. They have no existence outside of it. No 'head' or anything else for us to project ourselves into; only a story. And yet we can and do empathize with them and feel deeply moved, even motivated by their exploits. It is my contention that the situation is fundamentally the same in relationship to real people. We empathize and identify with others by way of their stories, stories which emerge in discourse between us.

This narrative mode of intersubjectivity is not 'second best' to something which might be more intimate because everything that I have discussed in both this chapter and the one preceding it suggests that actors relate to themselves by means of narratives too. Indeed, I have just argued that the I only knows itself as 'me' and that the me is a character in a story that the I tells about itself. We know others as we know ourselves; by way of stories. We do not learn about ourselves by looking inwards. Our conscious experience is intentional consciousness of objects external to us, a bond to the world. To inspect the contents of our consciousness is to inspect the objects in the world of which we are conscious. We can only make sense of ourselves by reflecting upon our actions within the contexts that lend them an intelligibility, that is, to set them within a narrative. Relationships are built and intersubjectivity, at least in this empathic sense of the word, is achieved by way of the building and sharing of stories.

In a similar way, as White (1992, 2008) notes, relationships themselves are storied. We collectively build relationships by building and telling stories of 'we' or 'us', exchanging and integrating accounts of how we met and what we have done together; accounts which indicate what we mean to each other, how far our relationship extends and perhaps also where its boundaries are. And these stories are intersubjective in the respect that they are crafted between the parties to them. The parties may not agree. They may argue about 'what really happened' and may have a different sense about what their relationship means but that meaning has to be constantly negotiated and renegotiated between them in and through stories.

Recognition and the public 'me'

The I constructs a me by assuming the role of the other and turning back upon their self. There are two aspects to this process, one involving form, the other, content. Learning to assume the role of the other is a practice or technique, at once imaginative and disciplined, which allows the actor to stand back from their own actions and thoughts and to subject them to a critical, reflexive interrogation. The actor can play devil's advocate against their self. This might involve the actor challenging their self in ways that others would not and in relation to thoughts and issues that others are unaware of. The actor borrows the form of the other's role, not necessarily its content. They can imagine what the other would say if the other knew what they know.

However, they may also internalize the content of others' views, coming to view their self as others view them. As Smith's (2000) above-cited references to 'mirrors' and Cooley's (1902) notion of the 'looking glass self' both suggest, we are all to some extent dependent upon others for information about ourselves. We are in many respects our own 'blind spot', unable to perceive attributes that are clear to others. Moreover, judging our abilities and dispositions may necessitate intersubjective conferral. When learning to do something, for example, we may need to ask experts if our performance or 'answers' are correct. We can see perfectly well what we have done but, as we are still learning, don't know if it is right and don't feel able to rely upon our sense that it is.

As I noted in Chapter 5, the exaggeration involved in early labelling theories has generated an aura of suspicion around the 'looking glass' conception of self but this conception is important and labelling theory, when formulated in a modest way, is important too. We do not passively absorb all that others reflect back to us about ourselves. We can, within our 'internal conversations', subject others' judgements of us to critical reflection and may decide that their judgements of us are wrong or unfair. Furthermore, as I discuss in more detail below, we actively present ourselves to others and seek to control the flow of information surrounding ourselves in an effort to, amongst other things, manipulate the view that others have of us. But we do depend upon feedback (explicit and tacit) from others in our efforts to construct a me because so much of what matters about ourselves is only perceptible to us by way of the mirror image reflected back to us in the reactions of others.

Also important in this context is the recognition or approval of others. It is widely acknowledged in both social science and philosophy that human beings strive to be recognized and valued by others. Having achieved a sense of ourselves by taking the role of the other we strive to have that self validated by others and perhaps also to establish our superiority over them – a precarious business, as Hegel's (1979) various reflections on 'lordship and bondage' testify. It is not enough for a human being to define their self in a particular way, according to this idea. Our awareness of the perspectives of others generates a felt need for that definition to be acknowledged and recognized by others. I am aware that I exist for others, that they too entertain conceptions of me and thus that my 'me' is, in some respects, a public phenomenon. The feedback which others offer with respect to myself is not merely a source of information for me, therefore. It variously feeds and starves, consummates and thwarts a desire that I have to realize myself, my me, intersubjectively. As Hegel puts it:

> [S]elf-consciousness exists in and for itself when, and only by the fact that, it so exists for another; that is, it exists only in being acknowledged.
>
> (Hegel 1979: 11)

The value and reality of my me, for myself, is dependent upon its value and reality for others (particular and generalized) to whom I am related. Smith puts a further intersubjective spin on this when he claims:

> The love and admiration which we naturally conceive for those whose conduct we approve of, necessarily dispose us to desire to become the objects of the like agreeable sentiments. . . . the anxious desire that we ourselves should excel, is originally founded in our admiration of the excellence of others.
>
> (Smith 2000: 166)

There is an intersubjective reversibility involved here. The value of the regard of others is apparent to us from our own regard for them. Knowing what it is to admire another, we want to be admired and, indeed, to be able to admire ourselves by assuming the role of others who admire us.

Presentation and privacy

The desire to be recognized fuels a range of actions, including both acts of conformity and status contests which might be socially destructive – again Hegel's (1979) 'fight to the death' springs to mind. It also fuels the strategic conduct that Goffman (1959) refers to as 'presentation of self'. In what remains of this chapter I want to trace some of these possibilities.

Much of what I have discussed with respect to intersubjectivity so far, in both this chapter and the previous one, has challenged the Cartesian notion that human subjectivity is private and thus only available to the individual herself. This is true at a philosophical level but at a sociological level we are both inclined and required to keep aspects of our subjective life private. Reflective thought, for example, presupposes language, which is a public resource and a social structure (see Chapter 5), but having learned to speak out loud and read out loud we learn to do so to ourselves and silently, effectively concealing our reflections from others and rendering them private. The self is not by nature private but it is privatized through social experience. There may be good strategic reasons for this. Like a poker player we may not want to show our hand until it is to our advantage to do so; or, rather, we learn through experience to play our cards close to our chest. Equally, however, we may be required by norms of politeness to do so. Indeed the norms of politeness and civilization that have emerged in recent centuries within western societies, notwithstanding a degree of 'informalization' in the period since the 1960s, have involved the privatization of a whole range of behaviours and aspects of life, putting them behind closed doors and rendering them unsuitable topics of conversation (Elias 1984, 1996; Wouters 1986). As Elias (1984) notes, the 'civilizing process' has involved the institution of a variety of social control mechanisms which, in turn, encourage self-control. From infancy onwards we learn to be discrete, to edit and filter what we say publicly about ourselves, and thus to render ever more aspects of our experience private.

In addition, since even the closest actors are not conjoined, what we know of one another is largely dependent upon acts of disclosure and what Goffman (1959) refers to as 'the presentation of self'. At one level Goffman's work on self-presentation is Durkheimian. Selves, perhaps on account of our modern 'cult of the individual' (Durkheim 1915), are 'sacred' objects and are oriented to as such within interaction. All parties to an interaction strive to maintain the self-integrity or 'face' of one another. Multiple rituals and resources are identified by Goffman as facilitating the achievement of this aspect of social order.

At another level, however, self-presentation is strategic and oriented to the achievement of advantage. With varying degrees of self-awareness, actors, both directly and indirectly, manage the flow of information regarding their selves so as to project a favourable and advantageous representation of their self. They strive to have a particular version of self recognized and validated.

At another level still, it is evident that, for Goffman (1961), this capacity to control information about oneself, to present oneself, is itself integral to our sense of self. This is particularly apparent in his discussions of situations in which such control is lost, situations where identity is 'spoiled' and, more specifically, in total institutions which undermine the actor's capacity to control self-presentation (Goffman 1961). Total institutions remove the capacity for self-presentation on two levels, for Goffman. First, they remove the trappings and props of self-hood. For example, inmates have regulation haircuts and uniforms, and are denied the right to personal possessions. They cannot build and project a distinct identity. Second, the total institution is 'totalizing' in the respect that every aspect of the individual's life is lived within it, with a strong information flow between different contexts of interaction. If an inmate misbehaves during breakfast this will be conveyed through a network of both guards and fellow inmates, such that it follows the individual throughout the rest of the day. The inmate lacks the power to edit incidents out of their story and thereby compartmentalize particular episodes and, indeed, particular identities. This, for Goffman, is one of the most difficult aspects of the total institution for the inmates. The inmate loses control over their 'self'.

What this suggests and what Goffman (1959) discusses more explicitly in *The Presentation of Self in Everyday Life*, is that most of us, most of the time, have the capacity to control information flow across the boundaries between the different circles in which we mix, and thereby to keep separate the identities which are specific to these circles. We tell different stories of self in the context of the different circles in which we mix. This might be strategic, in part, in the sense referred to above. Stories of self might be framed and edited so as to confer advantage. But it is also functional. Insofar as different circles cluster around different interests and purposes, the interests which their members have in one another vary too. They do not need to know everything and may have neither the time nor the inclination to learn.

This control over information flow, which is integral both to the construction/ maintenance of identities and to establishing the footing of interactions, is an integral aspect of the 'control' that White (1992, 2008) deems integral to social interaction and relationships (see also Chapter 4). Interaction and relations require that actors take up identities in relation to one another and frame their encounter accordingly. Information control is a crucial element in this process and, indeed, to the survival and viability of identities more generally. The control necessary to stable and coherent interactions and identities is, amongst other things, control over information flow.

Secrecy and disclosure in social relations

According to Simmel (1955), moreover, control over information flow is integral to the maintenance of relations. The interactions which give rise to and reinforce social relations are based in part upon disclosure but no less upon withholding information and the more general management of information and impressions. The front stage settings of social intraction, to borrow a metaphor from Goffman (1959), often only work successfully on the basis of 'backstage' activities which necessarily remain hidden. Concealment is necessary if interactions and relations are to achieve what the parties to them want to achieve. Furthermore, many beneficial social activities and practices, such as economic competition, demand a degree of secrecy if they are to be effective.

Secrecy and information flow also enter in Simmel's view, introduced in Chapter 3, that relations involve 'forces' of both attraction and repulsion. To form a relation with another involves bringing them closer to us but also holding them at a specific distance, a process which is played out in terms of information and self-disclosure. Relations won't work if the other knows everything about self. In part this harks back to my earlier point about information overload and the functional specificity of ties. The shopkeeper at the end of my road does not want to know my life story. I do not have the time to tell them, nor they the time to listen. Alternatively, I might undermine the authority and distance that I need in order to do my job if I reveal too many of my own worries and insecurities to colleagues or students. Even and perhaps especially in intimate relations, however, secrecy is important according to Simmel. Secrecy, he argues, maintains a tension in relations which is important to them. It keeps partners interesting to and interested in one another. Moreover, it affords space for imagination and fantasy, as actors project ideals onto one another. This point echoes conventional wisdom about relations – that an element of 'mystery' helps – and also anticipates more recent theories of 'narrativity', which suggest that it is the 'gaps' in a narrative that sustain our interest and draw us along it. Even a trivial fact can become exciting when an individual feels excluded from it, precisely because they are excluded and do not know that it is trivial. Withholding and the sense of not knowing generate a pleasurable tension in relations. If alter knows that ego has a secret then she will generally 'have to know' what it is and a game will ensue in which she will try to persuade ego to disclose.

Balance is important, however, as Simmel's references to both attraction and repulsion suggest. Too little information or too great an indication that (potentially) relevant information is being withheld may create bad relations and suspicion. Socially competent actors enjoy not only the competence to manage the information flow regarding their self but also to recognize that others are doing this too. This is part of the 'mystery' that keeps social life interesting but it is destructive if excessive. Whilst keeping secrets adds necessary vitality (and seductive mystery) to all relations, Simmel notes, it also generates a social distance and perhaps distrust which can prove damaging.

It is for this reason that relationship building, as noted in Chapter 3, often involves a process of gradual disclosure and 'letting the other in', that is, making them privy to aspects of one's story that are not widely known. Not only does this make interactions easier and facilitate greater empathy, from which the disclosing actor benefits, but it symbolizes greater closeness between the actors and forms part of a trust building exchange. By disclosing suppressed and secret chapters of their self-stories, actors make their selves vulnerable to one another and thereby demonstrate their trust in one another.

Conclusion

This chapter has developed the discussion of intersubjectivity begun in the last chapter. I have discussed the process of taking the role of the other and also the narratives in which a sense of self and other and relations between self and other are constructed and furnished with detail. Our sense of self, I argued, does not pre-exist our sense of the distinct subjective lives of others. The two are co-constitutive. We can have no sense of self in the absence of a sense of the existence of others, distinct from the self. I also suggested that both our sense of self and our sense of the other are built up through stories which we co-create. In this sense, contrary to those accounts of 'the problem of intersubjectivity' which wonder at how we ever 'get inside' the heads of others, our relationship to others is rooted in much the same process as our relationship to our self. In neither case do we look 'behind the forehead'. The self with which we identify is not a being to be found in the flow of our 'inner experience', which is no doubt why Hume (1984) famously failed to find it there. The self is a character in a story, with which we identity. And we can identify with other selves, projecting ourselves into their stories, much as we can our own.

The focus of the chapter has not only been upon the self, however. The process of self is important because it is integral to understanding the symbolic dimension of interaction. Selves take shape within symbolic interaction and a large part of what the symbolic dimension of interaction involves is the negotiation, presentation and defence of selves – both our own and those of our interlocutors. A focus on the symbolic dimension indicates to us just how the identities of the actors involved in interaction emerge from and are reproduced through such interaction. Interaction implicates the identities involved in it and, as such, in most instances, identity issues must be attended to in interaction.

Likewise relations, which are formed, built up and maintained by way of interaction. Indeed I have suggested that relations have (collective) identities which are storied in much the same way that individual identities are. Relations too rest in a sense and a story of who 'we' are, how we met and what we are about. Actors build up a sense of their relations through stories of those relations as, indeed, they build up relations by gradually (and selectively) revealing further aspects and incidents of their individual stories to one another. This is not the whole story of either relations or interactions, however. We have yet to consider what I referred to in earlier chapters as the exchange–power dimension of relations and interactions. That is the focus of the next chapter.

7   Exchange, sociability and power

In the preceding chapters I have discussed various dimensions of social interaction and I have sought to establish its irreducibility. Interaction involves emergent properties and some of these properties act back upon actors such that the latter are as much products of interaction as producers of it. We become linguistic, strategic, trusting, empathic (etc.) inter-actors by virtue of an interaction history in which we acquire and maintain these (variable) properties. Interaction shapes actors, making them capable of more sophisticated and complex interactions, which both shape them further and shape the wider network of interactions and relations comprising the structures of the social world (on structure see Chapters 8, 9 and 10). Moreover, network structure and the durable relations it entails both constrain interaction, such that each 'part' of the process affects every other part.

In this chapter I consider a further dimension of this interaction process: 'exchange'. As 'dimension' implies, 'exchange' is not a type of interaction so much an aspect of it. Some interactions are strongly focused around exchange. In other cases it is marginal. It is present in much interaction, however, and like the other dimensions discussed in this book, it manifests emergent aspects which render it irreducible and which shape those who engage in it. A reflection upon exchange will not only further enrich our understanding of interaction and relations, therefore, but also further bolster the contention that they constitute the *sui generis* basis of social life and thus the proper object of sociological inquiry.

As in other chapters my discussion of exchange is a springboard which allows me to consider much else besides. In this case, it allows me to briefly reconsider 'recognition' and to introduce Simmel's (1971) important notion of 'sociability'. In addition, it allows me, in the context of a discussion of coercion, to revisit the theme of conflict. More centrally still, however, the discussion of exchange leads directly into a discussion of resources and power.

The chapter begins with a brief outline of exchange theory, followed by a reflection upon Simmel's (1990) contention that economic exchange is a historically specific and variable social form. Anticipating the criticism that 'exchange theory' presents an amoral account of social relations which reduces them to an instrumental focus, I then consider (amongst other things) Simmel's (1971) conception of 'sociability' as a way of rebuffing these claims. I argue that relations of sociability are perfectly consistent with the exchange perspective and yet, by definition, are pursued as ends in themselves. Furthermore, acknowledgment of this fact should encourage us to think more laterally and less reductively about the exchange dimension. Finally, the chapter turns to power, considering forms rooted both in exchange (or more precisely exchange interdependency) and coercion. My concern here is both to bring 'power' into our consideration of relations and interactions, as it is essential to them, and also to outline a genuinely relational model of power. Many sociologists are inclined to think of power in substantialist terms, as a 'thing'. We need to guard against this and exchange affords a persuasive way of doing so.

Exchange

Human beings interact, in some part, because we need or want things from one another. We are interdependent. What we want need not be material. Indeed it is very often not. We might want recognition, stimulation or just company. But we want something. From this point of view interaction can be seen as an exchange of 'goods', a point which has been developed and extended, quite extensively, in the context of 'exchange theory' (Homans 1974; Blau 1986; Emerson 1962; Thibaut and Kelley 2007). In a study which anticipates exchange theory, Simmel (1990: 82) claims that 'most relationships between people can be considered as forms of exchange.' Having made this claim, Simmel devotes most of his attention to economic exchange, a form of exchange which he deems different from the others. However, other more-developed exchange theories have elaborated upon the manifold forms of non-economic exchange which weave the social fabric. From information, through support, to gossip, sex, domestic chores, deference, flattery and much besides, exchange theorists argue, interaction mobilizes and transfers goods and resources between actors. And this seems to be *a*, if not *the* point of interaction. We interact with others, in some part, to secure goods that we value.

Or rather, we form relationships upon this basis. When we interact with another for the first time or even the first few times we often have little idea whether and to what extent we will find the interaction rewarding, nor is that question necessarily on our mind. Although we can and sometimes do deliberately seek out specific alters or categories of alter to interact and form bonds with, as the concept of 'networking' suggests, many first meetings, though influenced by our lifestyles and therefore not random,[1] are entirely accidental from the actor's point of view. We 'happen' to meet in the course of doing something else. Over time, however, we will find interaction with some alters rewarding and others not so and, the theory claims, we will tend to gravitate towards those we find rewarding, initiating further, iterated interaction with them. Furthermore, we will tend to withdraw from relationships if and when the goods they provide dry up (although of course relationships might involve the exchange of multiple goods and might centre upon different goods at different points in time as, for example, friends become lovers, colleagues become friends etc.). Interactions may be 'accidental' but relationships, with the repeated interaction they entail, are not. Chance interaction gives rise to more durable relations where parties to it discover a possibility for mutually beneficial exchange, and this constitutes an incentive for further interaction.

In many cases, moreover, actors in relationships come to depend upon one another for certain goods, whether support, fun or something more material. As such interdependency is a further dimension of relations deriving from exchange. Actors are not self-contained entities. They need one another both to survive and to realize their wants and plans. I will suggest later that interdependency is a basis from which power emerges in social relations.

Exchange theory is often criticized for being narrowly utilitarian in its conception of actors and their relations. I will be revisiting this criticism at numerous points in this chapter in an effort to indicate that it need not be conceived in this way. As a first step in this direction, however, I want to suggest that exchange theory affords a valuable means of drawing out the purposive aspect of human relations. Insofar as relations are entered into voluntarily they must be 'about' something. We enter into them for a purpose. At one level this is all that exchange theory is arguing. To say that we enter into relations and interactions because we find them rewarding is simply to say that we act purposively in interactions and relations, that interaction has a point. If exchange theory allowed only a narrow range of possible rewards of interaction then we might have recourse to criticism but, on my reading, it doesn't. It invites us to explore the range of possible rewards that might be achieved both in human relations in general and in any particular relationship or set of relationships that we are analysing.

Furthermore, as such it also affords us a way of distinguishing relations. Some are focused upon material rewards; some perhaps upon status; others on sex; others still upon friendship or fun. Far from closing down our conception of human relations or reducing them to a common formula, exchange theory invites us to consider and classify their differences.

Conceiving of exchange in terms of purpose also draws out some of the similarities between exchange theory and Mead's (1967) symbolic interactionism, which is also premised upon the notion that human interaction is purposive. Mead is actually quite explicit in claiming that some interaction is based upon economic exchange, as I discuss further below. He makes an important contribution to our understanding of exchange relations. The somewhat wider definition of exchange that I am suggesting here is also commensurate with his general perspective, however. Mead stresses that interaction dynamics issue from the manner in which parties to an interaction affect one another: what they do to and for one another. Although exchange is not the only manifestation of this, it is one important dimension.

Resource mobilization and social integration

Although exchange theory is not tied to a crude material definition of the goods exchanged in social relations, it is important to recognize that crude material goods (or 'resources') play a very important role in the structure and dynamics of the social world. A further strength of exchange theory is that it both recognizes this fact and affords a useful and relational way of theorizing and exploring it.

The exchange perspective posits a vision of the social world in which resources are constantly being mobilized through exchange. Many perspectives in sociology attach significance to resources but that significance is taken for granted and it is often not clear how, within these perspectives, resources enter into our actions and relationships. Actors are said to 'have' different levels of resources and these resources are said to affect their life chances but exactly why and how is left vague. Exchange theory, by contrast, situates resources within interactions and relationships in which they are exchanged. As such resources become a crucial element in the very definition of interaction and relationships, and are seen to be woven into the fabric of the social world, a fabric which is constantly rewoven as resources are exchanged and circulate through social networks. Moreover, as I argue below, this allows for a properly relational conception of the value of social resources, rejecting the tendency amongst some sociologists to treat objects and services as valuable in and of themselves.

Exchange is important, according to exchange theory, because it binds the social world together by *making actors interdependent* – a view which echoes Durkheim's (1964) argument in *The Division of Labour*. The social world hangs together and achieves integration, to the extent that it does, because actors need and depend upon one another. Their lives interlock. Furthermore, according to Mead (1967), the social integration achieved by way of such material interdependence often precipitates further forms of integration and solidarity. Actors typically begin trading from a narrowly self-interested perspective, according to Mead. They trade because they want something from one another. Trading triggers a communicative process, however, in which actors learn about one another, learn to adopt one another's perspectives, and form moral bonds. In this way what Mead calls *the economic process* can begin to merge with and trigger what he calls *the religious process*:

> If you are going to carry on the economic process successfully, you have to come in closer and closer relationship with the other individual, identify yourself not simply in the particular matter of exchange, but finding out what he wants and why he wants it, what will be the conditions of payment, the particular character of the goods desired and so on. You have to identify yourself with him more and more.
>
> (Mead 1967: 298)

> In carrying out these activities the individual has set up a process of integration which brings the individuals closer together, creating the mechanism by which a deeper communication with participation is possible. . . . the two processes ['economic' and 'religious'] taken by themselves tend to bring about the larger community even when the persons have not any ideals for its

realisation. One cannot take the attitude of identifying himself with the other without in some sense tending to set up such communities.

(Mead 1967: 297)

Of course resources, their exchange and ownership are also a major cause of conflict and, as I argue later in the chapter, a basis of power in relationships. Mead recognizes this. His perspective on social life is, in many respects, centred upon conflict. His point, as I interpret it, however, is somewhat akin to Simmel's (1955) perspective on conflict, as discussed in Chapter 4. That is to say, he believes that exchange is a genuinely social form, which socializes those party to it and which may evolve into something other than or perhaps rather bigger than itself, giving rise to other relational dimensions. Like Simmel, Mead believes that concrete social relations comprise a tangle of sometimes conflicting elements and accents which variously rise to and fall from prominence within them across time. Thus relations of self-interested exchange may give rise to other, more cooperative and 'we focused' relations, just as more cooperative and 'we focused' relations may retain and/or collapse into more self-interested relations of exchange. The key point for now, however, is that exchange is a process which can draw actors into closer relations, collapsing the distance which it initially involves and perhaps drawing actors into closer, solidaristic bonds.

This argument maps onto and informs a widely cited distinction in the social networks literature between what are variously referred to as 'bonding and bridging capital' (Putnam 2000), 'brokerage and closure' (Burt 2005) and also 'strong and weak ties' (Granovetter 1973, 1983). Mead's 'religious process', in essence, involves the formation of strong, transitive[2] ties underwritten by shared beliefs and collective identities. It does not imply religion, as such, but rather, as in Durkheim (1915), fundamental tribal groupings. Economic ties, by contrast, are weaker and intransitive.[3] They are motivated by self-interest, at least in the respect that actors engage entirely for the purposes of securing goods by means of exchange, and they tend therefore to reach outside tribal groupings. Indeed, they 'bridge' (Putnam 2000) or 'broker' (Burt 2005) between these otherwise 'closed' and tightly 'bonded' groupings. That Mead should have distinguished between these two types of ties and hinted at the network figurations they entail is significant, not least because these types and figurations are central to contemporary debates on both social capital and the small world networks discussed in Chapter 10 (Prell 2009). More significant still, however, is the fact that he envisages a social process in which weak exchange relations give rise to stronger and more solidaristic bonds, effectively enlarging the social group.

Exchange, for Mead, is a mechanism which can lead to the formation of solidaristic bonds and a fusion of groups. It creates and enlarges 'society'. Of course it is just one mechanism and is counteracted by others which lead to schisms, conflict and so on but it is clearly an important one and one which operates on different levels, from children in a playground whose exchanges of goods and services lead to pacts between their gangs, to nations whose relations of plunder, piracy and warfare give way to trade or exchange (see below), which in turn encourages the formation of trading blocks and even international political bodies. Exchange has a socializing influence. As we will see below, Simmel (1990) adopts a similar view.

Value, forms and justice

Thibaut and Kelley (2007) claim that the subjective value of whatever is exchanged in social relations, the value goods have for individual actors, is established by way of comparison. They suggest that actors compare (1) current exchanges with past ones; (2) their own exchanges with those of other actors whom they know and perceive to be in a similar situation to themselves; and (3) any particular exchange with other exchanges that might be available. An actor might compare the deal that they get with a present employer, for example, with the deal they had in a previous job. They might compare their marital arrangement with that of their friends. And they might compare their current gym buddy with other possible gym buddies in their network.

Note that what goes on in the dyad between two people, on this account, is shaped by the wider network of the agent, both past and present. What might in some circumstances strike an actor as a good deal, or perhaps rather a fulfilling relationship, might seem less so if it comes in the wake of other relationships which were more fulfilling or if an actor's friends have an even better deal or if the actor has lots of other options open to them, some of which are better. Judgements of value are made relative to reference groups, which is to say networks. This latter point, which crops up again later when we discuss power, is a good example of the way in which dyadic relations are shaped by the larger network to which they belong. The value of what any alter has to offer is determined in some part by the wider availability of that good in ego's personal network.

Thibaut and Kelley only scratch at the surface of the relational roots of value, however. In an important reflection which supports a relational interpretation of exchange, Simmel (1990) notes that exchange relations are generative of the values they involve and, in this sense, *sui generis* phenomena. We tend to think that the goods which we exchange have value prior to and independently of exchange, he argues. We assume that the objects or services that we bring into an exchange relation already have value. This is not so, however. Value, he argues, is a function of the difficulty we experience in securing objects. Objects must be attainable to have value for us but the extent of their value is a function of the difficulty we experience in securing them or the price, in the broadest sense of the word, we are prepared to pay. Even objects which we objectively need to survive are not experienced as valuable if we experience no difficulty in getting hold of them. Air doesn't strike us as valuable, for example, however essential it is to our survival, because it is freely available to us.

This is the principle which underlies labour-based theories of value. Labour adds value because it is a cost we pay, in physical exertion, for an object. But the principle applies equally to exchange, and exchange is no less essential to the production of value. Exchange, like labour, makes objects available to us but only at a cost. The value of whatever is exchanged is determined by the price which the buyer is prepared to pay.

Moreover, this underlies the role of scarcity in the production of value. It is not scarcity *per se* which effects value, Simmel argues, but rather the fact that we can modify scarcity by making rare objects available, at a cost, to those who desire them: 'only exchange makes scarcity an element in value'. Moreover, scarcity is not literally a matter of the existing volume of a given resource but rather of our ease of access to it: 'objects are not hard to get because they are scarce but rather they are scarce because they are had to get' (Simmel 1990: 100). There may be more than enough gold in the earth for everyone on the planet, for example, but if the costs of extraction remain high because the process is difficult then gold remains scarce – and valuable. Thus, and this is the key point, *value is an emergent property of the exchange process and we cannot decompose that process into its component parts without losing what is essential to it. Exchange relations are irreducible.*

Simmel's argument here is effectively an argument for a relational conception of value over a substantialist conception. Value lies not in the object of exchange but rather in the use of that object within exchange. In this respect he anticipates other more recent arguments in the sociological literature regarding different types of 'capital'. In an important discussion of 'social capital', for example, Coleman (1990) argues that this resource is not constituted by patterns of connection, as such, but rather by their 'facilitative functions'. Actors 'have' social capital, insofar as it is meaningful to talk in this way, to the extent that their connections with others facilitate certain forms of action for them that would otherwise be impossible, more risky or more difficult. Likewise, scholars in Bourdieu's tradition have argued that his various 'forms of capital' (chiefly cultural, social and symbolic) refer not to individual possessions *per se* but rather to their value when mobilized in particular 'fields'. 'Educational qualifications', for example, are not valuable or constitutive of 'cultural capital' in and of themselves. They count as capital only insofar as they function within a particular field, such as the employment market, and their value is always relative to the field.

Exchange as a social form

It is not just value that is emergent for Simmel, however. Exchange itself is an emergent social form. His first key claim in this respect is that exchange has replaced piracy and robbery, historically, as a means of securing goods. Where once actors simply took what they wanted from others, often by force, they now bargain and offer something in return. He therefore perceives exchange as having both normative and conventional aspects. To enter into exchange is to enter into a conventional pattern of interaction in which the other is recognized as a being who deserves something in return for what they give. This same historical pattern is repeated in human ontogenesis, moreover. Infants learn that they cannot simply take what they want but must either do without or enter into fair exchange.

Doing this entails the internalization, as self-discipline, of external social control, Simmel continues (see also Elias 1984). We can only enter into exchange to the extent that we have acquired the self-control to refrain from simply taking what we want and to orient to the conventions and norms of exchange. Furthermore, acquired self-control is important in relation to the fixing of value. It is easy, Simmel claims, to be overtaken by infantile impulses for immediate gratification which tend to unduly elevate the value of whatever we might want right now. When children want something, he observes, they momentarily prioritize it above all else. It becomes, temporarily, the be all and end all. Mature exchange entails the capacity to control these impulses, taking a more detached view of value and perhaps also mobilizing a transitive schedule of preferences akin to that referred to in rational action theory – which is not to say, of course, that we are ever entirely mature or rational in our exchanges. To learn to exchange is to learn to resist the demand for immediate gratification and to put our current wants into perspective. This is an important observation as it suggests that a further property of individual agency – namely the tendency to act in accordance with a transitive ranking of preferences – is acquired by way of interaction. Insofar as we follow a transitive ordering of preferences, and that is clearly an ideal that we attain to varying degrees, we do so because we have learned to do so, overcoming the more immediate tendency to overvalue immediate and momentary wants.

Also important in this context is the role of cultural reference points in the establishment of value equivalence. Mature exchange entails that actors orient to intersubjective judgements of the value of the objects exchanged, again subordinating infantile acquisitive impulses which tend to inflate the value of immediate wants from an individual, subjective point of view. I touched upon this above when I noted, with reference to Thibaut and Kelley (2007), that actors establish the value of objects of exchange by way of reference groups and comparisons. They can't assess the value of an object when taken in isolation and need some sort of external reference point. Simmel (1990) develops this further by reflecting upon the rationalization entailed in the emergence of monetary and pricing systems. Modern societies, he maintains, tend to standardize value. Moreover, he observes that the tendency for trade to occur in public spaces in pre-monetary economies is integrally related to this need for intersubjective verification. Actors exchange in public, before witnesses, in order to 'test' the terms of their agreement. Value is a collective, intersubjective, rather than a private and subjective, judgement.

Finally, Simmel is keen to insist that, as with all social forms (e.g. 'language, custom, law, religion'), economic exchange is a collective rather than an individual invention. All social forms, he argues, 'evolved as inter-individual structures, in the interaction between the individual and the multitude, so that their origin cannot be attributed to a single individual' (Simmel 1990: 99). Social forms such as exchange do not emerge because they are functional for society (which is not to deny that they may be socially functional) but neither can they be reduced to the properties and inclinations of atomized individuals. They are shaped, often over protracted periods of time, by the dynamics of interaction within and between given communities.

Simmel's account is speculative. It is not beyond criticism and its bearing upon exchange in a broad sense is open to question as it is explicitly focused upon economic exchange (which, as noted, Simmel distinguishes from exchange *per se*). It is useful, however, because it raises issues that we can bring to bear on social exchange and, more importantly, forces us to recognize that exchange is a social form, shaped by the network of social relations in which it is embedded and irreducible to its individual parts, i.e. actors and the objects or services they exchange.

Exchange and justice

Simmel's reflections on the normative basis of exchange lead into a theme that has been key for some exchange theorists and contentious for others: justice. Parties to exchanges expect to be treated justly and often feel a duty to treat others justly too. This claim is contentious for some exchange theorists because it doesn't follow logically from the key premises of the theory and is, in that respect, an 'add-on'. More reductive versions of exchange theory are reluctant to embrace it for that reason. However, there are good reasons, not least in the form of experiments and other empirical studies conducted by exchange theorists (e.g. Molm 1997), to think that issues of justice are important in social exchange and we must therefore attend to it. Actors want to feel that they are being fairly treated in exchanges and may refuse to exchange under conditions which they perceive to be unjust even if this refusal is damaging to their material interests.

These claims about justice suggest that actors approach exchange situations, even ones which they don't conceptualize as exchanges, with particular expectations about what they should receive in return for what they give. Where do these expectations come from? The accounts in the exchange literature vary but most hinge, to reiterate a point from earlier, upon a notion of comparison and reference groups. Present may be compared with past. If my previous line manager let me sneak off early on a Friday in return for maximum effort during the rest of the day, it might strike me as somewhat unfair that my current one won't; likewise, if my current manager used to let me but now refuses. Similarly, I may compare myself with others who are in a similar positions. Children do this all the time: 'but Paul's dad lets him, it's not fair!' Such comparison may be specific (e.g. to Paul and his dad) or to a more abstract reference group or generalized other ('but all kids these days are allowed to!'). Finally, we compare our situations against formal norms, including but not exclusively, laws.

This point about comparison is interesting because it resonates with my claims in both this and earlier chapters about the referential function that others play for us in orienting our sense of reality. Actors often want to act in ways which are fair, reasonable, which 'make sense' and so on but they cannot determine in isolation whether or not their actions fit these descriptions because the criteria involved are necessarily intersubjective. Their only point of reference is wider practice.

Moreover, it follows that we are only bothered about these issues because we are intersubjectively attuned. To want to be treated fairly is to want to be treated as others are treated and that can only be an issue for a being who experiences the world as populated by other experiencing beings.

Sociability and recognition

One of the criticisms that some people have of exchange theory is that it seems to demean human relations by reducing them to crude utilitarian considerations and, in doing so, paints a picture which is at odds with most people's experiences of (most of) their relationships. The theory seems to suggest that we only interact and form relationships with others because of what we can get out of them. Others are means to our ends and, as such, interactions and relations appear to lack any moral basis, at least in respect of Kant's (1993) golden moral rule: that others should be treated as ends in their own right rather than means. I disagree with this criticism on three grounds.

First, as I argued above, there is a normative aspect to exchange. We do not simply take from others. We give and take, treating the other as a partner rather than a resource. We might drive a hard bargain, seeking our own advantage, but we nevertheless treat the other as a being to be bargained with, a rational being who is open to persuasion and capable of defending their own corner. This accords with a Kantian definition of moral relations. Exchange relations are moral. They entail respect for the other and emergent norms.

Second, exchange theory does not necessarily entail that we conceptualize or otherwise consciously think about relationships in cost–benefit terms. The point is that whatever we might think about our relationships we are inclined to pursue pleasure and avoid pain, and this means that we will tend to initiate interactions with others who, in the past, have given us pleasure or otherwise proved to be rewarding contacts. That we do this might completely escape our attention and is not necessarily 'deliberate', at least not insofar as that implies deliberation. If we accept this then the fact that exchange theory feels counter-intuitive is no objection to it. Exchange theory explores tendencies in behaviour that may escape our attention even as we engage in them.

Third, it is very difficult to explain human interaction and relationships at all unless we concede that we are attracted to others by something and that 'something' is all that exchange theory is asking us to recognize. There must be some purpose to interaction, something rewarding about it, otherwise it is either a random and inexplicable happening or the caused effect of something preceding it, neither of which are very appealing options. This purpose might not always be exchange of goods. Some relations centre upon conflict and some might be based purely upon empathy, duty or the sheer fact of unavoidability. But as pure forms, devoid of any exchange element, these are exceptional bases of interaction and they don't represent any more appealing a basis for human relations than exchange. I do not want to think that most of the people who interact with me do so because they feel sorry for me or duty-bound or because I just happen to be there. I want to think that they interact with me because they want to; because I am attractive to them in some way. And that very fact of 'attraction' suggests 'reward' and thus exchange. To be attractive to another is to have something to offer them.

Of course I don't want to think that they are only friends with me because they want to benefit from my fabulous wealth or play on my *Nintendo* but exchange theory does not require that. They might want something that I am only too happy to give and to take as the basis of our relationship – perhaps they find me fun and have an enjoyable time in my company. There are two issues here. The first centres upon identity and recognition.

Identity and recognition

I might not like the idea that the other is my friend on account of my wealth because I believe that I have other qualities which ought to suffice and because I believe that our relationship is built upon something else. In this respect recognition and identity may be part of the package involved in exchange, and integral to the way in which we 'story' (see Chapter 6) and define our relationship. Part of the deal in our relationship might be that you, to my face at least, verifiably recognize me as the sort of person that I want to be and uphold the definition of our relationship that I demand. Indeed, parties to any kind of meaningful relationship will always demand recognition from the other in any of the exchanges in which they engage, whatever else is being exchanged between them. Quite how this achieved – mutual consent, deceit, power or coercion – will vary but, as noted in Chapter 6, recognition is central to human relations and identities and, as such, is likely to be integral in most instances of exchange.

Sociability

The second issue centres upon what Simmel (1971) calls 'sociability'. The exchange perspective can make us uneasy because it can seem to suggest that relationships are necessarily instrumental, always means to ends which lie beyond them. We are happy to accept that some relationships, particularly economic relationships, are like this but we don't want to think that all relationships are like this. In my view exchange theory does not require this and we have reason to believe that it is not always the case. Interaction and relationships can be rewarding in and of themselves. Simmel's account of sociability illustrates and theorizes this.

Interaction can be pleasurable in its own right, Simmel notes. It is akin to and perhaps literally the kin of 'play'. We might entertain one another with stories, for example, building and releasing tension as the plot twists and thickens and thereby generating cathartic pleasure. We might play games, from teasing and flirting to friendly competition and mock battles, which are again cathartic (see also Elias and Dunning 1986; Huizinga 1950). And we make one another laugh. Such interaction is rewarding in itself and, Simmel (1971) argues, through exposure to it, beginning with childhood play, we develop a taste and even a need for it. By learning the pleasures of social interaction we become (more) sociable beings.

Simmel is quite clear that sociability need serve no purpose outside itself. Indeed, although he concedes that its pure form is an ideal type which is usually only imperfectly achieved in practice, he claims that it only works to the extent that external matters, whether 'public' or 'private', are kept out. To interact sociably is to interact for the sake of it, for the pleasure of interacting. 'Flirting' only remains sociable, for example, to the extent that it is a pleasurable game in itself which is dissociated from the aim of having sex – although, of course, sex is a form of interaction which is pleasurable in its own right and often an end in itself too. Likewise, conversation loses its sociable form if and when it is used to serve purposes external to it, whether social or personal. The person who replies to a friendly 'how's things?' with a tale of woe immediately negates the potential for sociable interaction inherent within the question. They bring a serious tone to the interaction and make demands (for sympathy or aid) which are not consistent with sociability. Sociability demands that actors bracket out external (to the interaction) considerations and, to reiterate, interact for the sheer pleasure of doing so. Importantly, Simmel suggests that a degree of equality between 'players' is necessary if this is to occur because marked inequalities are difficult to bracket out and tend to inhibit the playfulness necessary to sociability.

What Simmel captures here is the 'something' beyond instrumental benefits that provide incentives for interaction and relationship formation. But what he describes is entirely compatible with the exchange perspective. We form relations with others, in some instances, because they are fun to be with, interesting or because they make us laugh and we get on. In other words, because they service our need for sociability. Moreover, the exchange is more likely to be one of like-with-like here (i.e. we 'pay' for their 'services' by servicing their need for sociability too) because, as Simmel (1976) says, sociability works to the extent that it is mutual. If you can't or won't 'play' with me then I can't play with you. We must both orient to the conventions of sociability and be sociable to one another if sociability is to be achieved. Sociability is a mutual achievement. Of course you may derive less satisfaction from my scintillating conversation than I derive from yours, and you may therefore expect more from me than sociability. You might conclude our sociable evening by asking to borrow my football season ticket, making it clear that future evenings of fun depend upon it. But this is by no means necessary. Sociability may be all that is required in a relationship.

We may feel that sociable interactions are avenues for the expression of our real and natural selves. Against this, however, Simmel reminds us that sociability is a social form, shaped by conventions. It demands of us, as noted, that we leave certain aspects of our selves and lives 'at the door', a skill which we must learn like all others. Moreover, sociability, as a social form, changes across time. The conventions and demands of sociable interaction are in constant evolution. Those of contemporary Britain are different to those of its Victorian equivalent, for example, as indeed are those of contemporary aristocratic circles from those on council estates.

Exchange and power

Exchange relationships, as noted earlier, involve interdependency. Interdependency, in turn, is a basis of power (Elias 1978; Emerson 1962; Molm 1997). If I depend upon you for something then you have a lever with which to influence my conduct. You may not be aware of my dependency or your own power but the very fact that you have what I want affords you a hold over me and will affect my behaviour towards you in a way which (generally) is to your advantage. Insofar as ours is a relationship of interdependency, however, then I provide you with something that you want or need and I too, therefore, have a lever to pull. There is a two-way power-balance in our relationship (see especially Elias 1978).

The balance of power in a relationship may be even. If i depends upon j to the same extent that j depends upon i then there is power in the relationship but neither party is advantaged by it. Each can influence the other but only to the same degree. To the extent that one or the other is more dependent, however, then there is an imbalance of power. If i needs j more than j needs i then j has the upper hand.

Many factors affect power imbalances. In the simple case i may simply lack any of the goods that are high on j's list of priorities. Even if j does value i's goods, however, relations may be imbalanced, not least as an effect of exchange networks. If j has an alternative supplier for the same goods that i can supply, then i is at a disadvantage. Perhaps j prefers k, such that i is forced to work harder and offer more. Perhaps j has no preference but i and k are aware that they are in competition and seek to outbid one another.

Of course this only applies if i and k supply the same good to j and collectively have more to offer than j wants. Indeed, if i and k are not supplying the same good and their respective contributions do not impact negatively upon one another then, although they may still be involved in the same *social network*, technically they are not involved in the same *exchange network*. *Exchange networks only exist where exchanges of goods between multiple actors impact upon one another*. These conditions are not uncommon, however, from love triangles to competitive economic markets, and the notion of exchange networks is clearly important therefore.

Of course if i and k form an alliance then the power balance shifts again. Though working on a different problem and in a different tradition McAdam (1982) makes this point in his discussion of power and social movements. Social movements are often assumed to be mounted by 'powerless' actors, he notes, but this is incorrect. Such actors cease to be powerless when they combine forces and pull on the 'levers' available to them, the obvious example being workers who enjoy little individual leverage in relation to their employers but can force the hand of the latter by means of collective strike action. If workers join forces then they can change the balance of power in the employment relation.

The advantaged party in a power relation may act strategically. Cognizant of their advantage they may seek to exploit it. In an early formulation of this power–dependency theory, however, Emerson (1962) argues that strategic conduct is not necessary because effects of power are induced structurally if all actors pursue rewards in the manner predicted by exchange theory. If j stands to achieve greater rewards by exchanging with k rather than i, for example, then she will tend to do so, thereby inducing i to offer her more. This happens independently and irrespective of j's intentions or awareness. Her decision to exchange with k may be subjectively oriented towards k, not i, but it affects i all the same and serves j's interests vis-à-vis i insofar as it induces i to offer j more.

This power dynamic can be found in relationships of all types and at different levels of social organization. That is one of its strengths. Insofar as the social fabric is woven by multiple iterated relations of exchange then power is integral to its evolving structure. From children struggling to fit in with peers, through lovers taunting and teasing one another to international trade deals and political pacts, the same basic mechanism is at work. Actors pull one another's strings by withholding or threatening (however tacitly) to withhold the goods that the other depends upon them for. Exchange and particularly networks of exchange generate power.

Defined in this way, power is genuinely relational. It is not possessed by one party or another but rather located within their relationship. What gives j the advantage in her relationship with i only does so because i wants but doesn't have it. It may proffer no advantage in any of j's other relationships and j's relationship with i may be the only one in which she enjoys any advantage. An individual may enjoy a considerable advantage in one relationship, to the point of exerting complete domination, and yet be disadvantaged and dominated in all of their other relationships. They are not powerful or powerless as individuals but are rather positioned within exchange networks such that they enjoy advantage in one and disadvantage in the rest. Moreover, as noted above, power does not generally derive from dyadic structures but rather from the triadic or more complex exchange networks in which they are embedded, e.g. when i's dependence upon j for x is lessened by her relation to k, who can also supply x, the balance of power between j and i shifts back in i's favour. This applies as much to children in the playground, whose 'other friends' detract from the power of any one friend, as to companies who can bargain for a better deal because they have access to another supplier.

In addition to the balance of power, general levels of dependency in a relationship may vary too. Depending upon another for 'gossip' will usually carry less weight than depending upon them for a wage, for example. This level of dependence, which Emerson (1962) dubs 'average power', varies independently of the balance of power. Average power may be high, as when resources integral to survival are exchanged, but that does not entail that it is imbalanced. Actors may be equally dependent upon one another for resources necessary to their survival. Likewise, low average power can be balanced or extremely imbalanced. I may depend upon you to water my plants when I am on holiday but have nothing to offer in return or we may each perform this service for one another. When average power is lower, Emerson continues, it has less effect. I might choose to sacrifice my plants if you demand too much in return for watering them but I have less choice with respect to resources upon which my life depends.

Peer pressure, normative norms and behavioural escalation

Peer pressure can be explained by reference to exchange power. If we seek approval from specific others but they only give that approval on condition that we behave in particular ways then this generates a pressure for us to act in those ways. We must act as they wish if we want to secure the approval we seek. Our peers may deliberately manipulate this mechanism but, as before, this is not necessary. They may simply admire certain forms of behaviour over others and grant their approval and recognition accordingly. In such situations actors learn vicariously what to do to win approval without anybody intending to teach anybody else anything, let alone intending to pressure others into forms of action.

Similarly, local norms might emerge and operate in this way. If most of the girls in a particular network are prepared to sleep with a boy on their first date, for example, then girls who don't might find themselves labelled deviant and might experience difficulty getting dates. The majority generate a statistical norm by virtue of their behaviour but they also establish a 'going rate' for sexual favours and thereby a 'normative norm' which boys orient to. Even if her boyfriend applies no pressure she knows that she isn't offering what he could get from others, and is thus taking a risk. Likewise her boyfriend will experience pressure because, amongst other things, he knows that he is accepting less in his relationship than his friends are getting in theirs, a fact which might cause him to lose status in their eyes because it looks weak.

If we grant this point then we can also see that and how dynamics of behavioural 'inflation' or escalation might kick in. If, for example, some members of a network seek elevated status within it by way of law breaking but find that their behaviours tend to become the norm, the going rate for basic status within the network, they may feel the need to step up their law breaking in order to maintain their distinction. This sets a self-perpetuating spiral of escalation in motion, in which those seeking distinction must constantly do more to maintain their position.

In this case power in the group is genuinely diffuse within the network but is affected by the dynamics between three analytically distinct but potentially overlapping subgroups: (1) those who up the ante in pursuit of distinction; (2) those who follow them, pulling the norm up behind them and thus nudging the first group into ever more extreme behaviour: and (3) those who bestow recognition and status on groups one and two. Groups one and two each exert power over the other in this example, but only by virtue of their respective pursuits of recognition from group three. Group three may not be a separate group of course. It may simply comprise members of groups one and two. If it is separate group, however, then it is in a powerful position, attracting ever greater efforts to impress for the same level of basic recognition.

However, its power is at least partly rooted in the competition between groups one and two. As in the earlier example, group one are only motivated to give more to group three because group two constitute an alternative source of titillation for group three. If groups one and two were to form a pact, deciding not to compete for the attentions of group three, they could thereby lessen the power of group three over them.

Power and justice

I noted above that actors engaged in exchange typically orient to issues of justice. The *prima facie* implication of this is that partners to exchange gravitate towards a fair arrangement and might invoke justice in an effort to counter the effects of power imbalances in their relations. However, drawing upon experimental data, many exchange theorists argue that subjective expectations about justice in exchange relations tend to reinforce power imbalances. Experimental exchange relations which have been designed to be unfair are often perceived as fair by those who are party to them, irrespective of whether they are the losers or the winners. Molm's (1997) experimental work, which is discussed further below, for example, suggests that both the advantaged and the disadvantaged parties to exchange in conditions of power imbalance tend to perceive the conditions of their exchange as just. Likewise, in work which draws upon Mead (1967), Della Fave (1980) has argued that individuals tend to develop self-conceptions which are consistent with their social rewards, such that the disadvantaged often see themselves as undeserving. Whilst conceptions of and concerns for justice might provide a basis for resistance to power, therefore, this is less likely when power relations have become established. Conceptions of justice, as my earlier discussion of reference groups and comparison also suggests, tend to be rooted in the *status quo* and where that *status quo* is unjust they can therefore serve to legitimate inequities.

This is not to deny that actors may achieve awareness of injustice and may revise their self-concept accordingly. It does happen. McAdam's (1982) interesting work on 'cognitive liberation' in the black civil rights movements in the US, for example, focuses precisely upon this process of redefinition. My point is only that injustice is not necessarily recognized as such and that experimental evidence, at least, suggests that conceptions of justice are often formed around the *status quo* and therefore do not always challenge it.

Coercion and power

Heath (1976) has argued that the basic logic behind the exchange theoretical definition of power also supports a further, complementary but different definition, centred upon coercion. My leverage over you need not derive from the fact that I have something you want, he argues. It may equally derive from the fact that I can punish you in ways that you do not want. Physical violence, name calling, sulking and malicious gossip are all examples of the kinds of punishment that may be involved.

Coercion, in this context, involves punishment intended to induce a change of behaviour. Random violence is not coercion. Neither are unintended negative externalities. And neither, in and of themselves, are constraint or execution. To coerce another is to get them to do something by virtue of a threat of punishment. Harming another without seeking to change their behaviour does not meet these criteria. Neither does killing them, physically preventing them from behaving in particular ways or otherwise directly manipulating their body without the mediation of their conscious 'consent' (e.g. by dragging or drugging); though, of course, 'consent' is only given under duress in coercive situations and the actor only acts 'willingly' because they are sufficiently fearful of the alternatives. We have other concepts to capture these other uses of violence. 'Power' is best reserved for relations in which one party, in virtue of their capacity to affect the other(s), exerts a pressure upon the other(s) to act in ways which serve their own interests. One is reminded of Foucault's (1982: 220) claim that power relations presuppose that 'the "other" (the one over whom power is exercised) be thoroughly recognised and maintained to the end as a person who acts'. Power does not bypass purposive behaviour. It works upon and by means of it.

Power, in this case, centres upon 'punishments' rather than 'rewards' but the logic is the same. Indeed, as Heath notes, the two blur because the withdrawal of rewards can be construed as a punishment and the withholding of punishments a reward. Notwithstanding this, however, experimental work[4] by Molm (1997) suggests that these two bases of power do play out differently in practice.

In her early experiments Molm found that coercion did not seem to be effective as a source of power in exchange relations in the way that 'exchange power' – that is, power arising from unequal levels of dependency – was. Later experiments allowed her to discern that this was because it is not widely used, especially as relationships develop over a series of exchanges. There were two aspects to this lack of use.

First, coercive power does not work 'structurally' in the way that reward power does. As noted above, actors who have the upper hand in exchange relations, being in possession of something that the other wants more than they want anything from the other, do not need to consciously use or even become conscious of their advantage in order to benefit from it. Others who desire their resources will actively court them and, particularly where there is competition for those resources, will offer them favourable terms. Molm consistently found evidence of this in her work. Coercion is different, however. It requires the actor to do or threaten something painful to alter in order to force a change of behaviour. This sheer fact of having to do something, Molm maintains, reduces the likelihood of coercive power coming into play.

Second, Molm found that actors in her experiments were generally not inclined to use the capacity for punishment available to them in the context of exchange relations. The only way that she could induce actors to use coercion routinely was by designing the games in her experiments such that coercing others was unavoidable if the actor was to pursue their own gains and avoid punishment themselves – in effect she coerced them to coerce. If they could pursue reward in exchange without recourse to coercion then they generally did. Coercion is less often in play, from this point of view, because actors actively prefer not to use it.

Molm's next batch of experiments sought to explore this further and to establish why actors prefer not to use coercion. A number of experiments established that it was not because coercion is ineffective. Early proponents of learning theory suggested that punishment is ineffective because it generates resentment and resistance, and similar views are made by some strategic and game-theoretic analysts; coercion is said to lead to escalating cycles of conflict and other such unproductive outcomes (see Schelling 1981). More recent learning theory has pointed to the efficacy of punishment in bringing about behaviour change, however, particularly when accompanied by rewards. And Molm's work echoes this. When coercion was used consistently and contingently, only to punish behaviour which the coercer sought to change and always when the coerced failed to comply, it was very effective – though, of course, Molm's experimental subjects may not have known this, certainly not in advance of their participation.

Molm therefore sought to test out a number of further explanations for her subjects' reluctance to use coercion. Her experiments suggested two broad types of explanation. The first relates to ideas regarding 'bounded rationality' and 'risk aversion' in uncertain contexts. Actors seek to improve their position through exchange, she notes, but not to maximize their outcomes. If gains can be made without coercion, therefore, even if coercion would increase rewards, a non-coercive approach is often deemed more preferable. More importantly, actors afford potential losses greater significance than potential rewards when weighing up their options[5] and consider both the effort involved in administering coercion and the possibility of retaliation to be likely costs of a coercive strategy. Potential gains have to be much greater and/or much more likely than potential losses before actors are inclined to pay the likely administrative and retaliation costs of coercion, and most do not believe that they are. Actors imagine that coercion will be very costly, in terms of the effort required to execute and enforce it and the retaliation it will provoke, and that whatever gains are made will not outweigh these costs. For this reason, she argues, actors are reluctant to resort to coercion. It is deemed too risky and potentially costly.

Exploring this point further, Molm argues that coercion is the more likely strategy of partners to an exchange whose bargaining power is otherwise quite weak, especially if their returns in an exchange are dropping, and especially if and when they drop to a negligible level where the actor has little to lose by trying coercion. What we can't get by exchange, whether fair exchange or unfair, in other words, we may try to get by coercion. The implication here, somewhat counter-intuitively, is that coercion is a strategy of the 'weak'. We must qualify this claim, however, by noting that we are referring to weakness in exchange relations not to weakness *per se*. If an actor has little to offer in exchange for what they want and their want is sufficiently strong, then they are more likely to use coercion to seek to secure it. But the fact that their exchange power is weak does not mean that their coercive power is. Indeed, given that coercion may provoke retaliation, it is the more likely strategy of a weak exchange partner who nevertheless has access to stronger coercive means. The bully who finds someone smaller than themselves and the mugger who carries a knife exemplify this. The terrorist network who take on a powerful nation are a more complicated case as their coercive power, as such, does not match that of their adversary, but their invisibility arguably undermines much of their adversary's coercive power and they fit the picture in all other respects. They have little to bargain with so they resort to force.

The second reason why coercion is seldom used, Molm continues, is that it tends to be perceived as unjust. Those on the receiving end are certainly likely to perceive it as unjust and, as a consequence, to retaliate (although Molm's work, as noted above, suggests that retaliation is often short-lived when coercion is used consistently and conditionally to change specific patterns of behaviour). Those in a position to use coercion tend to recognize and anticipate this such that, as noted above, they deem it too risky. In addition, however, Molm found that even those in a position to use coercion (which in the case of her experiments meant use of a financial penalty) were reluctant to do so because they deemed it unfair. Actors preferred to pursue their goals in what they perceived to be a just manner and, as noted, only resorted to coercion when the rules of the games Molm constructed left them little alternative.

As a final point on coercion, note that moral proscriptions against its use increase the effect of 'exchange power'. Exchange power assumes more significance in our society because and to the extent that coercion is deemed illegitimate. If coercion was acceptable then actors who lack the goods to profit from exchange would have alternative means of securing what they want from those in possession of them, and those in possession of them would enjoy less of a power advantage from the fact of possessing them. This takes us back to Simmel's (1990) abovementioned observation, that exchange, as a social form, has supplanted piracy and robbery and works to the extent that it has supplanted them as legitimate options.

Relations and mechanisms of power

The exchange–coercion[6] theory of power is only one of many available in the social sciences and is, in some respects, quite basic. It is important, however, on a number of grounds. First, it is genuinely relational. It does not locate power with an individual but rather in the relations between actors. This is appealing because it fits with the general argument of this book but it is also important because it resonates with the general observation that the same actor might enjoy political domination in one context, whilst they are subordinate in another. Furthermore, as we know that relations may involve exchanges of a range of goods and may evolve over time, such that the salience of certain goods rises and falls, it allows for the fact that power may have multiple bases within the same relationship and that power balances may shift over time. As colleagues become friends or friends become lovers, for example, the basis of their relationship, what is exchanged between them, changes and so too does the balance of power in their relationship. Likewise, the power balance in a relationship may lie in one direction according to one of the sets of goods exchanged in it and in the other according to another set.

Second, the exchange–coercion model avoids the pitfalls of what Hindess (1982) calls 'capacity–outcome' models of power, whilst also avoiding the problems of his suggested alternative. Capacity–outcome models, which Hindess shows to be common in political sociology, entail that power is seen as the capacity of an actor to bring about a particular outcome, a definition which Hindess problematizes on the grounds that outcomes are never assured and can be unpredictable. The defeat of the Americans in Vietnam is his example. America was and is perceived to be a 'powerful' nation, he argues, and Vietnam a power- less nation. One might have imagined, before the event, that America 'had the power' or 'had the capacity' to subdue this much weaker nation, that is, it had the 'capacity' to secure a given 'outcome'. But it didn't. Outcomes are decided in practice, Hindess argues; they are the result of a process, and it makes no sense to suggest that actors enjoy the capacity, in advance, to bring them about. This is a critique of substantialist approaches to power which conceive of it as a 'thing', a property or possession of actors.

Hindess's suggested alternative is a concept of 'arenas of struggle' in which actors fight it out with various obstacles and with the possible intervention of third parties. This concept is important because it introduces both interaction and process into the picture. However, it effectively dispenses with the idea of 'power' and with the sense that parties to a struggle may be relatively advantaged vis-à- vis one another. Outcomes are decided in practice but we throw the baby out with the bathwater if we fail to consider that and how some parties to a struggle have greater leverage than others.

The exchange model of power allows for this. It makes no claim about the likelihood of certain outcomes and certainly does not associate power with the capacity to secure given outcomes. Outcomes, for exchange theorists, are contin- gent upon interactions, as they are for Hindess. But interactions are affected by the relative levels of dependence (and coercive means) between actors and some actors clearly are advantaged in some instances by the balance of these levels.

It is perhaps also worth noting here that Hindess's Vietnam example, which resonates with contemporary situations in Iraq and Afghanistan, is an example of coercive power. In some respects, from an exchange point of view, the Americans were not in a strong position in relation to the Vietnamese because they did not have any strong bargaining chips. They resorted to violence because they appeared to lack alternative 'levers'. They could only threaten to cause pain and in doing so they had also to bear the considerable costs of both keeping up their campaign and withstanding retaliatory attacks.

The third strength of the exchange model is that it explores the mechanisms of power. It seeks to explain why some people do what others want them to, suggesting that this is because others are in a position to offer rewards and pun- ishments which may prove decisive. We can understand why i obeys j; it becomes intelligible to us, if we know that i is more dependent upon j than j is upon i for whatever goods are exchanged between them. The workings of power are laid bare; we know that i obeys j because not doing so will cut them off from their supply of valued goods.

I return to power in Chapter 10, where I consider the 'technologies' that allow it to be deployed relatively effectively across large networks and territories. In this respect what I have said here is far from complete. It is a beginning, however, and is important as a beginning, to reiterate, because it identifies power as a property of relations, rather than actors, and explores its mechanisms.

Conclusion

This chapter, which concludes my attempt to tease out some of the key aspects of social interaction and relationships, has covered a lot of ground. The key under-lying argument, however, has been that many social relations and interactions centre upon the exchange of 'goods', albeit sometimes goods which are intrinsic to the process of interaction itself, that this tends to create interdependency between actors, and that interdependency is a basis of power.

As a source of power, exchange may equally be a source of conflict. However, the chapter has also considered the integrative effects of exchange, the fact that exchange, based upon limited self-interests, can exert a socializing effect which leads to more solidaristic relations. Our conclusion, in this respect, can only be to agree with Simmel that relations are complex, multifaceted and involve 'forces' of both 'attraction' and 'repulsion'. Exchange draws us towards others but also, in other respects, distances us from them and encourages us to draw back (e.g. into self-interest).

As in the earlier chapters, I have also sought to demonstrate in this chapter how relations and interactions are irreducible and how they shape the actors who participate within them. There is no exchange without actors but exchange transforms those who participate in it, in various ways, both temporary and more durable. Furthermore, the value of what is exchanged, like the meaning of what we say, emerges in the (exchange) interaction and does not exist independently of it. Again we see that, whilst the social world cannot be 'rolled up' in a teleological whole, neither can it can be decomposed into its parts without us losing much that is important about and characteristic of it. The social world cannot be reduced either upwards or downwards to unified wholes or disconnected parts. It is a network of dynamic interactions and relationships.

8   Structure, agency and social worlds

In the preceding chapters I have attempted to tease out and explore the strategic, symbolic, affective, conventional and exchange dimensions of interaction and relations. In this chapter I develop the picture that has emerged in this discussion in three overlapping ways. First, I reflect more deeply upon convention and draw two further foci to the analytic foreground: networks and resources. All three concepts have been implicated in what I have argued in earlier chapters. They are indispensable for an understanding of interaction and relationships. But they are also indispensable for an adequate conception of social structure. Each is or belongs to a key aspect of structure.

My second concern in the chapter is to draw this structural aspect out, demonstrating that and how relational sociology engages with both the issue of structure and the so-called structure/agency dichotomy. In particular I engage critically with the 'solutions' to the structure/agency problem posited by Giddens (1984) and Bourdieu (1992). I am not persuaded that there is a 'problem' of structure and agency in sociology. Giddens and Bourdieu derive the 'structure/agency problem' from their respective engagements with French structuralism and, to a lesser extent, functionalism. This hardly pre-empts the sociological field. More significantly, however, their respective 'solutions' to the 'problem' draw upon the sociologically deficient model of structure posited within French structuralism, a model devised originally to analyse language rather than society, and they reproduce its deficiencies, not least of which is its inattention to social relations. Giddens (1984) removes 'relations' altogether from the definition of structure and Bourdieu, as noted in Chapter 3, theorizes relationality very oddly. In both cases social structure is rendered strangely asocial and located within rather than between actors. Furthermore, their respective conceptions of 'rules' and 'habitus', whilst appealing in many respects, are deficient in others.

Social life involves both agency and structure and one cannot say much more than that in general theoretical terms but structure is something more than what Giddens and Bourdieu each take it to be. Actors interact in purposive ways, bringing their desires, preferences, intelligence etc. to bear (agency) but they necessarily do so in a context of opportunities and constraints (structure) deriving from (1) their connection to and interdependency with others, in various forms, and the further connection of their alters within a network, (2) the resources they have available to them and (3) the sedimented weight of the past, embodied in conventions, as it bears upon their present.

My third concern builds upon this. It centres upon what symbolic interactionists have referred to as 'social worlds' (Becker 1982; Hall 1987; Martin 2006a, b; Shibutani 1955; Strauss 1973, 1993). Networks, conventions and resources figure prominently in discussions of this concept and I want to use it to draw them together, showing how they interlock, and also to inject more sociological content into them and into my accounts of both interaction and social structure. 'Interaction' has remained relatively abstract in my discussion so far. There has been little mention of the concrete contexts which generate and are simultaneously occasioned by it, or of the purposes and interests, in both the economic and the psychological senses of that word, which drive it. The concept of social worlds foregrounds these aspects of interaction, alongside networks, conventions and resources. Furthermore, in doing so it allows us to address the issue of structure in a relatively concrete way too. 'Structures', as I discuss them, are always structures of specific, concrete social worlds, and worlds always manifest a structure. The chapter begins with an account of the structure/agency dichotomy.

The structure/agency dichotomy

The structure/agency dichotomy is often conflated with the individualism/holism dichotomy which was discussed in Chapter 2 of this book. This is understandable as the two overlap. The 'holism vs individualism' debate raises issues regarding agency, for example, as holism precludes any role for individual (or collective) agency, and individualism seeks both to rescue it and make it foundational. Furthermore, in what must count as the classic formulation of the structure/agency dichotomy, Giddens (1984) attacks functional explanation in a manner resonant of individualistic critiques of holism. There is a difference between the two dichotomies, however. The easiest way to the heart of this difference is via Marx:

> Men make their own history but they do not make it just as they please; they do not make it under circumstances chosen by themselves but under circumstances directly encountered, given and transmitted from the past. The tradition of all the dead generations weighs like a nightmare on the brain of the living.
>
> (Marx 1977: 300)

Marx was, fairly or not, the target of Popper's (2002) critique of historicism, discussed in Chapter 2 (see also Popper (1992)). And some Marxist writers have employed crude forms of functionalist explanation. The above quotation is not about holism and individualism or functions and historical destiny, however. It is about structure and agency. There are two key differences.

First, where holism seeks to explain events in the present by reference to *the future*, that is, teleologically, by reference to functions or destiny, Marx is discussing the impact of *the past* upon the present. He is claiming that we are born into sets of relationships which pre-exist us, have their own distinct form and constrain us, at least insofar as others maintain them through their actions. In addition, he is suggesting that our ways of thinking, perceiving and acting betray a clear historical trace. We are historical creatures through and through, inside and out.

This is not just a matter of constraint. Even as he criticizes capitalism Marx famously celebrates all that it has achieved and all that it makes possible. It is a structure of opportunity as much as constraint. Moreover, he is clear that the traditions which 'weigh' upon our 'brains' serve equally as 'shoulders' upon which we stand, to borrow Isaac Newton's expression. We inherit the intellectual and technological achievements of our predecessors, in the form of a culture that we learn, and we build upon it, achieving much more than we would otherwise be capable of. Our actions pick up the thread of a 'story' begun way back in the midst of time. History never starts again from scratch.

Second, Marx's position admits both agency and structure, whereas holism and individualism are mutually incompatible principles of reduction. If my action is explained by reference to its social functions then there is really no room for agency to make a difference. All that happens is pre-ordained to happen, whatever the actor may think. My action can be shaped by the past, however, in a way that does not preclude agency. The past, in the form of both conventions and configurations of social relations, can influence and shape my action without wholly determining it.

Agency appears twice in Marx's account: (1) 'Men' (sic) are deemed to make their own history, albeit starting from an inherited position, and (2) the past which weighs upon them is a sediment of the interactions of previous generations of social actors. Structure may enable and constrain agency for Marx but there is no structure without agency, both past and present. History is always necessarily a matter of both structure and agency, as interactions in the present pick up the story begun by those in the past. Where 'holism' and 'individualism' are mutually exclusive, 'structure and 'agency' necessarily presuppose one another. Moreover, where holism and individualism are reductive principles of explanation, structure and agency are (entirely compatible) properties of the social world which need not in any way be thought of in reductive terms.

I am tempted to say that 'structure', for Marx, is the product of past interaction but this would be misleading since his point is that history is a continuous process with no finished 'products'. Structure is always in-process. Patterns emerge and endure within the flow and they are important because they constitute opportunities and constraints which shape the possibilities for its (immediate) future, but they are always a part of the flow, never fixed or external impositions upon it.

At the same time as he poses the structure/agency dichotomy, Marx resolves it. There is little else that one can say, in general, about structure and agency than that we make our own history but only ever on the basis of the history sedimented both within conventions and the structure of relations in which we are embedded. I do not believe that other contributors to the debate have been able to conclude with anything more decisive than that.

However, it is not obvious exactly what the components of structure are in Marx's account. I would suggest that they are *relations* (of production), *conventions* ('tradition of dead generations . . . etc.') and *resources* (capital), and I will be developing a concept of structure along those lines myself, but Marx does not really specify his model for sociological purposes. More problematically, recent 'solutions' to the structure/agency 'problem', notably Giddens' (1984) structuration theory and Bourdieu's (1977, 1992) theory of practice, have popularized a deficient and one-dimensional conception of structure, thereby generating a problem in this area. Their concepts of 'structure' strip it of relational content. We need to put relations back into structure. One of my aims in this and the following chapter is to do just this.

I have already outlined a number of objections to Bourdieu's relational sociology, in Chapter 3, and I develop this critique further in Chapter 9. For this reason I tilt my critique in this chapter towards Giddens. As there are certain key similarities in their respective approaches, however, it will be necessary to make reference to both.

Structure and structuration

Giddens (1984) formulates his position, to large extent, in response to French structuralism, an approach rooted in Saussure's (1959) linguistic theory. Saussure famously focuses upon the structure of language (*la langue*), bracketing out an analysis of speech and communication (*la parole*). Furthermore, he brackets out considerations of historical change and process (the *diachronic* dimension of language) which, as Volosinov (1986) and others note, derive from speech, in order to capture its structure at a particular point in time (its *synchronic* dimension). As such he does not need a concept of agency (or linguistic interaction). The agent is deleted from consideration. Giddens was writing at a time when many French structuralist writers were following this example and applying it more widely in social science. Levi-Strauss (1969), who extended the model into anthropology by focusing upon the rules underlying kinship, for example, claimed to 'dissolve man' (sic) (Levi-Strauss 1966). Likewise Althusser (1969), who argued that scientific Marxism displaces any reference to 'man' or historical subjects by way of such structural concepts as 'mode of production' and 'social formation'. Actors only enter the Althusserian picture as supports of structural functions and their subjectivity is reduced to the status of an ideological effect (Althusser 1971). And Foucault (1970), who sums up the structuralist aspiration in the conclusion to *The Order of Things*, wrote: '[M]an is an invention of recent date. And one perhaps nearing its end' (387). The rise of structuralist methods, Foucault continues, allow us to 'sense the possibility' of shifts in the structure of our knowledge (*episteme*) which, if they come to fruition, would 'erase' man 'like a face drawn in the sand at the edge of the sea' (ibid.). Foucault's 'man' is not Giddens' 'agent' but Giddens' formulation of the structure/agency debate is partly an attempt to challenge this 'dissolution of man'.

Structuralism deletes agency by limiting the range of questions it addresses to those which can be answered without recourse to it. If, to stick with the linguistic example, one is not interested in speech and communication and one is prepared to bracket out questions of process and historical change, then certain structures can be analysed without reference to agency. Agency has to be actively repressed in this process because linguistic structures can only be accessed through examples of speech (Merleau-Ponty 1964; Volosinov 1986). Likewise, it would be disingenuous to assume that the structures derived are anything but snapshots of a relational figuration which is always in process and constantly evolving. But there is no reason why the machinery of language cannot be described independently of an account of the speakers who mobilize and, over time, transform it. The problem only occurs if one wishes to engage with speech (i.e. interaction) and/or historical process and change. This is a problem for sociology, however, and thus for Giddens, because sociological interest in structure is generally coupled with interests in interaction and change. Sociologists, as members of the social world they analyse, know it to be dynamic and in-process, historically. Static snapshots of structure are important but only ever part of the story, a part which must be treated with caution precisely because it abstracts from praxis (interaction) and brackets out time, freezing the social world in a moment.

Giddens' structuration theory is an attempt to put agency and change back in. He defines 'structure' as involving rules and resources but, following Wittgenstein (1953) more than Saussure, argues that these rules and resources must be mobilized with skill and competence if they are to work in practice. They do not speak for themselves, either literally or figuratively. Whilst actors follow rules, doing so requires initiative and agency. Moreover, it is in the 'play' of speech and communication that rules and resources are changed or 'coherently deformed', giving rise to the change that is recorded in diachronic accounts. Structure and agency are mutually implicating for Giddens. Structures structure action but action reproduces and modifies structure, facilitating its survival.

This solves the 'structuralism' problem but from a relational point of view it raises another, no less serious problem. Giddens adopts Saussure's conception of structure, modelling it upon language. He deems the rules and resources comprising structure 'virtual'; that is, he claims that they are internalized by actors and only ever manifest indirectly in practice by means of their observance and use by social actors. This reconnects structure with practice but it excludes any consideration of the *relations* that are central to *social* structures qua social. Social structures, in virtue of being 'social', involve multiple social actors and sets of relationships between those actors. As such they do not exist virtually, *within* actors but rather *between* actors. Social structures are, amongst other things, social networks. Capitalism, as a social structure, for example, involves a population of workers, tied by an employment relation to a smaller population of bosses who compete with one another in a market.

In Giddens' defence he does offer a concept of 'systems' which makes reference to relations but it is not at all clear why he separates 'structure' and 'system' in this way. Why analyse rules and resources in separation from relations, especially when this takes the 'social' out of one's definition of 'social structure'? Moreover, he never does anything with the concept of 'system' such that hiving 'relations' off from 'structure' effectively amounts to a way of ignoring them. *The key relational criticism of structuration theory, therefore, is that its concept of 'structure' fails to engage with the concept of social relations and is thereby curiously asocial. Giddens individualizes structure. He places it within the individual qua internalized rules and resources.*

Furthermore, compounding the problem, he gives insufficient consideration to the fact that social action is ordinarily interaction. Whatever order is evident in social life and whatever patterns endure do not come about in virtue of isolated individuals following rules and mobilizing resources for their own independent purposes but rather by means of engagement between actors who affect and influence one another. Order and the patterns of social life that invite reference to 'structure' are not the aggregate effect of individuals each following pre-existing rules but rather of actors negotiating with, influencing, coercing and otherwise interacting with one another. This is not to deny that actors do, indeed, internalize rules etc. but rather to suggest that the effect of those internalized rules is always necessarily mediated by actors' interactions. Although Giddens recognizes that actors interact, his Saussurean conception of structure blinds him to the importance of interaction in relation to the 'constitution of society'. He at least appears to suggest that the ingredients of order and structure are all contained within the individual, in the form of virtual rules and resources.

Bourdieu has a stronger position on the face of it. He offers three key concepts through which to analyse social structure: (1) *habitus*, which serves the same role in his account as internalized 'virtual rules' plays in Giddens' account, but which is posited, in part, as a critique of the concept of rules (Bourdieu 1992); (2) *capital*, which serves the same function as 'resources' serves in Giddens account, but is not liable to the same criticisms (see below); and (3), more significantly for our current purposes, *field*, which is intended as a relational concept. Bourdieu, who formed his theory, like Giddens, in response to the limitations of French structuralism, includes relations in his account by means of the concept of fields. This is certainly an improvement and is to be welcomed but I noted in Chapter 3 that his concept of relations, as applied to 'fields', is deeply problematic and tends to bracket out any focus upon concrete interactions and bonds. *Actors have no direct relations to concrete others within fields, as Bourdieu conceives of them, and as such his 'social space' too is curiously asocial, comprising atomized individuals or at least individuals whose relations to one another are deemed theoretically uninteresting and subordinate to structure.* Furthermore, the concept of habitus, like Giddens' 'virtual rules' and resources, locates structure within the actor as an internalized disposition. Structure is deposited within the individual, in the form of habitus, and then externalized by them in their actions. Whatever the differences between Giddens' 'rules' and Bourdieu's 'habitus', and I discuss these differences below, both suggest that the structured patterns of behaviour partly constitutive of 'social structure' are secured by way of stable dispositions located within individual actors.

The point here, to reiterate, is not that Giddens and Bourdieu fail to recognize that actors interact or prove capable of improvisation, innovation, strategic manoeuvres etc., but rather that they attach no explanatory significance to interaction and conceive of improvisation etc. as individual achievements. Interaction isn't allowed to make a difference to structure. At most it is mediated by structure. There is little sense that actors make and remake the social world *together*, in ways that are irreducible to them as individual actors. To draw a musical analogy, actors are portrayed as soloists and there is little sense that they ever jam (see also Barnes 2000).

Moreover, meaning, insofar as it enters into these accounts, is similarly located within the rule-following actor. There is little recognition of intersubjectivity or its significance (see Chapters 5 and 6, and also Crossley 1996). As Mead (1967) argued many years ago, 'meaning' does not reside within the heads of actors or in the materials of communication but rather between actors. The meaning of what I say consists in some part in how you respond to it and what effect it has upon you. As we discuss, moreover, present utterances refine the meaning of earlier ones. Meaning is intersubjective and co-constructed. This applies to explicit verbal interaction but also, equally, to all interaction. The meanings of what we do in situations involving others is and has to be negotiated with those others. There is no sense of this in structuration theory where the seeds of meaning, along with the seeds of order, are located in the internalized dispositions of the actor.

I return to this critique later in the chapter when I discuss both conventions and Wittgenstein's (1953) critique of the concept of rules. First, however, we must push our examination of structuration further by way of a reflection on Giddens' (1984) deficient conception of 'resources'.

Resources

Archer (1995) has criticized Giddens for deeming not just rules but also resources 'virtual'. She points to the material existence of many key resources, and questions the sense in which they can be deemed 'virtual'. My car is a resource, for example, but it is not virtual and I cannot internalize it. I suspect that the reason Giddens deems resources 'virtual' is that he is thinking of cultural resources (e.g. the vocabulary we mobilize in speech) rather than, in this case, material possessions and goods. And there is some room to defend his position by arguing that, for example, money and the monetary value of goods is dependent upon our 'agreement' and is in that respect virtual. He may even argue that resources, as possessions, depend upon a concept of property which is, again, virtual. This wouldn't fully answer Archer's critique, however, because possession of material resources entails more than just agreement over who own what. It entails physical access and (in the final instance[1]) control. We use and use up resources. Furthermore, any agreements regarding value or ownership are agreements *between* members of a social world not agreements *within* their heads.

In addition, the concept of resources, and more particularly the notion that resources are unevenly distributed through a population, suggests a further aspect of social structure that Giddens (1973) was sensitive to in his early work but which is not captured by the notion of virtual rules and resources which are internalized and reproduced by individual actors. That some actors are rich in resources and others are not, to make the point crudely, is a crucial structural aspect of social life. Many of our key structural metaphors, from 'pyramids' through 'strata' to 'social distance' and 'fields of force' are based on these ideas. And of course many have argued that such inequities exert a key structuring force (opportunities and constraints) upon social interaction. Structure as a distribution of resources is neither virtual nor internalized within actors. It exists between them.

Finally, the value of resources, which is essential to their identity as resources, is in many instances necessarily relational. If I were shipwrecked on a desert island, for example, any coins that I managed to salvage from my sinking ship would be worthless in the absence of others prepared to accept them in return for other goods. Even if I were not alone I would need to persuade Friday to accept my coins as currency before they would be of any value. The value of coins presupposes agreement between actors. It is an emergent property which cannot be individualized. Of course some resources would have a use value. I could always throw my coins at predatory animals to scare them off and, in that respect, would be advantaged by having them. But use value does not pre-empt the concepts of either value or resources. Exchange value is very important to a properly social account of 'resources' and it presupposes exchange relations.

Rules, habits and conventions

In what follows I will be developing an alternative notion of social structures centred upon 'social worlds'. As a way into this, however, I want to explore the concepts of rule and habitus in a little more detail and also to (re)introduce a further concept, convention, as used by Becker (1982), which is preferable to either. I begin with a definition of rules and habitus.

'Rules' are not all of a kind. In particular we must distinguish 'regulative' from 'constitutive' rules (Hollis 1995). This distinction is not always clear cut but in essence regulative rules serve to regulate activities which exist independently of them whereas constitutive rules enter into the very definition of a particular activity. The rule prohibiting noise in a library is an example of a regulative rule. One could have a library in which people were noisy. It might not work very well but it would still be a library. If I were to designate an empty room in my department as 'the library', however, without putting any books or other 'reading resources' in it, then I have broken a constitutive rule regarding libraries. There is no library without books and critics will say that I do not know what a library is.

To some extent this is a distinction between moral rules and rules of meaning. Acts which break regulative rules aren't typically meaningless. They are just wrong (assuming that the rule is legitimate). Acts which fail to follow constitutive rules, by contrast, may appear meaningless, at least insofar as we try to make sense of them in terms of constitutive rules that they fail to follow and cannot find another set of constitutive rules through which to make sense of them. Calling an empty room a library might make sense in the context of a joke, for example, or perhaps as a political statement about university funding but if I am not joking or protesting then my action makes no sense.

Note that in this sense constitutive rules are interpretive devices for making sense of what others are doing. They are not just rules that we follow (or don't) in the course of our actions. Note also that it is to some degree impossible to talk about right and wrong until we have established what set of constitutive rules are supposed to be applied to a situation, at least insofar as the establishment of meaning is concerned. Calling a bookless room a library isn't right or wrong in itself. It depends what the actor is doing: joking, making a political point or making a statement of fact.

Constitutive rules may have a moral aspect, however. Students in my department might be angry about my 'library', for example. They might tell me that I cannot call a bookless room a 'library'. Their anger may stem, in part, from what they take to be my breach of a variety of regulative rules. Perhaps they feel that I have *deceived* them by claiming to provide something that I am not providing and have thus broken the rules regarding honesty between students and teachers. But if I were to take the view that I can call whatever I like a library this would provoke moral indignation and sanctions in its own right. They would say that *I have no right* to disregard the agreed upon rules of language (or meanings of words) and that *I ought* to comply with them. They would deem me either bad or mad. We are expected to adhere to constitutive rules and are punished or at least called to account when we do not.

Bourdieu (1977, 1992) formulates the concept of habitus in the context of a critique of 'rules' as formulated in the (structuralist) work of Levi-Strauss (1969), which analyses patterns of marriage and kinship in terms of an underlying rule-structure. He posits four criticisms of Levi-Strauss's rules.

First, he argues that at least some of these rules belong to an official picture of the social world and are often subverted, circumvented or observed only in the breach in practice. When asked about their practices by a social scientist, actors will often give a normative account of how they are supposed to behave, Bourdieu contends, and they may believe this to be a faithful account as they do not observe their own practice in detail, but practice very often differs from official representations of it. This is a damning critique because Levi-Strauss, as noted above, purports to 'dissolve man' in favour of an analysis of the rules which determine her action. Rules, Bourdieu is arguing, do not determine anything. Actors routinely deviate from and play with rules and we therefore cannot dispense with them.

Second, and relatedly, Bourdieu finds the concept of rules too rigid to account for the way in which actors act. Actors pursue their own ends in strategic ways, for Bourdieu; they do not slavishly follow rules. Moreover, they often improvise and innovate. Again, agency is central.

Third, he notes that where rules are not aspects of an official picture of the world posited by lay members, they are intellectual constructs devised by analysts in an effort to make sense of what they observe but which, qua analytic constructs, do not belong to the actor's frame of reference and, as such, cannot enter into an explanation of their action. Most of us are unaware of the linguistic rules identified by Saussure (1959), for example, and it is questionable, therefore, whether we could really be said to be following such rules when we speak or write. As Merleau-Ponty puts it: 'Saussure may show that each act of expression becomes significant only as a modulation of a general system of expression and only insofar as it is differentiated from other linguistic gestures. The marvel is that before Saussure we did not know anything about this, and that we forget it again each time we speak – to begin with when we speak of Saussure's ideas' (1961: 81). A 'rule', in other words, is just a convenient way for an analyst to describe a regularity in practice. It is not a real element in the domain analysed by the analyst and cannot be invoked, therefore, as a causal mechanism. This begs the question of how regularities in practice can be explained and Bourdieu answers that question by reference to habitus. 'Rules' are not real and explain nothing but habitus are and do.

Levi-Strauss (1963) seems to get round this objection by insisting that rules are unconscious, but for Bourdieu – quite aside from the difficulties involved in the notion of unconscious rules[2] – this exemplifies a problematic intellectualism that runs throughout structuralism. Levi-Strauss constructs his rules on the basis of an interpretation of empirically observed practices which are considerably less regular and considerably more messy than his construct. 'Rules' are derived from practice. But this process of abstraction is forgotten and the temporal ordering of events reversed as 'rules' are invoked to explain practice, as if they pre-existed and caused it. The structuralist, qua intellectualist, confuses her model with the reality she purports to be modeling.

Finally, Bourdieu notes that rule-based explanations underdetermine action and succumb to problems of infinite regression. Rules have to be applied correctly, that is, in the right way, in the right context etc., which begs the question of how actors are able to apply them correctly? How do actors know when and how to apply a rule? There could be rules about this too but that just moves the problem one step on (how do we know when and how to apply those rules?) and so on to infinity.

Habitus are, at one level, a means of bringing this regression to a halt for Bourdieu. Actors do not have recourse to endless sets of rules, he argues; rather they enjoy a practical mastery of different forms of practice, a practical sense of how to act, which steers their conduct. Habitus are these forms of mastery, this practical sense, acquired through practice. Moreover, like the skills of the footballer or some other skilled game player they do not preclude innovation, improvisation or strategy. Rather they enable such forms of action. A habitus is a 'feel for the game' which allows an actor to respond in a strategic and potentially innovative way in a particular field without having recourse to conscious thought or reflection. It is not unconscious, however, merely a pre-reflective disposition whose reality is empirically manifest in action itself.

Bourdieu's critique is impressive but insufficient and flawed. In the first instance, it is noteworthy that he doesn't dispense with the concept of rules altogether. He just deems them less fundamental. Marriage rules exist but they do not determine marital practice because actors' interests enter into practice and they bend and circumvent the rules, albeit generally in ways which allow them to demonstrate some token observance. More importantly, his notion of a 'feel for the game' implies a 'game' which, in turn, implies rules (both constitutive and regulative) of the game. Actors are, by virtue of their habitus, skilled players of a game, but the status of this game, qua game, is never adequately explored and it implies that rules must enter into practice at some point. Games involve rules, both constitutive and regulative.

In talking about 'games' Bourdieu implies that engagement between actors involves some level of agreement between them about what they are doing and what is permissible. Without this, even conflict and competition would be impossible and social life would descend into chaos. As Bourdieu himself notes, actors in conflict must at least agree about the source of their disagreement and that it is worth fighting over. Actors playing a game must agree about the game they are playing. They must agree about what is involved and what is permitted. The concept of rules seeks to capture this sense of agreement in a way that 'habitus' does not.

We can elaborate this point by way of an argument by Winch (1958). Engaging in an earlier round of debate regarding 'rules' and (in this instance) 'habits', Winch concedes that the two concepts do more or less the same work. However, he claims that 'rules' is preferable because it indicates that there are right and wrong ways of acting, thus tapping into a normative texture that is integral to social life. Moreover, he maintains that rules are integral to the meaningful nature of social life. The earlier example of the bookless library illustrates this point. The sense that libraries have books is not just a sediment within my habitus nor even the habitus of all actors in my society, taken as individuals. It is a sense that we share and that we enforce between ourselves. Heads of sociology who try to get away with bookless libraries are called to account and subject to sanctions. This is a matter of social norms but equally of meaning. If libraries do not necessarily contain books then it is not clear what a library is, what makes it different from a room. The term loses any meaning. To be meaningful a word must demarcate something. It can't refer or apply to everything since, in doing so, it applies to nothing in particular and has no meaning. There must be rules as to its use. Even anarchism, as Winch points out, entails some rules. Advocates of law and order and a strong state cannot call themselves anarchists, whatever free play we might allow in the term, otherwise 'anarchist' fails to demarcate anything and loses any meaning. The concept of rules, Winch argues, better captures this sense of right and wrong than habit. Habits can be good or bad but not right or wrong and, as such, they do not suffice to capture the important moral and meaningful texture of social life. Note also that this hints at an intersubjective dimension to rules which is not present in relation to habits or habitus. Rules do not exist within actors but rather between them.

As we have seen from Bourdieu's critique, discussed above, however, 'rules' is a problematic concept too. Neither habitus nor rules adequately captures the regularities that they purport to theorize. As an alternative I propose the concept of 'conventions'. I draw strongly from Becker (1982) here but also from Wittgenstein's (1953) critique of the concept of rules. I begin with this critique. It centres upon rule adherence: what is it to follow a rule?

Wittgenstein, rules and conventions

Rule adherence, as Wittgenstein (1953) understands it, is not akin to repetition of a set pattern of behaviour. Rules have to be applied and therefore *understood*. To follow a rule entails that we go beyond the limited set of examples and illustrations from which we learn the rule and extend or apply it in new circumstances. His illustration focuses upon sequences of numbers which follow a distinct pattern (rule) which a social actor is required to continue. I might be presented with the sequence 2, 4, 6, 8, for example, and asked to continue it, following the rule that is in play here. Assumedly I would continue 10, 12, 14 etc. One difficulty with this, drawn out in Kripke's (1982) interpretation of Wittgenstein, is that it is not always possible to grasp what the rule is. In the above case it seems that the rule is 'add 2', such that I would continue 10, 12, 14 and so on, but it might be 'add 2 until you get to 8 then start subtracting 2 until you get back to zero'. How would I know? I will leave this point for the moment and focus upon the inference that Wittgenstein wishes us to draw: that following a rule entails understanding. Rule following is intelligent and not mechanical behavior. We must understand a rule in order to follow it. I must, for example, grasp what is happening in the number sequence in order to continue it. I cannot simply reiterate the numbers presented to me by way of the example, i.e. 2, 4, 6, 8.

This begs the question of what it is to understand a rule. Wittgenstein's first response to this question is that understanding a rule is not an intellectual or discursive operation. It does not suffice to understand the rule in the above example that I can stipulate that one must 'add 2'. In the first instance this merely shifts the problem one step on. We may now ask what it is to add 2. Furthermore, reciting the formula is not actually following the rule and may therefore exist independently of the requisite understanding. In the example above, the correct continuation of the sequence '2, 4, 6, 8' is not 'keep on adding two' but rather '10, 12, 14 . . .'. This is salient because I may be able to formulate the rule without understanding it. To give a more plausible example, I might recite the formulas and rules of calculus without actually being capable of implementing them, in which case it would be fair to say that I do not really understand them. Conversely, I may understand rules, in the sense that I follow them perfectly, without being capable of formulating them discursively. Most social actors can speak and write grammatically, for example, without being capable of explicitly formulating the rules that they are following.

Similarly, to return to a point from Chapter 5, Wittgenstein rejects the idea that understanding consists in a psychological experience of any kind, e.g. a 'click of comprehension' or an 'aha' moment. Feeling that one understands something and actually understanding it often fail to coincide and are therefore distinct. It is not uncommon for an individual to say 'now I get it', moved by a feeling that they do indeed get it, only to find that they don't. Conversely, understanding something does not necessarily involve a feeling of any sort. When we speak or write, for example, we do not generally do so with a feeling that we are correctly grasping the rules of grammar even if we are. And even when we first learned to follow the rules of grammar we may not have had such a feeling.

So what does understanding involve? For Wittgenstein the answer lies, in the first instance, in embodied competence. To understand is to be able to go on, to complete the number sequence properly, to do calculus, to speak and write grammatically. Understanding and thus rule following are embodied practices.

Merleau-Ponty (1962, 1965) makes a similar argument. Understanding, for him, is embodied competence and, insofar as it is acquired, 'habit'. Moreover, in an argument which parallels Wittgenstein's denial that understanding consists in feelings, he argues that we do not and cannot know what we understand by way of introspection. If I want to know whether or not I understand something I do not look within myself for a sign. Rather I try to do something in an effort to see if I can indeed do it. My knowledge of my own understanding derives from reflexive observation of my practices.

There is a problem here, however: how do I know that my practices are 'right' and that I have, indeed, understood? How do I know that my attempt at calculus is correct? This is a fundamental issue for Wittgenstein and one which touches upon aspects of his famous 'private language argument' (at least as interpreted by Kripke 1982). To test my understanding I need some sort of criteria against which to measure it and those criteria must be external to me. Judging my own performance against internal criteria (setting aside the problem of what they might be) is, as Wittgenstein puts it, akin to buying a second copy of the same morning paper in an effort to check the veracity of the first. Indeed we come back to the issue noted above: that something seems right to me is not the same as it actually being right. So what criteria do I have?

For Wittgenstein the answer is 'other people'. I understand if, over a series of instances, others accept my practice as correct. I know that I understand calculus because, over successive iterations, I approach problems in the same or a similar way to others and derive the same answers. But how do we know that others understand? Here we get to a crucial point. For Wittgenstein, the rule itself consists in agreement between social actors as to how to 'go on' in specific situations. This is not agreement in opinions or explicitly held views, however. It is agreement in what he calls 'forms of life'. What Wittgenstein means by 'forms of life' is open to interpretation. It may be that they have a biological component. At various points Wittgenstein seems to indicate that other animals are wired differently to humans and that this is significant to the issues he is addressing. He notes, for example, that 'If a lion could talk we could not understand him' (1953: 223). Furthermore, he observes how the human tendency to look in the direction that another is pointing, which clearly plays a key role in communication, is often not found in dogs, who study the finger. Notwithstanding this, however, 'forms of life' have a clear social dimension. They are conventions or, rather, agreement in forms of life is another way of saying 'convention', as Becker's definition of convention – 'earlier agreements now become customary' (1982: 29) – makes clear.

There is a twofold sociality involved here. Rules are (1) negotiated by actors, in practice, that is, in interaction, on the basis of conventions which are themselves (2) sedimented residues of earlier agreements arrived at in practice. 'Agreement' need not imply active and willing consensus in either of these instance. To reiterate, we are not talking about opinions but rather about what people do. And of course actions can agree and such agreements become institutionalized on the basis of coercion. Actors can enforce their ways of doing things, as when colonial powers establish their language as the official language of the society they have colonized. Note also, however, that conventions are neither static nor determining of conduct. They evolve with the dynamics of the social world, as inter-actors adapt, and actors may elect to interact in unconventional ways. Doing so, according to Becker, is often costly, not only in the sense that it might attract sanctions but also because conventions tend to make action easy and abandoning them therefore introduces difficulty. A musician, to take one of Becker's examples, may elect to abandon Western tonal scales, musical instruments (which embody conventions) and forms of writing music. It is not impossible. But it is very difficult, especially if the musician wants others to understand and like her music, because others 'read' and appreciate music by means of the conventions that the musician is electing to reject. A musician who wants to revolutionize music, therefore, must seek to revolutionize music audiences too.

'Convention' provides a better basis for our conception of structure than either rules or habitus, not least because it combines aspects of both without succumbing to their major problems. Convention implies the embodied know-how suggested by habitus, for example, but also the agreement and normativity suggested by 'rules' and integral to meaning.

Convention is just one aspect of structure, however. Following the above discussion I suggest that structure involves *conventions*, *resources* and *networks*. In the next chapter I consider how these various elements of structure overlap and interpenetrate. In what remains of this chapter, however, I provide a preliminary sketch, drawing upon the concept of 'social worlds' as developed by symbolic interactionists and by Becker (1982) in particular. 'Worlds', as Becker defines them in *Art Worlds*, are constituted through interaction focused upon particular objects of mutual interest or concern, interactions in which actors mobilize resources and networks of relations and interdependency. In worlds inter-actors draw upon conventions, both general and specific to the world in question, which facilitate coordination, communication and the co-production of meaning.

I use the concept of worlds to explore structure because I believe that structures should be thought of not as 'things' in their own right but as properties of something else which 'has' or manifests structure, in this case dynamic and evolving social worlds. Worlds entail structure, they are structured, but they also entail interactive dynamism, qualitative content and a concreteness and processual nature that is often missing in abstract discussions of structure. To analyse 'structure' is to abstract from this rather richer social reality. This is an important and often necessary step to take but we should not mistake the abstraction for what it abstracts from and we need concepts which operate at a lower level of abstraction, a more concrete level, if we are to do sociological justice to the relational, social world.

Social worlds

Social worlds are networks of interaction demarcated by their participants' mutual involvement in specifiable sets of activities. They form around sports, art forms and genres, pastimes, occupations, locations, conflicts and controversies, and projects, anything that can become a focus for collective interest and action. Worlds are networks whose members manifest a shared orientation towards specific conventions and common adherence to a shared framework of meaning. They are generated by interaction but also function as a context and environment which shapes interaction. As actors 'enter' a world, interacting with others whom they recognize as members of it, they shift their orientation and perhaps also their identity, thereby collaboratively (with the other) (re)generating their part of that world. They orient to the world and in doing so bring part of it (back) into being. Moreover, as Shibutani (1955) in particular suggests, worlds serve as a reference group for their members, providing them with standards against which to measure normality, success, failure etc. They might be very small, in terms of the numbers of people involved and the geographical area spanned, as in the world of a particular family, neighbourhood or circle of friends. But they might equally be global, as in the world of international political relations.

The boundaries of a social world, according to Shibutani, 'are set neither by territory nor by formal group membership but by the limits of effective communication' (1955: 566) and by 'differential association', that is, by patterns of who interacts with whom about what. Worlds are networks. They 'come into existence with the existence of communication channels' (ibid.: 567) and extend to all who plug into those channels. To be in a world is to interact with others within it. Worlds equally centre upon the content of interaction, however, and the identities adopted by parties to them. To enter a 'criminal world', for example, it is not sufficient to interact and form bonds with criminals. Criminality must in some way enter into those interactions and the identities adopted by both self and other. I might know many criminals but unless criminality in some way forms a part of our interactions I remain outside the criminal world to which they belong. Communication need not be face-to-face, however. Shibutani insists that it may be by way of periodicals or newsletters, a list to which we might now add websites, blogs, Twitter etc.

The networks which constitute worlds are not only communication networks. They are equally networks of resource mobilization. Actors pursue and exchange resources and goods in social worlds, sometimes deploying them in pursuit of other, further goods. Some of these goods and resources are generic across most worlds – money makes most worlds go round, for example – but some may be specific to a particular world. The ability to 'spike' a tree or disable a mechanical digger (human capital) may have little value outside the world of radical environmental protest, for example, whilst sociological datasets from the 1960s probably have little value outside the social worlds of academic sociology and history.

Connecting with interactionist work on 'careers', Shibutani adds that a world is an 'order . . . which serves as a stage on which each participant seeks to carve out his career and to maintain and enhance his status' (1955: 567). By implication this suggests that some worlds involve a division of labour, with positions or roles which actors move between, generating a career path and also a status hierarchy. This concept of careers again points us to the networked character of worlds. Paraphrasing Hall (1948), for example, Becker defines careers as:

> the patterned series of adjustments made by the individual to the 'network of institutions, formal organisations and informal relationships' in which the work of the occupation is performed.
>
> (Becker 1952: 470)

Furthermore, anticipating important work on 'vacancy chains' from within the network analytic tradition (see White 1970), he notes that a key contingency which can shape an individual's career trajectory is the movement of others in their network, with the consequent opening up of positions that this generates. Actors enjoy an opportunity to move into certain positions in a social world as others vacate those positions. Without movement further up the chain, opportunities are limited.

Similarly, Hall (1948) identifies a network-related career contingency when he discusses the role of the 'inner fraternity' of an occupational network in allocating jobs. Career trajectories, he observes, depend at least as much upon who the actor knows within a given world as what they know. Contact with important others in a world constitutes an important advantage. Again, however, this is world specific. Friendship with an Oxford don is of little use if one is seeking fashion advice or an opportunity to fence stolen goods.

Social worlds start to sound like occupational worlds in these accounts but this is only one area of application. Interactionists have used the concepts 'world' and 'career' to explore individual trajectories and forms of social organization which are far removed from the formal economy and occupational structure. And they insist that worlds can assume radically different forms. Strauss (1973), for example, claims that worlds might be tiny or huge; local, national or international; geographically anchored or dispersed. Some are public, he notes; others are covert or scarcely visible:

> Some are so emergent as to be barely graspable; others are well established, even well organised. Some have relatively tight boundaries; others possess permeable boundaries. Some are very hierarchical; some are less so or scarcely at all [etc.].
>
> (Strauss 1973: 121)

The point is not that anything goes or that these variations do not matter. On the contrary, Strauss is encouraging us to reflect both upon the ways in which worlds might vary and upon the likely consequences of such variations. This need not preclude identification of the key components of worlds, however, and in particular those elements which lend them structure. *Art Worlds* is invaluable in this respect.

The structure(s) of social worlds

As defined by Becker (1982), social worlds have three crucial components: networks, conventions and resources. They are networks, constituted by way of interactions and relations which draw upon specific conventions and which involve, in many cases, the exchange of resources which are often unequally distributed across members of the network. These three concepts, networks, conventions and resources, have all been discussed to some extent in the preceding chapters. They are important elements of social interaction. But they are also the basic components of social structure. Social worlds are social structures or rather social worlds are structured and social structures are interesting to us, as sociologists, insofar as they are structures of social worlds.

'Social structure' has two aspects as I use it. First, it implies that social interactions and relations are patterned rather than random. They manifest a structure which we can seek to describe and analyse. We see this in networks in the form of patterns of connection. Some networks are very dense, others sparse; some are centred upon key hubs, others are decentred; some manifest a clear core-periphery distinction (see Chapter 9), others don't and so on. This is illustrated in Figure 8.1 which demonstrates different patterns of connection between the same set of 10 hypothetical actors (the graph was drawn using the Ucinet software (Borgatti, Everett and Freeman 2002)).

We see structure in conventions in the respect that the way in which actors interact with one another betrays a pattern. The way in which friends interact, for example, is different from the way in which colleagues interact or doctors and patients or lovers. Each has a pattern which makes it recognizable and dis-tinguishes it. To talk of convention is, amongst other things, to identify such distinctive patterns within interaction, patterns which are iterated both across time and, in some cases and to some extent, across different pairs of interactors.

We see structure in relation to resources, most obviously, by way of their distribution. Some resources might be normally distributed within a population, others manifest a Pareto distribution etc. And individuals can be located and clustered in accordance with the amounts and types of resources they possess. Bourdieu's famous correspondence maps, which locate individuals, their practices and/or occupations etc. within a 'social space' constituted by a scatterplot whose axes measure both the volume of the sampled actors' capital resources and also their ratio of cultural to economic capital, is an obvious example of this (see Chapter 3). Social space is structured, for Bourdieu, and demonstrably, visibly so in the respect that certain practices and groups tend to cluster together in it.

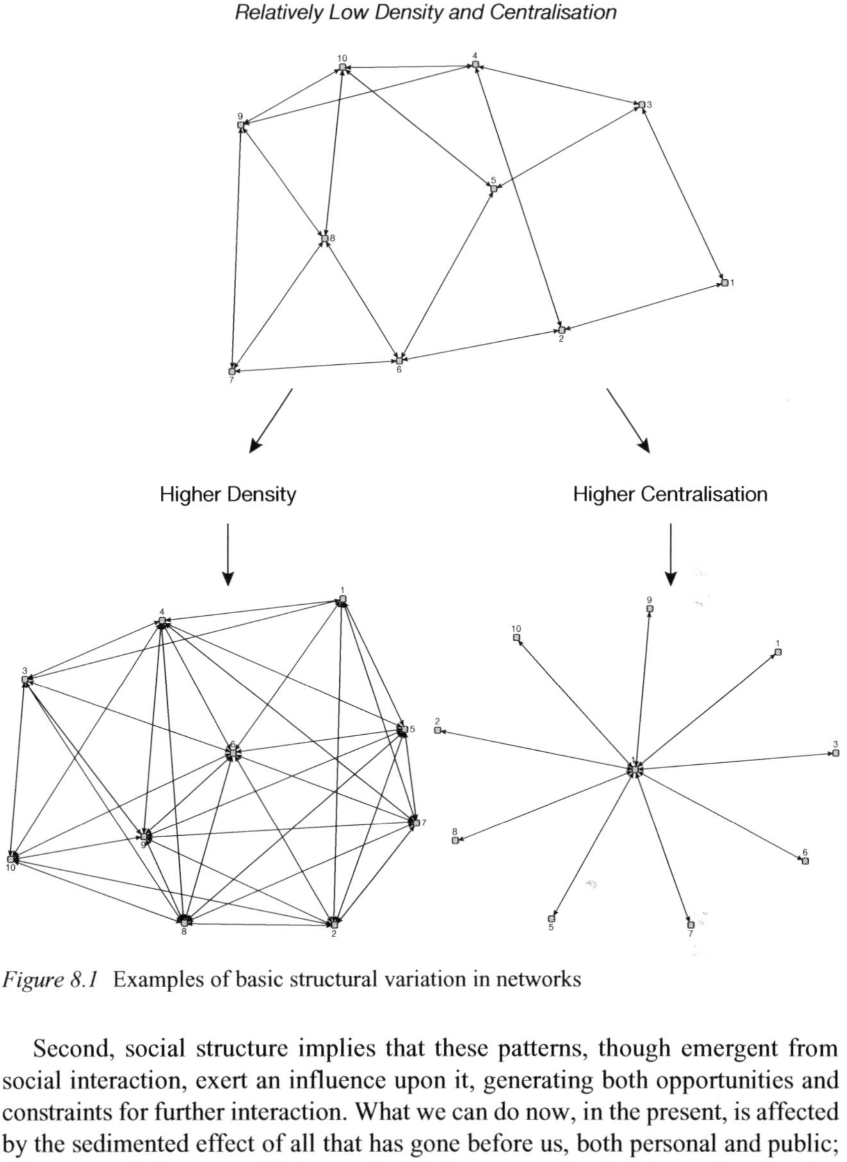

Relatively Low Density and Centralisation

Higher Density   Higher Centralisation

Figure 8.1 Examples of basic structural variation in networks

Second, social structure implies that these patterns, though emergent from social interaction, exert an influence upon it, generating both opportunities and constraints for further interaction. What we can do now, in the present, is affected by the sedimented effect of all that has gone before us, both personal and public; the traces of the past which remain in the present in the form of networks, conventions and (distributions of) resources.

I discuss the constraints and opportunities effected by structure more extensively in the next chapter. For present purposes it must suffice to say, in relation to networks, that who an actor interacts with (and doesn't), how many alters they connect with, whether those alters are themselves connected to one another and whether they belong to a particular 'circle', all affect opportunities and constraints for them. Furthermore, opportunities for collective action and the speed with which ideas, innovations and other resources diffuse and circulate within a world all depend upon how it is 'wired up', that is, upon network structures. Likewise, conventions facilitate organization and coordination, which is enabling, and, in the form of know-how, sometimes allow us to do what we would not otherwise be able to do; but they can also channel our actions in particular directions, if only because it is always easier to follow a convention than to depart from it, blinding us to other options. And they can prove resistant to change. Choice, as I have argued elsewhere, necessarily presuppose habit and thus convention, but it is necessarily always shaped by it too (Crossley 2001). The opportunities and constraints which stem from the distribution of resources are more obvious. Many lines of (inter)action presuppose access to certain resources.

Structure does not determine action, however. Constraints and opportunities are not causes. Purposive interaction remains central to my account, as does the deliberation and reflexivity which, as my discussion of Mead in Chapters 5 and 6 demonstrated, emerge within it. Even when actors work entirely within the parameters of established social structures, which is certainly not always and perhaps not often, the details of what happens are determined by them in their interaction, whether consensually, coercively or however. The situation is akin to a football match in which everyone plays in accordance with the rules, in established teams, with pre-determined resources, but the precise course and outcome of the game are unknown in advance and depend upon what players collectively do and how they interact.

Of course the situation is different to football, in part because we never start a new game afresh, wiping the score board clean, but also because the game evolves as we play it, in virtue of the way in which play it. As Wittgenstein (1953: 39) notes of language games, in some we 'make up the rules as we go along' or 'alter them'. Indeed transformation of a world can become a focus of the world itself and thus integral to its structure. As such a world, like a language:

> can be seen as an ancient city: a maze of little streets and squares of old and new houses, and of houses with additions from various periods; and this surrounded by a multitude of new boroughs with straight regular streets and uniform houses.
>
> (Wittgenstein 1953: 8)

Social worlds are patchworks of old and new, always open to modification, change and addition but at the same time containing aspects which have endured across time. Their structures are always in process, always potentially changing and becoming.

Worlds are further removed from games, moreover, in the respect that both change and resistance to change may be relatively deliberate on the behalf of 'players', especially when those players are dis/advantaged by the current structure of the 'game'. Shaping the game to best suit one's interests, in both senses of that word, might be part of the game – a metagame within the game. Furthermore, participation in some 'games' can be imposed upon players, by other players, such that withdrawal is impossible and refusal to play counts merely as a move within the game. Note, however, that worlds are not necessarily conflict ridden or competitive and those that are may be so only in certain of their aspects. Conflict and competition characterize only some parts of some worlds.

Finally, note that I use the plural, 'structures'. Although I do not rule out the possibility of an ultimate structure of structures (a universe of worlds) and I believe that relations between worlds are very important, I believe that it is more fruitful for sociologists to explore the various ways in which different social worlds are structured and linked. Any given world may be structured in different ways and different social worlds most definitely are. The purpose of sociology, or one of them, is to explore these diverse structures.

Conclusion

I began this chapter with a brief reflection upon the structure/agency 'problem', arguing that there is no problem, as such, because interaction necessarily entails both the initiative and intelligence of purposive actors (agency) and the constraints and opportunities (structure) constituted by way of their interdependency with one another (networks), their resources and the conventions they have both created for themselves and inherited from historical ancestors. The social world necessarily involves both agency and structure in some balance – and there is every reason to suppose that the balance shifts relative to specific situations.

There is a problem, however, with the concept of structure developed by Giddens and Bourdieu in their respective 'solutions' to the agency/structure 'problem'. In their work social structure is often curiously asocial in character, affording no place to interaction and concrete relations. Moreover, whilst their respective conceptions of rules and habitus are interesting and insightful, neither quite suffices to capture the aspect of structure that they purport to investigate.

Drawing upon Wittgenstein (1953) and Becker (1982) I suggested that the concept of *convention* might be better suited to capture this aspect, and I suggested that convention is one of three aspects of social structure, the other two being *networks* and *resources*. I have also warned against an abstract focus on 'struc-ture', however, suggesting that structures are always structures *of* something or other. Structures are not 'things'; rather, they are properties. More specifically, I have suggested that we might think of them as properties of dynamic and evolving 'social worlds' which emerge from the interactions of actors who con-verge around foci of common interest. Worlds manifest a structure by virtue of their networked character and the role of conventions and resources within them. In the next chapter I expand upon this argument, exploring networks, conventions and resources in more detail.

9 Networks, conventions and resources
The structure(s) of social worlds

In Chapter 8 I argued that social structures are best conceived as structures-of 'social worlds', as defined in interactionist sociology. In addition to the shared interests of their members, I argued, social worlds comprise social networks, conventions and a distribution of key resources which are mobilized and exchanged in interaction and which lend worlds a structure. In this chapter I elaborate upon this position by way of a more detailed examination of networks, conventions and resources. The aims of the chapter are threefold. First, I aim to pin down the meaning of networks, conventions and resources more precisely than in the previous chapter, to explore the place of each in the constitution of the other, and to discuss further why I believe that the combination of these elements, in the context of social worlds, merits the label 'social structure'. Second, I aim to make my case more concretely, and with examples. I argued in the previous chapter that the concept of social worlds allows us to draw our debate to a more concrete level. Here I hope to demonstrate that. To that end I draw upon some of my own empirical work on both the world of a local gym and the world of UK punk and post-punk music in Manchester and London in the latter part of the 1970s.

My final aim is to introduce the notion that worlds themselves are linked and form a network by virtue of the actors who belong simultaneously to more than one of them and move between them. This argument is important, I suggest, because it contributes to an understanding of key social divisions and of broad divisions in lifestyle, of the type described by Pierre Bourdieu (1984), amongst others. In effect it affords a more relational and social way of understanding the patterns of division and distinction that Bourdieu identifies than he himself offers.

The chapter opens with a discussion of networks, particularly as conceived in the tradition of social network analysis (Scott 2000; Wasserman and Faust 1994). I then consider the claim that social structures are networks of roles, rather than individuals, a claim which is problematic but worthy of discussion. I elaborate this claim first by considering 'blockmodelling' methods in network analysis which purport to identify and analyse roles, and then through a consideration of the conventions involved in roles. This is followed by a broader and more general discussion of conventions and their significance for 'social structure'. After a brief discussion of 'official' and 'unofficial' structures, the focus then shifts to resources, before I turn to connections between worlds and their sociological significance. All network graphs used in the chapter and all network measures taken have been produced with the Ucinet software (Borgatti, Everett and Freeman 2002).

Social worlds as social networks

A social network, for present purposes, comprises a set of social actors and a set of relations between certain of those actors. It can be represented graphically, as in Figure 9.1. What counts as a 'relation' will vary. In social network analysis we select the relations we examine in accordance with the issue and indeed the 'world' we are investigating, always allowing for the fact that multiple types of relations might be salient in the same world and that the same pair of actors might enjoy multiple types of (or 'multiplex') relations.

Defined thus, networks have variable properties and sometimes form particular structural configurations. I offer some illustrations of this below. For present purposes, however, note that the significance of these properties and figurations is that they generate specific opportunities and constraints for the actors involved in them. This is why it is legitimate to think of them as social structures.

This might happen at the individual level, when, for example, certain actors are better positioned within a network for certain forms of action than other actors. Equally, however, it may be that the global properties of the network affect all actors within it in the same way and to the same extent, affecting their capacity to pursue individual and/or collective goals. Likewise, although networks do not cause actions, certain figurations may, for example, 'encourage' harmony or conflict, at least in the respect that they variously facilitate or inhibit the generation of trust, cooperation, good communication etc. Finally, between individual positions and the network as a whole it is often possible to identify sub-networks within a network (e.g. a 'core' and a 'periphery') whose presence has effects both within and beyond the boundary that demarcates them.

As a first illustration of these points consider the rise of the world of punk rock in the UK in 1976 and more especially two of its most widely celebrated local manifestations in London and Manchester respectively (Crossley 2008c, 2009). There is plenty of evidence in relation to both cities of the various factors that are commonly cited as explanations for the rise of punk: economic decline; dissatisfaction with the commercial music scene, which was deemed both organizationally corrupt and aesthetically bankrupt; and admiration for a variety of new and exciting musical forms, including especially those of a new wave of bands from Detroit and New York. In terms of these factors punk was equally as likely to have originated in Manchester as in London. But it didn't. It emerged first in London, raising the question of why? There are various reasons but I have suggested elsewhere that network structure is amongst them (Crossley 2008c). The individuals who were to play a pioneering role in London's punk 'world' were already densely connected before punk, making the collective action involved in the generation of their scene possible. Those in Manchester were not.

We see this in the graphs of the respective networks, as they were in mid 1976 (Figures 9.1 and 9.2). In these graphs individual actors are represented by small squares (vertices) and relations between them, which in this case are defined either as close friendships which predated 1976 or by co-involvement in musical projects, are represented by way of lines (edges) connecting the vertices.

Some of the differences between the two networks are evident from the graphs. The network in Figure 9.2 is much less well connected. In addition, however, we can, and in less clear-cut cases might need to, explore them further by way of the aforementioned network measures (for an extended discussion of these measures see Wasserman and Faust 1994; Scott 2000). In the first instance, note that the London network forms a single 'component'; there is a path of ties connecting every actor to every other. Everybody is linked, albeit often indirectly, to everybody else. Furthermore, if we take the shortest path between each pair of actors in the network and identify the longest of these shortest paths, we can derive the diameter of the network: in this case 3. The network spans 3 ties (degrees) at its widest point. The Manchester network, by contrast, is fragmented and involves a high number of individually unconnected actors (isolates). Most of the actors in the network have no path to most of the others and the diameter of the network, technically, therefore, is infinite. I will consider the significance of this shortly but first we can consider a number of further measures.

We can compare the densities of the two networks by, in each case, dividing the number of ties in the network by the number of ties that are possible given the number of people in the network. Density scores always range between 0 (minimal density, nobody is connected to anybody) and 1 (maximum density, everybody is connected to everybody else). London's is 0.2396, meaning that 23.96 per cent of all possible ties are realized. Manchester's is 0.0486, meaning that just 4.86 per cent of all possible ties were realized. The London network is therefore much denser than the Manchester network.

Relatedly, we can record the number of connections of each actor in the network (each vertex in the graph), their 'degree', and derive an average. In London, average degree is 10.783, with a standard deviation of 6.025, meaning that every actor in the network has, on average, 11 contacts within it (although there is considerable variation around that mean). In Manchester the figures are 3.016 and 3.954 respectively. The would-be punks of Manchester, at this point in time, knew far fewer fellow would-be punks than their contemporaries in London.

These differences in network structure made a difference. The formation of a social world, in this case a music scene, requires coordination and mutual influence between actors. This is only possible within components, however. It does not happen, by definition, where individuals or clusters of individuals are not connected. Furthermore, it will be more likely where ideas, information, innovations and other resources have less distance to travel, which entails a smaller diameter and either high density or, to introduce a concept I discuss later, high centralization. Information and innovations are more likely to reach people and more likely to arrive intact when they have fewer intermediaries to pass through and thus less distance to travel. This applies to all resources. And actors can more

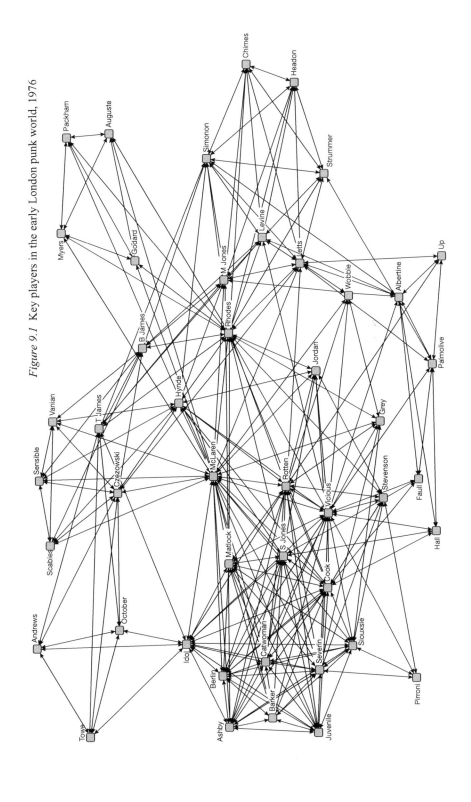

Figure 9.1 Key players in the early London punk world, 1976

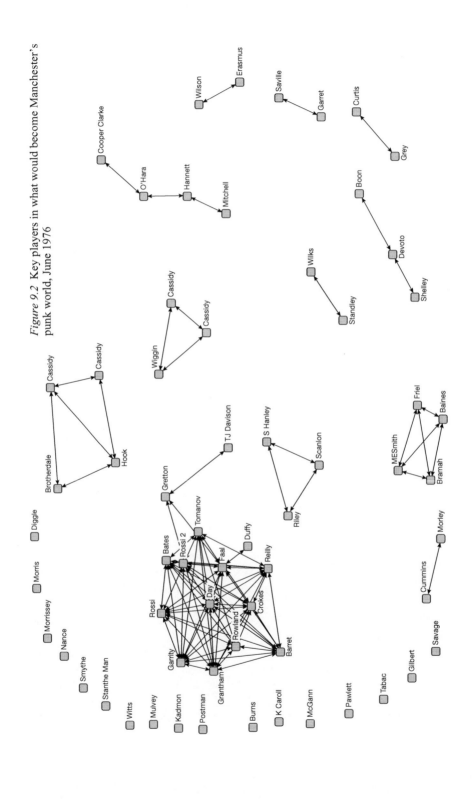

Figure 9.2 Key players in what would become Manchester's punk world, June 1976

easily find the alters and resources they require (e.g. they can more easily find a drummer or a bassist for their band) when information about the location of such resources has less distance to travel. If my friend's friend is a drummer with similar musical tastes to me then I am much more likely to hear of them than I am my friend's friend's friend's friend.

In addition, high density has been shown to be important in relation to the maintenance of deviant and distinctive cultural patterns (Bott 1957; Milroy 1987). Conventions are maintained to the extent that actors reinforce them for one another in multiple relations such that their maintenance is more likely in networks where most actors interact with one another (high density networks) or at least networks where the average number of ties (average degree) is high. The key studies which support these claims all focus upon the preservation of traditional cultural patterns in a context of wider social change (ibid.). There is no reason to suppose that the same is not true of new cultural innovations, such as punk, however. Indeed, there is every reason to suppose that it might be more important in relation to innovation, and especially controversial innovations, such as punk, which are likely to attract criticism and even attack (punks were both physically and verbally abused on the streets in the early days, and also vilified in the newspapers). As work in social movement studies suggests, dense networks provide more protection and support, as well as a sense of solidarity and *esprit de corps* for actors who are going against the grain (McAdam 1982; Crossley 2008a).

Extending this point, Coleman (1988, 1990) has shown that closed networks (or sub-networks), that is, clusters of actors who are densely tied amongst their selves but enjoy few meaningful ties beyond their cluster, provide fertile ground for the emergence of deviant sub-cultures and the incentive mechanisms which encourage their members to conform to their emergent conventions. Mutual influence is more likely to generate homogeneity where actors are influencing and being influenced in a closed network, he argues, because there is no external influence to dilute or detract from an emerging consensus. Furthermore, the rewards for compliance on offer to actors are more likely to be the only rewards available to them, and the sanctions for non-compliance are both less avoidable and perhaps also have more bite, creating a strong incentive to comply. In addition, for reasons discussed in Chapter 4, Coleman also deems closed networks more conducive to the development of trust, which, in turn, is conducive to cultural deviance (whether reactionary or avant garde) because it generates a safe space for experimentation or retrenchment. Actors are more likely to go out on a limb when they know that they can trust others to support them.

High average degree is important in this context too as it suggests that each individual gets the necessary support and encouragement to sustain their 'deviance' and, returning to Shibutani's (1955) contention, noted in the previous chapter, has a strong reference group. If many of my friends are punks and each person I meet tells me about this wonderful new cultural phenomenon I am much more likely to be drawn into it than if just one contact mentions it to me. Likewise punk fashion will seem much less odd. Indeed, not dressing as a punk might seem a little odd.

Note also that members of all of the early London punk bands[1] can be found in the network. Punk was not started by one individual or band but rather by a whole cluster of bands, and this was possible because the members of the various groups involved were connected to one another, influencing one another, moving between bands and passing on information about what one another were doing. Punk could only emerge as a movement and consolidate as a world because its protagonists and pioneers belonged to a common network.

Nothing is static in the social world, however, including network structures. Networks are always in-process. The differences between Manchester and London, described above, reflect a particular moment in time. Over time both networks evolved, or rather the London network evolved and the key Manchester players began meeting and forming their (constantly evolving) network. The Manchester network evolved rapidly during the late 1970s by virtue of a number of mechanisms that I have examined in detail elsewhere (Crossley 2009). Figure 9.3 shows the network of the same actors depicted in Figure 9.2, as it stood in early 1980. And Figure 9.4 illustrates the network between a bigger population of actors involved in the Manchester scene at the same point in 1980. Figure 9.4 is a more comprehensive map of the Manchester scene in 1980.[2]

We could develop this argument and analysis further but the point has been made. I want rather to open up a number of other network-related aspects of the world we are examining: fracture, conflict and power. Commentary upon both the Manchester and London worlds suggests that, whatever solidarity and *esprit de corps* there may have been between actors, there was also a degree of internal conflict, rivalry and perhaps also hierarchy. Personal testimonies in both cases often refer to an 'inner circle' of self-appointed elites who set themselves apart from the rest. This is relative, of course. All of the actors I have included in both networks were key players and part of an 'inner circle'. However, some were more 'in' than others.

We can explore this by way of a 'core-periphery' analysis. The version of this routine that I use here seeks out an inner circle by trying out different ways of bifurcating the network and exploring relative densities within and between the partitioned groups. If we can find an internally dense group with few ties to the outside and especially if those on the outside are poorly connected amongst their selves, it seems reasonable to assume that there is a split within the network between a core 'inner circle' and a more marginal periphery. The results of this routine as applied to both London (Figure 9.1) and the bigger, later Manchester networks (Figure 9.4) are given in the table in Figure 9.5. There are marked core/periphery structures in both cases.

The significance of this, to reiterate, is that such divisions may be both a cause and a consequence of conflict or tension within a world. Those in the periphery, as in the cases I analysed, might feel peripheral and excluded (because they are). As a consequence they might feel resentful towards those in the core and might act upon this, initiating conflict.

I was able to explore this in more detail, ethnographically, in work that I did on interactions amongst members of a circuit training class in a private health club

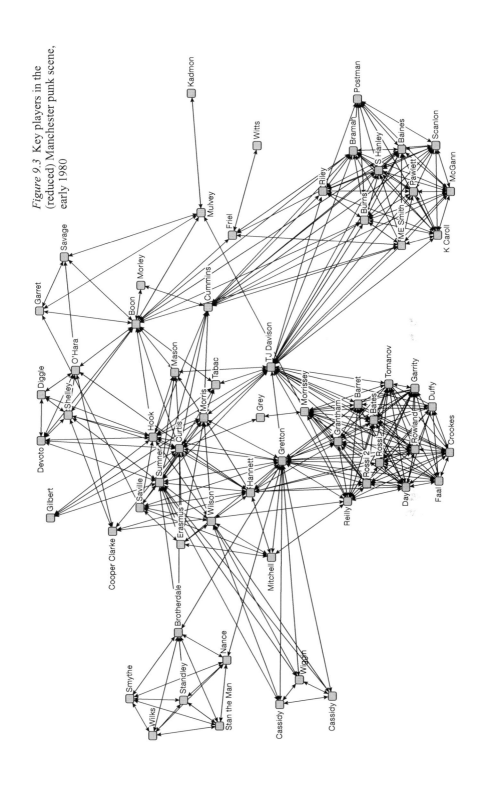

Figure 9.3 Key players in the (reduced) Manchester punk scene, early 1980

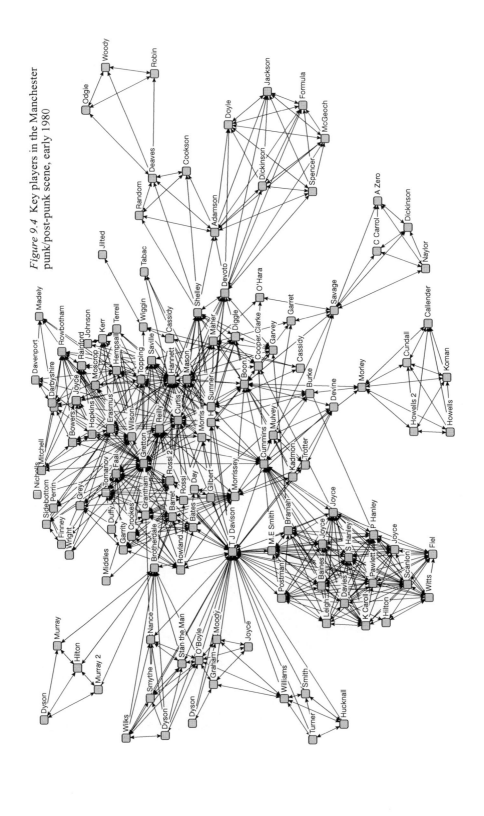

Figure 9.4 Key players in the Manchester punk/post-punk scene, early 1980

	London			Manchester		
	Core	Periphery			Core	Periphery
Core (n=16)	0.858	0.140		Core (n=28)	0.503	0.074
Periphery (n=30)	0.140	0.179		Periphery (n=121)	0.074	0.060

Figure 9.5 Density within and between core and periphery

in Manchester, some of whom enjoyed strong relations with one another outside the class whilst others did not (Crossley 2008b, and for background 2004a, 2006b). Although I didn't use the concept of core and periphery in this work I found a clear distinction between a core in-group and a peripheral out-group and I was able to explore, in some detail, how the activities of the core, which were internally beneficial for them, had what economists call 'negative externalities' upon the periphery, which the periphery resented and, in small ways, sought to resist. In particular the core tended to take liberties in the class, showing off to one another, messing about and gently subverting the order and routines of the class in a way which inevitably impacted upon the periphery, who were often unhappy about this and grumbled individually but who lacked the density and solidarity as a group (because they were not a group) to act collectively to do anything about this. There was a subtly coercive power balance in the class, rooted in the 'strength in numbers' enjoyed by the core. They enjoyed a freedom of action in the class because they were supported by others who applauded their actions and egged them on. Challenging them would have involved challenging the whole group to which they belonged.

I do not mean to suggest that the core were free and the periphery constrained. Core members were, for example, expected – even pressured – to support fellow core members and perhaps also to partake in collective pranks, whilst periphery members were not. In this respect it was core members who were constrained. My point, rather, is that the constraints and opportunities varied in accordance with network position.

Figure 9.6 visualizes this network and also shows comparative density scores for the core and periphery (nodes in the core are coloured black and those in the periphery white). Ties are assigned in this graph on the basis that actors (1) interact with one another outside the class and (2) realized those relations within the class by way of what Goffman (1971) calls 'tie signs' (Crossley 1995). These data were assembled through my participation in a series of events which brought actors together (circuit classes, post-class saunas and post-sauna 'sessions' in the pub and local curry house) over a number of months (for more detail see Crossley 2008b).

It is important to emphasize that the core-periphery structure identified here, though it affected interaction, was itself built up through a history of interaction and was sustained through ongoing interactions. When a core–periphery takes

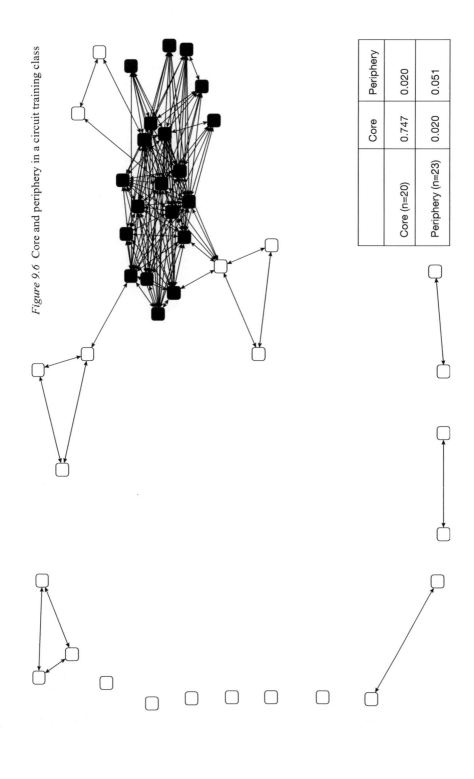

Figure 9.6 Core and periphery in a circuit training class

	Core	Periphery
Core (n=20)	0.747	0.020
Periphery (n=23)	0.020	0.051

shape it can be difficult to break it down. There is a tendency towards self-perpetuation, a path dependency, not least because the core–periphery boundary can acquire symbolic significance for the actors involved such that interaction across it attracts negative sanctions. But of course it can be broken down and might equally change as an unintended consequence of interaction. Structure is not magical or fixed for all time. It is relational and always in process. Even when a figuration endures it only does so by virtue of its constant iteration in interactions which could always take a different course and transform or modify it.

Central actors

It is not only subgroups, such as core and periphery, which can be distinguished within a network. Actors have different positional properties. The most obvious example of this is centrality. Some actors are more central than others. Centrality can be measured in many different ways. The most common ways are (1) *degree* (how many connections does each actor have?), (2) *closeness* (what is the total path length connecting each actor to every other?), (3) *betweenness* (how often does the actor lie in the (shortest) path connecting every possible pairing of the others in the network?) and (4) *eigenvector* (do the actor's alters have a high degree?). By comparing actors' scores for one or more of these measures we can determine which is most central. And by analysing the distribution of the scores we can derive a measure of the overall level of *centralization* of the network as a whole: do we find, for example, that most of the ties in the network centre upon a small number of nodes, making the network highly degree centralized?

Centrality within a network can be important because it creates different sets of opportunities and constraints for actors. Those with a high degree of centrality, for example, have many contacts upon whom they may call for help or support. This is an advantage or opportunity. Conversely, they may find that they are subject to more and perhaps competing demands from others in the network in comparison to less central others. This is a constraint. Those with high closeness centrality are in a good position to organize the network because they have 'less distance to travel' to communicate with everybody in it, which is again an opportunity. But their accessibility to multiple others might equally prove an impediment or constraint. Perhaps they are too easy to get hold of or too visible. There is certainly more risk of information overload in this position. Likewise with high between-ness centrality, which is often associated with the role of 'broker'. Actors high in betweenness are in a good position to mediate between otherwise unconnected parts of the network, which leads to many advantages for them according to one school of thought within network analysis (Burt 1992, 2005). However, when one is trying to broker between warring 'tribes' the position can be very difficult and constraining. Central actors can become caught in the crossfire of a conflict.

I found an example of this latter possibility in the abovementioned health club research. I identified a strong example of what I called, building upon Burt's (ibid.) work, a brokerage-closure figuration: that is, a network which involved (in this case) three closed groups and also a smaller group of two people who brokered between them. The groups were identified by means of a hierarchical cluster analysis and a comparison of density scores within and between the clusters, similar to that used in the core/periphery analysis above (see Figures 9.7 and 9.8). Having identified on this basis what appeared to be a broker's cluster (Cluster 2) I sought to further confirm this impression by taking measures for the three most relevant centrality scores (degree, closeness and betweenness). The two members of Cluster 2, not surprisingly, came top for all three measures and were many standard deviations above the mean score in each case (see Figure 9.9). All of these measures suggested that I had a strong example of brokerage between relatively closed groups. According to Burt this figuration should bestow a number of important advantages both upon the network as a whole and, more specifically, upon the brokers. What I found, however, was that the groups began to compete with one another and, in particular, to compete for the loyalty of the brokers (who belonged to all groups), in a manner which became conflictual and created stress for the brokers (Crossley 2008b). The combination of brokerage and closure, in this case, engendered conflict and, especially for the brokers, a considerable amount of distress and discomfort.

It is important to emphasize again here that this figuration, whilst relatively durable over a period, was not immutable or given. It emerged out of interaction, acquired a durability and traction or path dependence for a period, before gradually evolving into something else. Indeed, some of my analysis of it was conducted retrospectively, after it had changed and, in particular, after the initially distinct closed groups had merged to a considerable extent. Network structure, like any other aspect of social structure, is always structure-in-process.

The metrics generated in network analysis are important but their value is often accentuated when used in conjunction with qualitative analyses which variously deepen, qualify and in some cases challenge their meaning (Crossley 2010a; Edwards and Crossley 2009; Edwards 2009). To illustrate this point I will return to my punks. Both of my punk networks contain actors with centrality scores much higher than their peers. Moreover, although there is no necessary correspondence between the degree, closeness and betweenness measures of centrality, the same actors tended to score highly for each. The three most central actors for the London network are named in Figure 9.10 and their scores for degree, closeness and betweenness centrality (which in each case came in the top three of the network as a whole) are given. Note that in each case they are many standard deviations above the mean for the graph as a whole.

In quantitative terms these three actors were more or less equally central. What this meant in practice, however, is neither straightforward nor obvious. Whilst the centrality of McClaren and Rhodes confirms archival and secondary accounts of their status as 'movers and shakers' in the early scene, who could and did use their centrality to their advantage, this is not true of Sid Vicious. Vicious's centrality, as I have argued elsewhere, had a different meaning to that of McClaren and Rhodes, not least because it was generated by a different dynamic (Crossley 2010a). McClaren and Rhodes had resources and this made them attractive to others in the scene. Others courted and sought to establish a link with them. This is why they

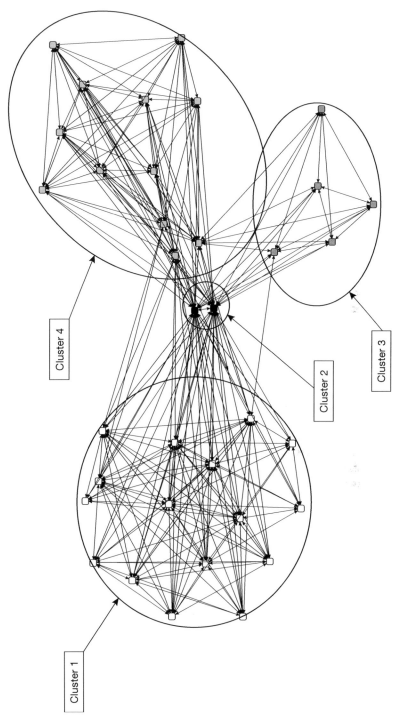

Figure 9.7 Brokerage and closure between health club classes

Cluster	Size	Internal density	Density of ties to cluster 2	Density of ties to cluster 3	Density of ties to cluster 4
1	16	0.767	1	0	0.052
2	2	n/a		1	1
3	5	1			0.1
4	12	0.97			

Figure 9.8 Cluster profiles (for Figure 9.7)

	Degree Centrality	Closeness Centrality	Betweenness Centrality
Mean	14.29	0.643	0.0176
S.D.	6.2	6.0.098	0.054
Key Outlier/Broker 1	34	1	0.229
Key Outlier/Broker 2	34	1	0.229

Figure 9.9 Centrality scores for the cluster 2 brokers (for Figure 9.7)

	Degree	Closeness	Betweenness
Malcom McClaren	29	0.738	0.203
Bernie Rhodes	24	0.681	0.164
Sid Vicious	25	0.692	0.116
Mean (for the whole network)	10.78	0.5927	0.02095
S.D.	6.092	0.0741	0.041

Figure 9.10 Central characters in the early London punk scene

have such a central position in the network. Vicious, by contrast, whilst popular, tended to flit between bands in an effort to find one in which he would fit. He lacked resources, such as basic musicianship, which didn't make him a great prospect for many of the better bands, but he kept trying and it was these efforts which generated the contact with others that gave him his centrality. His pattern of ties was similar or at least comparable to those of McClaren and Rhodes but the meaning of those ties and his status or identity within the network are very different and this makes a difference, not least in relation to the significance of his centrality.

None of this detracts, however, from the basic observation that social networks have structural properties – they are social structures – which generate potential opportunities and constraints for those involved in them. Furthermore, it points to the importance of a consideration of network structure in any analysis of the social worlds that, as noted earlier, are both the product and the environment of social interaction. Interactions shape and are shaped by both relations and networks (which are, in turn, mutually affecting). Networks are structures in and of the social world which create both opportunities and constraints for those involved in them. These structures don't drop from the skies. They emerge within the hurly burly of interaction within a given population but they can 'lock in', generating path dependence within the historical trajectory of interaction of that population. They emerge over time and may take time before they change to any significant degree.

Blocks, equivalence and roles

My contention is that all social networks are social structures (see also Martin 2009; Wellman and Berkowitz 1997). Some network-related theories disagree, however, and suggest something more specific. The anthropological theories of Radcliffe-Brown (1952b) and Nadel (1957) in particular claim that social structures are not networks of concrete individuals but rather networks of *roles*. I am not persuaded by this, for reasons I explain later. However, it is an interesting point which both allows us to push our investigation of the concept of social networks a little further and also to bring the concept of *convention* into play. Let us first consider how the concept of roles has been operationalized in some branches of social network theory.

The central elements of this operationalization are the concept of 'equivalence' and a method of analysis termed 'blockmodelling' (Lorrain and White 1971; White, Boorman and Breiger 1976; Boorman and White 1976). The idea is that a 'role' is a specific position in a network, such that actors who occupy the same role occupy the same or rather an equivalent position in a network. 'Equivalence' has been defined in different ways but there are two main formulations in the literature. The first, *structural equivalence*, entails that two actors are tied to exactly the same set of alters in exactly the same way within a network, irrespective of any tie they may or may not have to one another. If i and j are each connected to k, l and m, and only k, l and m, then they occupy a structurally equivalent position in a network, irrespective of any tie that they may have to one another. An obvious problem with this definition is that occupants of what we would ordinarily regard as the same role, in the same network, may have ties to different alters. Every sergeant major in an army will have privates whom they command and captains by whom they are commanded, for example, but the privates and captains in question may be different in each case.

The second equivalence concept, *regular equivalence*, captures this by suggesting that roles can be identified in networks if we can partition a network into clusters, each of whose members are defined by their having the same pattern of relations to members of the other clusters. We might partition a network into three clusters, for example, allocating to cluster 2 only those actors who take orders from one or more members of cluster 3 and give orders to a number of members of cluster 1. Cluster 3 membership, in turn, would be allocated only to those who give orders to a number of cluster 2 members and have no relation to any cluster 1 members. Cluster 1 members will be defined by their taking orders from certain cluster 2 members and having no relation to any cluster 3 members. How this happens in practice and becomes a blockmodel is complicated. For ease we will limit our focus to the procedure associated with the more problematic but more often used concept of *structural equivalence*.

We very seldom if ever find perfect structural equivalence in empirical data. People may have a similar profile of ties but not an identical profile. The first step in blockmodelling is to cluster or 'block' actors in accordance with these similarities. This can be done in various ways, using different clustering algorithms. Having done this, we then compare relative densities of ties both within and across clusters, much as we did when analysing core-periphery structures, and we decide upon a threshold value at which we were prepared both to call individual clusters internally connected and to deem relations between them absent or present (some algorithms, particularly optimizing algorithms, do this automatically as a part of the initial clustering process). We might, for example, decide upon a 0.5 density score, connecting those clusters between whom 50 per cent or more of all possible ties are present and also deeming those clusters with an internal density of 0.5 or above as (internally) connected. This gives us a new network, of clusters or blocks, which we can analyse in much the same way as we analyse any other network.

In a full-blown blockmodelling procedure we would consider a range of different relationships for the same set of actors, mapping the results onto one another. In a paper exploring the network of relations comprising the 'world system', as defined by Wallerstein (2004), for example, Snyder and Kick (1979) constructed a blockmodel out of networks based upon (1) trade, (2) military intervention, (3) diplomatic relations and (4) conjoint treaty memberships between nations. The four networks were combined in one blockmodel. In many instances, however, network data are often so difficult to get that the blockmodelling procedure will be used on one set of relations only.

For illustrative purposes I have blockmodelled my London punk network using the original CONCOR blockmodelling algorithm in the Ucinet programme (Borgatti, Everett and Freeman 2002). This produced an eight-block solution which, with the exception of one oddly placed actor,[3] resonates with the qualitative-archival evidence (Figure 9.11). Blocks 1, 5, 6, 7 and 8 each reflect membership of key bands – the Sex Pistols being block 1. Block 2 is the infamous 'Bromley Contingent', a group of close friends, including Siouxsie and Steve Severin (later of the Banshees), who were closely tied to the Sex Pistols. Block 3 reflects other friends and the wider entourage of the Sex Pistols. And block 4 comprises Sarah Hall and Jo Faull, who were romantically tied to Steve Jones and Paul Cook (of the Sex Pistols) and who belonged to the Flowers of Romance, an early band involving musicians who later went on to play in more famous bands. Blocks are linked in this graph if any of their members enjoy ties to any others. The density of ties both within and especially between the blocks is highly variable, however, as indicated in Figure 9.12, which displays the density matrix for the graph. Some

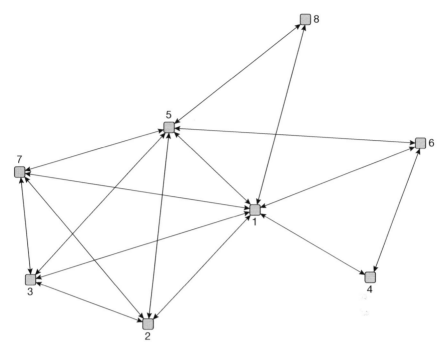

Figure 9.11 A blockmodel of the London punk network

BLOCKS	1	2	3	4	5	6	7	8
1 (n=6)	0.733	0.870	0.733	0.5	0.167	0.167	0.083	0.167
2 (n=9)		1	0.089	0	0.037	0	0.042	0
3 (n=5)			0.3	0	0.178	0	0.075	0
4 (n=2)				1	0	0.667	0	0
5 (n=9)					0.889	0.259	0.139	0.111
6 (n=3)						1	0	0
7 (n=8)							0.571	0
8 (n=4)								1

Figure 9.12 Block densities (for Figure 9.11)

of the ties between some of the blocks are relatively weak and some of the blocks
are not connected at all.

It is much easier to spot a structural pattern here, compared to the original
network, because we have 'reduced' the data. Of particular note is the very central
position of block 1 (comprising the Sex Pistols). Every block has a tie to block 1,
albeit a weak tie in some cases. Block 1 members are clearly important and

influential. It is also noteworthy that blocks 7 and 3 are each poorly connected within the network and have a relatively low internal density. We might surmise that these blocks are relatively marginal to the scene and, in contrast to block 1, lack any internal cohesion. Their members are united by their common occupation of a relatively marginal position but not through bonds to one another. This observation reflects an important aspect of blockmodelling. The technique is not intended to identify cohesive groupings – although they often emerge – but rather clusters of equivalently positioned actors who may form cohesive groupings but do not necessarily do so. I could continue my interpretation but this will hopefully suffice for illustrative purposes.

Blockmodelling, whether in accordance with structural or regular equivalence, is an invaluable tool for further detecting and analysing structure. I return to it in Chapter 10. However, I am not convinced that the 'positions' or 'equivalence classes' that it identifies can be equated with 'roles'. Most discussions of roles in the social scientific literature, including the literature that appears to have informed early work on blockmodelling (e.g. Nadel 1957), defines them by reference to mutual and conventional expectations about behaviour. Roles might entail network positions but they entail more besides. They entail conventions. Of course we could construct blockmodels on the basis of such conventions, recording relations as present only where they embody the conventions known to belong to the role. This would presuppose a knowledge of roles, however. It would not amount to a 'discovery' of roles. And that underlines the basic point that roles, as conventionally understood in sociology, are a function of conventions, at least as much as of positional equivalence in a network.

In the next section I explore this contention in more detail, drawing upon Radcliffe-Brown's (1952b) seminal account of social structure. Before I do, however, I should conclude by emphasizing that my reservations regarding block-modelling's adequacy as an operationalization of the concept of roles, first, does not apply to its operationalization of the concept of 'positions' – blockmodelling affords a powerful perspective upon the concept of position – and second, is less of a problem given the problems, discussed further below, with the concept of 'roles'. The concept of roles and the basis of role theory have been subject to considerable criticism in sociology since they were first introduced and whilst they undoubtedly tap into an important aspect of social life not fully captured by the concept of position, there is a good argument to be made for moving away from the idea of roles, whilst keeping the notion of position and seeking to fill in the gaps in other ways. Putting that differently, to say that blockmodelling is not very good at operationalizing a concept that is somewhat problematic in its own right may not be such a strong criticism. That blockmodels do not operational-ize the concept of roles very precisely does not matter, if, as I have said, they do operationalize the concept of position effectively, because the concept of roles is problematic and the concept of position arguably more useful.

Networks, conventions and roles

Social structures are social networks for Radcliffe-Brown (1952b), as noted above, but they are networks of roles rather than networks of concrete individuals. And roles are defined by institutions and rules, that is, by convention. Every social actor, he argues, is

> a complex of social relationships. He is a citizen of England, a husband and a father, a bricklayer, a member of a particular Methodist congregation, a voter in a certain constituency, a member of his trade union, an adherent of the Labour party, and so on. Note that each of these descriptions refers to a social relationship, or to a place in a social structure. . . . We cannot study persons except in terms of social structure, nor can we study social structure except in terms of the persons who are the units of which it is composed.
>
> (Radcliffe-Brown 1952b: 194)

Our identity at any point in time depends upon who we are interacting with and, no less importantly, which social world we are orienting to in our interaction. We have specific types of relationships which both demand different things from us and impact upon us in different ways. We always interact with others in a particular capacity (e.g. friend, lover, colleague, comrade, boss etc.) and the capacities or identities are enmeshed within complexes of conventions. To be a husband, for example, one must meet certain criteria (e.g. having gone through a ceremony of marriage) and one might also find oneself subject to certain regulative rules regarding fidelity, the division of domestic labour etc.

It is important to emphasize here that identities are relational and not just in the respect that they are 'done', collaboratively, in social interaction. To be a father one must stand in relation to a mother and a child. To be a worker is to stand within a particular set of social and economic relations to an employer. Marx's claim, noted in Chapter 2, that a slave is only a slave in relation to a master captures this point nicely.

For some writers, including certain of Marx's more 'anti-humanist' interpreters and also White (1992, 2008), these identities are a primary datum. These writers are inclined to reject any reference to an underlying actor who embodies the identity at a particular time, claiming that this invokes a notion of an underlying human essence, a strategy which is both reductionist and essentialist. The picture is more complex in my view, however. At a biological level, the human organism manifests specific characteristics that demarcate us as a species. There is nothing essential about this, however, and it is does not preclude a relational understanding. Our species characteristics are relatively durable across historical time but they are not given. They are the result of a long evolutionary process, which centres upon interaction between the organism and its environment. We are, biologically, in process. And they are sustained on a moment-by-moment basis by a complex web of biochemical and physical interactions. The human organism is not so much a substance as a network. For sociological purposes it is usually appropriate to 'black box' these relational dynamics, not least because evolution operates on a far broader timeframe than we typically do and the details of the biochemical interactions which constitute the organism lie beyond our professional competence, but we should not lose sight of this basic relational picture when making claims about what Marx (1959) called our 'species being'.

More importantly, on a psychosocial level, the social actor who emerges from the organism does so by virtue of interactions which endow it with various dispositions, including the capacity to speak and thereby think; body techniques which afford it mastery over its environment; tastes and preferences; etc. This social actor is not identical with any particular identity which it might adopt at a particular point in time, however. As Radcliffe-Brown (1952b) notes, we are all many different people (different identities) to different people and we behave and perhaps think differently as we move from one identity to another. But there are continuities across our different identity enactments. I speak English with the same accent irrespective of whatever identity I happen to be 'in' and no doubt betray many indications of my background and other identities as I do so. Moreover, one of the challenges of my life is to reconcile the demands and aspirations associated with my various identities, and one of the great opportunities I might have is to channel resources and goods from one of the worlds in which I interact into another, cashing in on the exchange.

This suggests that there is an underlying actor who manages these different identities but we must be careful not to assume that this underlying actor pre-dates the different identities that she manages. To the contrary, as both Simmel (1955) and Mead (1967) suggest, it is the process of taking different roles or identities which generates the reflexive actor who manages them. The 'perspective' of the underlying actor does not derive from outside the web of their relations but rather from the contrasts that emerge as, to use White's (1995) term, they 'switch' from one identity to another. Switching identities generates a meta-identity and a reflexive actor who can occupy that meta-identity, putting distance between herself and any of her other identities, so as to reflect upon and manage them. To learn to become a social actor, through social interaction, is to learn to manage and present identities, and it is the process of managing and presenting identities itself which gives the actor critical distance from their identities and a sense of an underlying self.

The actor is relational through and through, from the balance of interacting chemicals and organs and the evolutionary history (of interactions between organism and environment) that make her biologically human, through the childhood interactions that equip her to become an effective social agent to the ongoing interactions and relations that make her what she is in any given present. But she is never reducible to just this or that identity or role and supposing that she is can only ever result in bad sociology.

Returning now to Radcliffe-Brown, note that he defines roles in terms of a framework of rules:

> Social relations are only observed and can only be described by reference to the reciprocal behaviour of the persons related. The form of a social structure

has therefore to be described by the patterns of behaviour to which individuals and groups conform in their dealings with one another. The patterns are partially formulated in rules which, in our own society, we distinguish as rules of etiquette, of morals and of law. Rules, of course, only exist in their recognition by members of the society; either in their verbal recognition, when they are stated as rules, or in their observance in behaviour. These two modes of recognition, as every field-worker knows, are not the same thing and both have to be taken into account.

(Radcliffe-Brown 1952b: 198)

There are a few nuances in this passage that merit brief discussion. First, note the reference to 'reciprocal behaviour' and 'dealing with one another'. Discussion of norms and rules is often framed as if the individual adhered to them (or not) as an individual. To the contrary, insofar as they 'govern' anything, rules govern our interactions and relations with others. This is significant, because the others with whom we interact might be in a position to mobilize sanctions, providing an incentive for compliance. We don't need to be 'cultural dopes' in order to follow rules. We just need to be mindful of sanctions, both positive and negative.

Second, note that 'patterns are partially formulated in rules'. They are not fully accounted for by rules. Radcliffe-Brown doesn't elaborate upon his meaning here but his claim resonates with what I discussed in relation to rules (and particularly Wittgenstein's (1953) critique of rules) in Chapter 8. Rules are important in social life but they do not suffice to fully explain why we act as we do – they provide a framework within which there is often considerable room from manoeuvre – and they are grounded in an 'agreement in forms of life', that is, in conventions which cannot be reduced to rules.

Finally, note that rules are effective for Radcliffe-Brown to the extent that they are 'recognized by members of the society'. This doesn't mean that actors are necessarily consciously aware of rules when they follow them – as the reference to 'observance in behaviour' indicates – but it does keep actors in the picture. Rules do nothing for Radcliffe-Brown unless actors recognize them. Even if this recognition is pre-reflective, it consists in a tacit understanding and practical knowledge rather than an unconscious driver or cause. On this point Radcliffe-Brown resists the path taken by later structuralist writers, such as Levi-Strauss (1963), and agrees with our Wittgensteinian understanding of rules as inter-subjective products of human interaction which remain open to modification and change in the course of interaction.

The way that Radcliffe-Brown defines and discusses rules, though perhaps a little narrower than my conception of conventions (outlined and argued for in Chapter 8), and for that reason less preferable, overlaps considerably with it, such that, for present purposes we can regard them as equivalent (I will revert hereafter, therefore, from 'rules' to 'conventions'). What Radcliffe-Brown adds here, however, is a consideration of the way in which conventions enter into the definition of relationships and roles. All relationships, he is arguing, are shaped by convention. We have particular 'types' of relationship (e.g. collegial, marital, parental, sexual, romantic) and these types reflect conventions that we draw upon when forming relations. This is what he means by roles.

The relationship between conventions and relationships is not unidirectional, however. Knowledge of rules and conventions must be disseminated to be effective and dissemination presupposes networks of interaction. Conventions emerge through interaction and only become conventions for a population of actors insofar as those actors each interact with one another, carrying over what they establish in one interaction into the next. Homogeneity in conventions, as well as their systematic variations, is dependent upon diffusion and reinforcement within networks. We see this, for example, in relation to language. The rules and resources of language spread through contact between people, which is to say through networks:

> the spread of language, the unification of a number of separate communities into a single speech-community, and the reverse process of sub-division into different speech communities, are phenomena of social structure. So also are those instances in which, in societies having a class structure, there are differences of speech usage in different classes.
>
> (Radcliffe-Brown 1952b: 196)

Conventions might shape relations but they only exist as shared conventions (and, by definition, conventions must be shared) by virtue of their diffusion through networks of relations. Moreover, to reiterate an earlier point, sociolinguists have demonstrated that closure and (high) density within the network structures of linguistic communities is important if the peculiarities of such communities are to be protected from outside influence (Milroy 1987). Regional linguistic traditions are much more likely to be preserved and insulated from wider cultural change in the context of relatively closed networks.

The scope of these observations is not restricted to language, of course. They apply to all forms of human competence and convention. This is why theorists of social worlds attach such significance to networks, because actors cannot enter or belong to a world if they lack access to the meanings, competence, information and so on that animate it. And access entails contact (however mediated) with other members of the world.

It is important to grasp here how networks and conventions, as managed by competent social actors, serve to construct boundaries around a world and how worlds, in turn, 'cut' networks. The punks in my network interacted with many other people than just fellow punks, for example, but when they did they (assumedly) didn't enthuse about punk, passing on information about the latest bands, gigs and fashions; or if they did, these conventions, resources and this enthusiasm were not passed on. Although, as I discuss later in the chapter, there is always of flow of resources and influence between social worlds, there is equally also a degree of closure effected through identities and conventions specific to that world. The network of the punk world ended where actors ceased to engage in interactions constitutive of the punk phenomenon.

Having said this, world-specific networks are sometimes underpinned by and embedded within other networks which have played a role in their formation. The networks of the black civil rights movement, for example, emerged from and were embedded within networks of membership at black churches and colleges (McAdam 1982). Actors who became political comrades were earlier and often remained co-parishioners as well as perhaps neighbours and family members. One network grew out of another, not without some measure of change but not with so much change that they ceased to overlap considerably. As with the multiple identities referred to above, this both facilitates flow and interference between worlds as well as cautioning against any aspiration we may have to treat either identities or worlds as completely self-contained entities.

The actual and the general

Radcliffe-Brown's reflection on roles is further developed when he draws a distinction between what he calls 'the actual' and 'the general'. Empirical analysis, he notes, must necessarily focus upon the concrete particularities of relations between specific people (*the actual*) but what we are interested in is *the general*, that is, aspects of *the actual* which endure and outlive particularities. The British political structure is headed by the Prime Minister, for example, and a man called Gordon Brown currently occupies that position. If we want to study this part of the structure we must focus upon Mr Brown (or one of his predecessors) and the network of concrete actors in which he is embedded because the structure doesn't exist independently of this network. But Mr Brown is just the latest in a long line of actors who have occupied the position that he currently occupies and he will be replaced. What interests us is not Gordon Brown as such but rather the position he occupies in a configuration of relations which is more enduring than his individual term of occupancy.

The process of institutionalization is central to what Radcliffe-Brown is arguing here:

> [S]ocial institutions, in the sense of standardised modes of behaviour, constitute the machinery by which a social structure, a network of social relations, maintains its existence and its continuity.
>
> (Radcliffe-Brown 1952b: 200)

Institutions, as Berger and Luckmann (1971) note, exist where the conventions of a particular population outlive the concrete individuals making up that population at a given point in time and are continued by new members. In relation to social networks they often entail roles, positions or identities, such as Prime Minister, which individuals within a population can move between, creating what White (1970) refers to as a 'vacancy chain'. That is to say, as one person moves out of their position they create a vacancy, which another person may then fill, which may create a further vacancy if that person is moving from another position and so on. Thus, Gordon Brown became Prime Minister and was only able to do so when Tony Blair, the previous Prime Minister, vacated that position. His move into the Prime Minister's shoes required him to leave his post as Chancellor of the Exchequer, however, thus creating a vacancy there, and so on along the chain. It is the network of these institutionalized and mutually reinforcing, interacting positions which particularly concerns Radcliffe-Brown and which he designates with the term 'social structure'.

Unofficial structures

Roles and institutions are important but there is danger in what Radcliffe-Brown is advocating that we focus only upon the official relations of an institutionalized social order. Not all social worlds are institutionalized. At the very least, all come into being in a more fluid and ephemeral state, only then and only in some cases undergoing a process of institutionalization. I believe that even those which are never institutionalized, such as my above-mentioned punk worlds, are important and interesting. Furthermore, if we want to study institutionalization we need to to begin with worlds that are not institutionalized.

More importantly, the institutionalized rules and roles that Radcliffe-Brown is referring to constitute 'official structures' which are often embedded within emergent informal and unofficial network structures which are at least as important for an understanding of what is going on in a given social world. Consider Gordon Brown again. He occupies an official position in a network of official positions whose general form, whilst always evolving, is centuries old. Any politics textbook will, by way of a flow diagram, describe that network. But we do not need to look too deeply to see that what happens in the political world is constrained and facilitated not only by this official network structure but also by an unofficial structure of factions, alliances etc. between players within the official structure (and perhaps outside it too). The much discussed conflict between Gordon Brown's 'camp', when he was Chancellor of the Exchequer, and that of the then Prime Minister, Tony Blair, is a very obvious example of this. Whilst the formal ties between their offices remained more or less as they had for all other recent incumbents of those offices, they brought with them an interpersonal history of antagonism, encouraging a wider polarization within both the cabinet and the parliamentary party. The official institutionalized structure was meshed with an unofficial, more idiosyncratic and non-institutionalized, but still relatively enduring, unofficial structure, and that unofficial structure was important in shaping what happened.

Relational analysis must explore unofficial as well as official structures but isn't that collapsing *the general* into *the actual*? I do not believe that it is. The cliques, factions etc. which constrained/enabled the Blair premiership are not a part of the official structure of political life but they constitute irreducible structures and relational (network) mechanisms which crop up time and again in (different) social worlds. What emerged within and between the Blair and Brown camps happens frequently within all kinds of social worlds, institutionalized as well as non-institutionalized. Unofficial structures, their network figurations, properties and mechanisms, and the potential consequences and effects of these properties are equally if not more recurrent and general in social life than institutionalized roles. Thus an analysis of 'the Blair years' which focuses upon unofficial network patterns and dynamics is no less 'general' in scope than an investigation of official roles and role relations. Whilst it is important, therefore, to attend to processes of institutionalization and to institutionalized networks of (institutionalized) roles, it would be a mistake to limit structural and relational analysis to this.

We should also note, in this context, that the concept of 'roles', as defined by Radcliffe-Brown (1952b), Nadel (1957) and others, has been subject to considerable critique in the period since they were writing. Giddens (1984), for example, suggests that many so-called roles lack clear normative guidelines. It is often not clear what duties and expectations attach to them, if any. Furthermore, to return to an above point, actors may experience conflict between their roles – doing what is right as a father might conflict with one's duties as, for example, a husband or a worker. I can occupy several roles or identities at once and it is not always obvious, nor could there be comprehensive rules covering every eventuality to tell me, what identity or role should take precedence. When discussing curriculum issues in my faculty do I let my sociologist identity predominate or my 'employee of the university of Manchester' identity or my 'friend and colleague to the staff affected' identity or even my 'parent who empathizes with other parents and wants the best for their children' identity. These identities are not always, perhaps not even often in conflict, but when they are they demonstrate that the situations we are in could be taken in many different ways by different 'identities' and must be negotiated and made accountable (Barnes 2000).

In more recent work Giddens (1991) has suggested that this is particularly so in what he calls 'late modernity'. What it is to be a father and what one should do as a father, to take one of Radcliffe-Brown's example, are both much less clear than they may have been in the past, for example. Changes in divorce laws force a distinction between biological and social fatherhood, for example. And competing philosophies of parenthood proliferate, each offering very different guidance on the 'role' of the father.

Giddens draws the implication from this that the individual is very much thrown back upon their self. They have to decide for their self what type of father they will be. They reflexively construct their role. This may be so but, as noted above, roles are relational; they concern our dealings with others and are negotiated with those others, sometimes harmoniously but sometimes also through conflict and power. How a man plays the father role will be shaped by interactions with and between his children, wife, parents, parents-in-law and less directly perhaps also employers, friends, teachers etc. Unofficial structure is again very important here. In the absence of clear institutionalized prescriptions, the dynamics of unofficial network properties are more likely to exert an influence, if only because formal rules and procedures will not screen them out, allowing them to play a larger part in shaping what happens on the ground.

Nevertheless Giddens is right regarding the indeterminacy and ambiguity of roles in practice and this muddies the picture that Radcliffe-Brown and others paint. Individuals occupy particular positions by virtue of the relations they have with others, and these positions, in many cases, invite the ascription of an identity, but quite how that position and identity are fashioned into a stable (albeit changing) pattern of interaction and perceived duties and obligations is a matter of negotiation. The actor does not choose her role for herself but neither does she simply slip into a pre-designed 'role'. She must work her role out and possibly fight it out with her salient alters, all the time reconciling this role with the demands made upon her in other relational contexts. In this sense, to reiterate an earlier point, the actor cannot be subsumed within her role. Roles are made and re-made in interaction. Actors draw upon and orient to conventions in these interactions but conventions allow for innovation and improvisation and, in any case, do not determine interaction.

Conventional structure

Beyond the specification of roles and identities, worlds manifest a structure by virtue of multiple other conventions concerning the goals, means, justifications, rewards and criteria of evaluation deployed in interactions. One of the reasons why entering a new social world feels strange to us, as it often does, is that we are unfamiliar with and not attuned to these conventions. We fail to read the (inter)-actions of others through the lens of the convention which, to other members of the world, including the actor herself, lends it meaning. And we lack the embodied know-how required to respond appropriately and mobilize the appropriate conventions in our own actions.

However much punk fought convention, for example, the punk world was defined in large part by its musical and fashion conventions, and perhaps a conventional 'posture' of rebellion and disaffection. These conventions were partly specific to punk but of course, however innovative and different it may have been, punk, like any other social world, necessarily drew from the conventions of various other worlds which preceded it. The punk world did not emerge *ex nihilo* but rather through bricolage and what Merleau-Ponty (1962), writing about linguistic change, referred to as 'coherent deformation' of existing conventional structures.

Also important to the conventional structure of many worlds are the narratives which lend the members of that world a sense of its past and its future, bestowing meaning and often furnishing a set of significant heroes, villains and events which further specify that meaning and direct the actions of those involved. It is, as Coleman (1988) hinted, the collective adherence of members of the world to these conventions which lends certain actions and outcomes a value, thereby generating an incentive structure. Actors in a world know what to do to win the recognition of others and sometimes internalize those structures themselves to the point whereby accomplishment of the act and achievement of the outcome is reward enough.

In addition, the conventions of a social world are often embodied in physical objects, from tools, symbolic tokens and technologies through to architecture. Becker (1982) captures this point nicely when he discusses the various ways in which Western conventions of music are built into Western musical instruments. These instruments presuppose that actors will play them in particular ways, aiming to achieve specific results. Of course the objects do not determine conduct nor preclude innovation. As Mead (1967) notes, physical objects derive their meaning, for human actors, from the (usually conventional) ways in which those actors use them. Meaning is dependent upon use and use is negotiated between the actor and the object, in interaction. The physical characteristics of an object set limits to what we can do with it, and its affordances shape what we are likely to do with it, but there is always room for manoeuvre and, indeed, misunderstanding (relative to convention). However, for the most part, the materialization of convention within physical objects does tend to perpetuate those conventions, if only because, as with convention more generally, it is much easier to go with the flow and the benefits of doing otherwise are often far from being either assured or obvious. Conventions can become materialized.

Resources

Our discussion so far has only touched upon resources. They are important too, however. Many actions require certain resources for their successful execution and many worlds therefore involve the exchange and circulation of these resources. Actors interact by mobilizing and exchanging resources. As such, the network structures constituting the infrastructure of many worlds are, in one of their aspects, exchange networks. Networks are economies and, indeed, 'the economy' of a society, national or international, is a network and manifests the dynamics and properties that it does because of this (see Chapter 10).

We might also add that resources come into play and acquire their (exchange) value in interaction and networks. We discussed this with respect to Simmel (1990) in Chapter 6. Simmel makes a strong claim that value is constituted within relations of exchange. This is not to deny what Marx (1959) referred to as use value. Simmel's position does not preclude this possibility and it is important for any understanding of social worlds. But exchange is fundamental. It is, as Simmel noted, a key mechanism for making resources available and, as such, it bestows value upon them.

Convention too plays a role in relation to resources and their value, moreover. Monopoly money is valuable in the context of a game of monopoly, but only there. It's value rests upon the conventions which undergird the game or more precisely upon the activation of those conventions by players. The same applies to 'real' money (Searle 1995). The paper is more or less worthless in itself and only has value because actors agree to treat it as such. The value of the pieces of paper and chunks of mental that we exchange as money is a symbolic value underpinned by agreements in forms of life no less than the meaning of the words that we use is underpinned by such agreement. In different ways this is equally true of the various objects, skills etc. that are regarded as valuable within and sometimes between different social worlds. Some resources, such as money, have value in a wide range of worlds. Others, such as rare stamps, are specific but easily convertible into money. Others still, such as the obscure marks of distinction which attract prestige within deviant subcultures, have little convertibility and only a very narrow range but they have value within their world all the same. And many resources have this (exchange) value in virtue of convention.

The distribution of resources amongst the population of actors within a world can contribute to the shaping of the network structure linking those actors. In my punk worlds, for example, I found that well resourced actors often became significant hubs within the network structures involved because others, attracted by their resources, sought them out as lucrative contacts. Who controls or owns which resources will inevitably shape networks rooted in activities which require those resources and/or involving relations which entail their exchange.

And where we find exchange, to reiterate a point from Chapter 7, we find balances of power. To the extent that actors depend upon one another for resources and goods, their relationships manifest a balance of power. This balance may be even or uneven and levels of dependence, the importance of what we rely upon others for (what Emerson (1962) calls 'average power'), may be low or high. These are variables for analysis and investigation. But relations of interdependence are always, by definition, relations of power.

This is significant in relation to our understanding of 'positions' within a network. We might further embellish our understanding of positions by adding a consideration of actors' opportunities for controlling the flow of certain resources in a network and the power advantage this affords them in relation to certain others. Careful examination of many classic accounts of roles reveals a tacit focus upon exchanges of goods and resources. The duties and rights entailed in roles, as described by Parsons (1951), for example, are often rights to certain goods in exchange for other goods which they are obliged to provide. Rights and obligations are both rights and obligations to exchange, and rights and obligations, in some cases, regulating the terms of exchange. I have suggested, above, that these rights and obligations are often ambiguous and open to negotiation in contemporary societies. What I am now suggesting is that such negotiations will be influenced by balances of power rooted in the relative levels of dependency of each party upon the other. Actors who control highly valued resources are in a position to call the shots, relatively speaking.

I am not suggesting that those with the most (relevant) resources in a network 'have' power in virtue of this. As noted in Chapter 7, power exists in the balance of interdependence between actors. However, those who possess valued resources are more likely to be advantaged in their relations with others as a consequence of this, at least if those others want or need those resources and they are valued in the world in question. They are likely to experience fewer (or at least different) constraints to others and more (or different) opportunities. And the distribution of resources within a world is, if only for these reasons, a significant aspect of its structure. We might expect different dynamics in a world whose resources are normally distributed, for example, than one whose resources manifest a Pareto distribution.

Connected worlds

Hitherto I have treated social worlds as discrete entities but they are connected to one another by virtue of what network analysts refer to as 'overlapping memberships'. Each of us belongs to multiple social worlds, Radcliffe-Brown's above-cited quotation suggests. We are dads and husbands in families, professors in universities, customers in gyms, neighbours in neighbourhoods, citizens in political worlds and so on. This has implications for us individually, as a number of relational sociologists, most famously Simmel (1955) and Goffman (1959) have observed. Belonging to different social worlds develops our individuality. It allows different and perhaps conflicting dispositions to be given expression, nurturing them, and it affords us different vantage points upon our selves, different 'generalized others' from whose perspective to construct our 'me'. Each world affords us a perspective upon the others, relativizing and affording us a critical distance from them. Furthermore, moving between different worlds affords us a control over our identities and the information flow which partially shapes them, affording us a sense of autonomy and of control over who and what we are (this is what the inmate of the total institution loses, according to Goffman's (1961) famous analysis and that is one reason why life in the total institution is so hard). What is of more concern to us here, however, is the fact that actors who belong to different worlds constitute a tie between those worlds.

The worlds of my university, gym, home and neighbourhood are connected to one another and affect one another because I belong to all of them. I carry ideas and resources between them and I bring the effects of one into the other. These worlds are different. I behave differently in them, have a different identity in each and certainly 'edit' my contribution to each in terms of my understanding of what is appropriate to it. But there is always leakage and overlap.

At the most basic level, for example, I only have a limited amount of time to devote to each. The more I devote to one the less I have to devote to others. Likewise money; I earn it in my world of work and spend it in most of my other worlds but I only have so much to spend, such that spending more in one may mean spending less in the others. And should something happen to my work-based money supply, then my activities in other worlds will be curtailed. Even my mood may carry across. Work worries carry across into the home, unless a session at the gym manages to alleviate them, and likewise worries at home in relation to work.

Some worlds overlap in other ways. My university, for example, is a world in its own right. It is a large organization which competes in a market and in the world of British higher education, and which makes demands and frames my work experience accordingly. At the same time, however, being at work, I am involved in British, European and international sociological worlds, each of which is distinctive in some respects and each of which may impact upon one another.

I am constantly juggling the demands of these different worlds and, as such, maintaining a connection and some degree of harmony between them. Of course most worlds that are connected are not connected by a single actor but rather by multiple actors. Numerous actors traverse the same worlds, ensuring a connection and flow between them.

These observations shed fresh light upon functionalist concerns regarding the 'fit' between different institutional orders, concerns captured by Lockwood's (1964) concept of 'system integration'. The worlds of the economy, education, family etc. do not hang together, insofar as they do because 'the system' is in some way self-correcting or guided by an overarching *telos*. Rather, the system hangs together because social actors bridge the various worlds which it involves, carrying influences over from one to the other and striving to maintain some sort of coherent and fulfilling life in the process. If the worlds of work and family to some degree mirror and fit with one another it is because actors who straddle both (who will be in the majority in each) endeavour to keep these two aspects of their lives, these partitions in their personal networks, in harmony. Of course harmony is not assured. The demands of different worlds might prove irreconcilable and actors might be damaged in the process of seeking to reconcile them. Moreover, individual worlds can go into crisis, generating repercussions in other worlds, cascade effects and so on. Insofar as there is harmony between worlds, however, it is because actors span those worlds and pull them together in their actions.

Stratified worlds

Not all worlds are connected, however, or at least not to the same extent. Occupational worlds provide a useful way into this point as they both demand and allocate certain resources from their participants, which in turn tends both to presuppose connection to certain prior worlds and to shape subsequent involvement in worlds. Medical doctors, for example, must have a university degree, and so must have belonged to the world of higher education at some time. Furthermore, their salary allows them to live in certain neighbourhoods rather than others. They won't necessarily have other doctors as their immediate neighbours but they will tend to live alongside others who have similar salaries, which will in many cases mean others in occupations demanding graduate entry. If we were to construct a network map of worlds, therefore, we might expect certain occupations, neighbourhoods and universities to connect up in virtue of the flow of actors between them or perhaps, in a blockmodelling exercise, to form equivalence classes. If not directly linked, they would share a similar profile of connections to others.

Conversely, some occupations might be very poorly linked to certain neighbourhood worlds or to universities or indeed to those schools which 'feed' the universities. They might be linked to other neighbourhoods, if only by way of house prices, and might typically recruit actors with different educational backgrounds and profiles. Our network map might reveal only weak connections here, no connections or perhaps rather, as these occupational worlds would still connect somewhere, different patterns of connection and different clusters or blocks within the network.

I am speculating about a network of worlds, connected by people who move through them, but this is also a network of people who are in some respects (more) connected to one another by virtue of their belonging to the same or (structurally/ regularly) equivalent worlds, that is, worlds which have similar patterns of connection to other worlds. It is a two-mode network[4] in which worlds are connected in virtue of the actors involved in them and actors are connected in virtue of their involvement in the same worlds (for a classic statement on this duality in two-mode networks see Breiger 1974). This is significant on the actor's side as it points to a process of 'differential association'; that is to say, actors are more likely to meet and associate with other actors who move in the same (interconnected) worlds as they do or in worlds which belong to the same basic clusters of equivalently positioned worlds.

If we agree that access to certain worlds, perhaps particular occupational worlds but possibly other worlds too, affords actors differential access to certain resources which, in turn, affords them, to borrow an expression from Weber (1978), differential 'life chances', then what begins to emerge here is a sense of 'stratified worlds' and of closure and restricted access to those worlds. All worlds are not equal, in respect of what they can offer actors, and neither are they equally open, as the connection between worlds suggests.

What I am suggesting here addresses Bourdieu's (1984) well-known account of the association between certain lifestyle preferences and positions in social space as defined by ownership of cultural and economic capital (see also Chapter 3). Where Bourdieu theorizes this in terms of capital and, more especially, habitus, however, I am theorizing it in terms of worlds. I do not deny that habit (or habitus) is important. It is in many respects, as William James (1981: 125) argued, 'the great flywheel of society', which holds everything together (see also Dewey 1998). This should be clear from my discussion of convention. But Bourdieu, as noted earlier, often develops his argument in a curiously individualistic or atomistic fashion, each actor or habitus being formed in apparent isolation. This results in both a failure to adequately explain the clustering of lifestyle preferences in social space, and an explanatory account of individual habitus formation that is both vague and highly deterministic.

To caricature slightly, Bourdieu proposes that each individual habitus is forged by particular social conditions, specifically a portfolio of capitals, such that those actors who share a similar portfolio end up with a similar habitus: if i and j share similar types and amounts of capital, then Bourdieu predicts that they will share similar lifestyles and preferences, *irrespective of any contact between them*. This is why certain preferences cluster around particular points in his (correspondence) maps of social space (see Chapter 3). How this happens, the mechanisms involved, is never explained, however, and the account is further problematic because Bourdieu claims that there is no necessary relationship between specific locations in social space (i.e. portfolios of capital) and particular preferences. This is demonstrated by the fact that preferences move across social space in the course of history. Lifestyle practices once associated with the poor might, at a later point, characterize the wealthy or cultured and vice versa. This is problematic for his account because it makes it even more difficult to explain why actors located at the same point in social space would have similar habitus and engage in similar practices. If lifestyle choices, such as the preference for rugby over football, are only arbitrarily linked to positions in social space, then why do actors with similar resources tend to agree in their preference for, for example, rugby? Resources do not determine preferences, especially if the link between them is historically variable and therefore arbitrary. My argument is that we see these patterns because worlds tend to cluster and, in virtue of this, actors do too. This point needs to be unpacked.

Actors with similar resources tend to develop similar tastes and preferences, by my account, because they move in worlds which are strongly connected and therefore influence one another. They belong to a cluster of worlds, anchored upon certain key worlds, namely occupational, residential and educational worlds, the access to which is strongly conditioned by access to certain resources. Moreover, the circulation of resources between these worlds tends to close them off from those who are not already a member of them. Buying a house in a particular residential neighbourhood, for example, requires a given income. This tends to limit ownership to members of particular occupational worlds which provide the necessary salary. Occupational worlds, in turn, demand certain educational qualifications from their members, which are acquired from universities, which tend to recruit disproportionately from specific schools, which recruit from specific neighbourhoods, which, in turn, recruit from specific occupations and so on. Certain neighbourhoods, schools, occupations and universities, as worlds, therefore form clusters within the abovementioned network of worlds.

Furthermore, social influence runs through the connections which link these worlds. As actors move between home, school, university, work and neighbourhood they circulate particular ideas and influences. And those ideas and influences, which in many cases will only be transmitted in meaningful and relatively strong relationships, tend only to flow between (strongly) connected worlds. Influences circulating within highly paid occupational worlds are unlikely to be felt in the worlds of poor housing estates because nobody in a highly paid occupation is likely to live or have significant contacts with anybody on a poor housing estate. Likewise the emergent culture of the housing estate, generated by way of interaction between its denizens, is unlikely to find its way into any highly paid occupational worlds for the same reason. The worlds are, as the expression goes, 'worlds apart', but this is only significant because, as I have said, not all worlds are 'apart'. Some are connected and form clusters on the basis of their patterns of connection.

This entails that other worlds too connect to the basic clusters described above. If a preference for rugby takes shape in a particular cluster of occupational and neighbourhood worlds, for example, then the world of rugby is likely to connect with that cluster too. Our clusters involve core worlds of occupation, neighbourhood and education but also further worlds reflecting the fashions and preferences of the cluster at any point in time.

'Social space', from this point of view, is not only defined by volumes and profiles of capital, though these are important, but also by connections between worlds and, ultimately therefore, connections between actors. *Actors with similar profiles of capital tend to manifest similar tastes and preferences because they are more likely to meet, interact with and therefore influence one another.* Shibutani makes a claim similar to this in his seminal paper on 'social worlds':

> Variations in outlook arise through differential contact and association; the maintenance of social distance – through segregation, conflict or simply the reading of different literature – leads to the formation of distinct cultures. Thus people in different classes develop different modes of life and outlook, not because of anything inherent in economic position, but because similarity of occupation and limitations set by income level dispose them to certain restricted communication channels.
>
> (Shibutani 1955: 565–66)

Influence in interaction, moreover, shapes further influences. The most obvious example of this involves the mass media. The mass media are potentially open to us all and expose us all to the same influences. However, as is well known and clearly demonstrated through newspaper readership surveys, different 'clusters' of actors access different media and, as a consequence, expose themselves to different influences – they may, of course, also be selective in how they perceive and use those media forms. Which media we access is, in turn, influenced by the worlds to which we and the people with whom we mix on a day-to-day basis belong. There is relatively little discussion of stories from *The Mail* or the *News of the World* in sociology common rooms, in my experience, for example, and rather more discussion of stories from *The Guardian*.[5] Colleagues will tend to discuss media stories, collectively interpreting those stories for one another and, at the same time, generating expectations about the media sources that they respectively tap into. Thus, how we are affected by the media is affected by our peers, who influence the media that we expose ourselves to and how we interpret the ideas, information etc. which we encounter through these media.

I am returning here to my critique of Bourdieu from Chapter 3. Whatever claims he may make to relationalism, he employs a very odd definition of relations which systematically neglects concrete ties between actors. This is a fatal flaw in his argument because concrete ties and interactions between actors are necessary to explain much that he seeks to explain and, indeed, for making sense of the social world more generally.

Of course there are exceptions. Members of different occupations, with very different levels and forms of resources, do meet in the same workplaces; some schools have very mixed catchment areas etc. These more mixed milieus facilitate social influence across groups who are, in other respects, quite segregated, perhaps generating hybrid habitus or simply breaking down any rigid distinctions of lifestyle preferences and resources. I am not particularly concerned here to establish whether and to what extent worlds actually are segregated, however. It must suffice to say that the work in this area is very good, although the picture it suggests is much less clear cut than Bourdieu and his followers often suggest (e.g. Bennet *et al.* 2009). My concern is with the (relational) mechanisms that generate whatever level of cultural differentiation between socio-economic clusters we do find.

As a final point, note that my account not only explains the clustering and socio-economic profile of lifestyle preferences, insofar as we can find it, but does so in a dynamic and non-deterministic way. Actors aren't imprinted with a habitus by virtue of their location in social space. Their preferences are formed in the contexts of interactions and processes of mutual influence in which they are fully involved. In what follows in the next section I expand upon this position further.

Homophily

My contention, to reiterate, is that social influence, mediated by way of interaction, shapes what actors do and thereby shapes their tastes and other dispositions, their habitus. Insofar as habitus reflect the social influence of particular clusters within the network of worlds, however, they too can act back upon this process, reinforcing it. We see this in homophily, that is, the tendency for actors to variously seek out and bond more readily with those who are (more) like their selves.

Homophily is, in some cases, an outcome of what Feld (1981, 1982) refers to as network 'foci', that is to say, actors tend to meet up with similar others because their tastes and preferences draw them to the same places and events, where they are more likely to meet. On one level this might entail that all of the smokers in an organization are more likely to know one another because they meet 'behind the bike sheds' when having a crafty fag. The same process clearly operates on other levels, however, as when enthusiasts for a particular type of music are more likely to meet in virtue of their attendance at gigs, festivals and other such 'hangouts', political activists through their involvement in protests and meetings, football fans on the terraces and so on.

Of course actors generally attend such events without intending to meet likeminded others. They attend because they want to listen to music, protest, watch football or whatever. But they meet likeminded others all the same. And if their preferences, which guide their activities, reflect the influences they have experienced in the other networked worlds in which they mix, then the alters they meet are likely to belong to the same cluster of worlds. If enthusiasm for table tennis circulates through (and only through) the worlds of the wealthy and well-to-do, then those amongst the well-to-do 'infected' by it are likely to meet other wealthy and well-to-do individuals whilst pursuing their new passion.

Even when actors meet alters from very different worlds, however, the thesis of homophily suggests that connection may prove difficult on account of their lack of shared experience. They may find it more difficult to find issues of common interest to talk about, for example. They will orient towards different reference groups or 'generalized others', perhaps therefore finding one another's perspectives strange and for that reason disagreeable. They may find one another difficult to 'read' and for that reason difficult to trust and interact sociably with. Simmel (1971) argues that sociability is difficult to achieve across status divides because those divides encourage a formality in interaction which negates the playfulness integral to sociability. I would add to this that interaction across social divides is often more difficult because actors lack common points of reference and a background of taken-for-granted assumptions, which, in turn, makes it less playful, sociable and fun. Moreover, this might explain the formality referred to by Simmel because formality, in addition to marking status differences, is also a means of coordinating interactions in situations where we have no other intuitive feel for how the interaction should proceed. Indeed, in his history of manners, Elias (1984) argues that one of the drivers for the emergence of codified rules of interaction was an expansion of the social worlds in which actors were moving and the consequent increased probability that they would be interacting with others whom they did not know nor necessarily share a cultural background with. Formal codes emerged to help those now more likely to be interacting with strangers to do so successfully.

These obstacles to interaction reinforce the habitus that shapes them. Actors are more likely to gravitate towards those who are similar to them, which in turn exposes them most to influences which tend to reinforce the way they are. There is much research attesting to this power of homophily (McPherson *et al.* 2001).

Conclusion

The first part of this chapter sought to discuss the way in which networks, conventions and resources give structure to social worlds, both independently and in conjunction, generating opportunities and constraints for interaction. The relations which structure networks, I argued, are shaped both by convention and by the resources exchanged between the parties. No less significantly, however, conventions emerge from interaction and only take hold in a world to the extent that they are diffused through networks. Likewise, the exchange value of resources does not exist independently of their exchange within and circulation through networks, nor in many cases independently of conventions which bestow a symbolic significance upon them, money being the obvious example. In these ways networks, conventions and resources are co-constitutive.

Pushing this point I then considered whether network structures only count as 'social structures' where they are networks of roles (rather than networks of concrete individuals). Against this I suggested both that the concept of role can be problematic, insofar as it suggests greater consensus about rights, duties and responsibilities than is often the case, and that conceiving of social structure in terms of networks of roles can tend to reduce it to the official picture of a social world, paying insufficient attention to the various unofficial structures that we generally find. Actors occupy 'positions', I argued, which are constituted both by their pattern of ties to others (a pattern which they may share with others in an equivalence class) and by the resources they have available to them and can make available, through exchange, to others. Moreover, they orient to conventions and adopt role-based identities. But they carve out their 'role' for themselves in interaction with their relevant alters. Mothers, for example, must negotiate their role with the father of their child, with the child herself, with grandparents, teachers etc.

This argument bears some similarity to Giddens' (1991) arguments upon the negotiation of identity in 'late modernity' but crucially, where Giddens suggests that individuals reflexively work these things out for themselves, continuing the individualistic line of thought begun in his structuration theory, I am suggesting that these things are negotiated (and fought over) in interaction. Some mothers may be free to self-realize through their role, exploring exotic or therapeutic forms of motherhood. Others will be restrained by their resources, by other demands in the networked worlds in which they are involved or perhaps by partners upon whom they depend and with whom they therefore have an imbalanced power relation. And this is necessarily so because roles and identities are not 'about' the individual but rather about their relations to others. Motherhood, as a role and identity, for example, is 'about' a woman's relationship to her children and perhaps also the father of those children. Furthermore a mother is never just a mother and she must balance the demands of motherhood with the demands of her other involvements.

In the latter part of the chapter I sought to develop this position by considering how social worlds are themselves linked in a network by way of the multiple affiliations of their members. Every actor belongs to multiple worlds and is therefore a tie between them. I also suggested, however, that some worlds are more closely tied than others and I indicated that this might be a better way of thinking about the social distribution of lifestyles and tastes than the more individualistic model of Bourdieu. Of course people acquire tastes and the various forms of competence necessary to appreciate different cultural forms. These things do become embodied as habits. And actors are not 'candles in the wind', blown this way and that by the influence of others. But we are influenced by others; this plays a key role in the formation of our tastes and preferences, and it can engender both changes and stability in those tastes and preferences. Bourdieu's habitus, in itself, explains nothing and stands in need of explanation. Social interaction and patterns of homophily and differential association promise at least a start to that explanation.

10 Big networks and small worlds
The micro–macro dichotomy

In the last chapter I discussed the idea that social networks constitute important dimensions of social structures. In this chapter I want to address an objection that I believe some will have to this claim, namely that social networks might belong to small-scale 'micro-structures' but do not play a significant role at the 'macrocosm'. In other words, I address what is sometimes referred to as the micro–macro dichotomy. And I offer a relational solution to that problem, thereby completing the relational engagement with sociology's dichotomies that I began in Chapter 2.

The micro–macro dichotomy, if it is to be distinguishable from debates on individualism–holism (discussed in Chapter 2) and agency–structure (discussed in Chapter 8), is a problem of scale. How do we maintain consistency in our sociological understanding when some of us research small groups comprising 20 or so actors, others analyse national societies comprising many millions of actors and still others analyse a 'global order' comprising billions. Are the concepts, theories and techniques which prove so useful in relation to the analysis of small groups also useful for analysing and conceptualizing structure at the level of national and international populations?

The short answer is 'yes'. Whilst I accept that different jobs require different tools in sociology as much as in any other domain of practice, such that we should expect some variation in methods and concepts as we move from micro to macro, I believe that discussion of the macro-cosm is befuddled by recourse to unhelpful abstractions and reifications which are often attributed almost magical powers; 'the system' does this, 'capitalism' does that etc. Macro sociological thinking is often substantialist, conceiving of societies as things. Proper sociological understanding demands that we move beyond these quasi explanations, beyond substantialism, and that we look for relational mechanisms which work at the macro level. The 'macrocosm' is not different in kind from the microcosm. It is just bigger. It is a network of interacting, interdependent, mutually constitutive and mutually affecting actors. Size does matter, however, and the challenge we face is one of scaling up.

In this chapter I approach this challenge from three directions. First, I suggest that macro-level relations and networks are in some cases relations between and networks of actors other than human actors; they are networks of *corporate actors*.

It is not just human actors who interact and connect but also nation states, business corporations, NGOs etc. Human actors are involved in these corporate actors and we are all affected by their interactions but there are often good reasons, which I discuss, to pitch our analysis at the level of (networks of) corporate actors. And doing so scales our analysis and perspective up. Corporate actors are macro-actors and their networks and interactions constitute an important dimension of the social macrocosm.

A focus upon corporate actors also facilitates a consideration of the nested structures which, to some degree, bridge the micro–macro divide in practice (see also Coleman 1990). The large organizations that tend to qualify as corporate actors can be regarded as actors within networks in their own right but we can equally focus our analyses within them, upon the networks which compose them. These networks might involve human actors but they could involve smaller corporate actors which, in turn, can be broken down into a network of human actors in a process of successive nesting.

Having considered how a macrocosm might be generated through networks of macro (corporate) actors, I consider how certain types of relation have a similar effect. In particular I consider 'media of exchange', such as communication technologies, political technologies and money. These media are used in relations and interactions between both human and corporate actors. They do not alter the basic relational picture of the social world. But they make different, 'bigger' networks possible.

Finally, I focus upon network structure. This focus is itself broken down into three parts. In the first I briefly reconsider blockmodelling, which was introduced in Chapter 9. Blockmodels afford a way of analysing and detecting structure in large networks. In addition, however, I suggest that important models of 'macro-structure' can be rendered in blockmodelling terms. Blockmodelling can capture aspects of macro-structure and at least some macro-level theoretical descriptions of society can be rendered in blockmodelling terms. The second and third parts of this discussion centre upon different ways of accounting for what has been referred to as the '*small world effect*', that is, the surprising finding that the average distance between nodes in networks comprising hundreds of millions of nodes can in some cases be as little as six degrees. Insofar as this holds in the human world – and it is a question how far it does – the models proposed to explain it both allow us to think of the macrocosm as one huge network and also suggest mechanisms through which the coordination of this network and diffusion of culture and resources through it might be effectively achieved.

Macro nodes: corporate actors and nested structures

The first way in which relational, network ideas can be applied to the macrocosm is by way of a focus upon networks of what Coleman (1975, 1990) calls 'corporate actors'. The concept of a corporate actor entails that collectives of human actors, in certain combinations, might be treated as social actors in their own right. The British government, for example, might be deemed an actor in its own right, irreducible to the human actors who staff it and *a fortiori* to the 61 million British citizens whom it represents. It acts for its citizens in a variety of international contexts, deciding for them, but it is not reducible to them in the sense of being a simple expression of their aggregate will. Likewise, a trade union or business corporation might function as an actor within a particular context, making and acting upon decisions as a human actor might and representing its thousands of employees or members.

Such corporate actors interact and form relations, and their networks are an important aspect of what we mean by the social macrocosm. Nation states form trade and peace agreements, for example. They work as allies or compete and negotiate. Likewise large corporations, trades unions, political parties and (some) social movement organizations. These are 'big' actors whose actions often have 'big' consequences and their networks comprise a macro-level of social life.

How can collectives of human actors function as actors? Why should we treat them as actors and not reduce them to the human actors who staff them? The British government is not an actor, one might argue. It is a collective or network of human actors. One reason for treating corporate actors as actors in their own right, as Hindess (1988) has argued, is that they can make decisions which are irreducible to their members. The human actors involved within them may all cast a vote but the resulting decision is not simply an aggregation of these individual decisions. Different voting systems generate different decisions. Collective decisions are not a mere aggregation of individual decisions but rather depend upon the method by which those individual decisions are combined and counted. And this is just part of the overall process whereby decisions are made within complex organizations. Their systems of information gathering and other aspects of their internal organization all affect the way in which they decide and act, making them more than the mere sum of the individual actors who staff them. They do decide and act, however, entering into agreements, exchanging resources, declaring war etc., and as Hindess (1988) suggests, they thereby meet the criteria for a minimal definition of agency.

In addition, as Axelrod (1997) notes, corporate actors have a mandate to speak for others, whom they have the means to secure compliance from, and both own and control resources in their own right, resources which the individual human actors involved in them have no ownership of qua individuals. Politicians do not bargain with and deploy resources which belong to them individually, for example, but rather with resources owned by 'the government' or even 'the country' and only controlled by them to the extent that they enjoy an elected mandate to represent the government or the country; indeed, only insofar as they act in their capacity or role of politician. Corporate actors can make decisions to the extent that their representatives are in a position to mobilize the resources of the collective they represent and enjoy sufficient control over that collective to guarantee compliance to binding agreements. Again this renders the corporate actor irreducible to the human actors who staff it. Gordon Brown, to return to an example from Chapter 9, does not own and has no right to use UK tax revenue as a private individual or human actor, but as Prime Minister, executing a function within the corporate actor that is the British government, he does have that right. The government, as an actor, owns that money, not the individuals who happen to staff it at any particular point in time.

The other side of this is that corporate actors enjoy status and recognition as actors, often within law. They are actors, in some part, because others, usually other corporate actors, choose to treat them as such. The collective of individuals involved in the decision making process of the corporate actor could not, in and of themselves, function as an actor in the absence of this recognition, such that the corporate actor is relationally constituted and, again, irreducible. The UK government is an actor, in some part, because other actors, including other national governments and, in other contexts, UK citizens, recognize it as such.

Of course there are differences between human and corporate actors. Much of what we might want to include in a comprehensive conception of the human actor, including emotion and the capacity for spontaneous and pre-reflective action, cannot be attributed to the corporate actor. This is not a sufficient reason to abandon the notion of corporate actors, however. They are perhaps only actors in a limited sense, according to what Hindess (1988) calls a minimal conception of the actor, but they are actors all the same.

If we admit of corporate actors then, to reiterate, we can conceptualize at least certain aspects of the social macrocosm as networks of interactions and relations between such actors: between national states, NGOs and international political bodies, for example; between large business corporations and trades unions. In addition, we can posit that network structures, at least in some cases, nest within one another in a way which bridges micro and macro levels (see also Coleman 1990). Individual members of a trade union, for example, might be networked within and through their local union branch. They are nodes in a local union network structure and participate directly in decision making processes therein. Their local branch may then, qua corporate actor, constitute a node within a larger network comprising the national union. And the national union, qua corporate actor, may constitute a node within a general trades union council which itself functions, for some purposes and in some contexts, as a corporate actor within wider political contexts. Each corporate actor can either be broken down into the network of ('lower order') nodes which comprises its internal structure, or studied as a node in its own right within a wider network. Micro and macro are bridged by the nesting of and in corporate actors.

This is illustrated in Figure 10.1. The square nodes in this diagram represent human actors. They combine in networks which are also organizations, however, and which constitute corporate actors, represented as circular nodes, which also forge links with one another. In two cases these relations are also sufficiently organized to constitute a further nested layer of actors, represented by the ovals, who also interact and form a network (of three corporate actors). Networks nest within networks, telescoping from the micro- to the macrocosm.

A number of important studies of 'the world system', in Wallerstein's (2004) sense, demonstrate how a network analysis of corporate actors might work. Moreover, as they draw upon blockmodelling procedures, they also anticipate

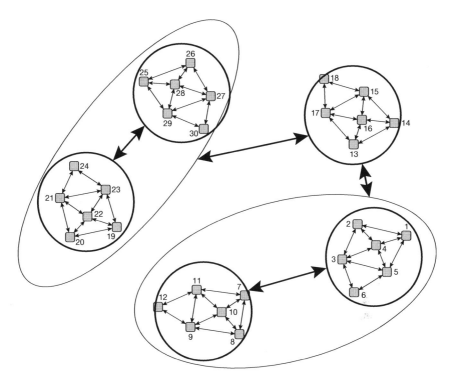

Figure 10.1 Corporate actors and nested structures

a further theme of this chapter. In an early paper, for example, Snyder and Kick (1979) modelled the relations between 118 nations, focusing upon ties based upon (1) trade, (2) military intervention, (3) diplomatic relations and (4) conjoint treaty memberships. The resulting four networks were combined in a blockmodel, and from the blockmodel Snyder and Kick were able to discern what they claimed was a clear clustering of 'core', 'semi-peripheral' and 'peripheral' nations in the world system. They were then, using regression analyses, able to show that position within this complex macro network had considerable economic and political effects upon the nation involved. More recent work by Smith and White (1992), whilst more complex in methodological terms and somewhat narrower in the range of relations studied, suggests a similar picture.

In these studies, network analysis, and in particular blockmodelling of relations between major corporate actors (nations), facilitates a proper empirical analysis of a key macro social structure on a global scale and demonstrates that the position of nations within this structure has significant effects. It facilitates an empirical test of world systems theory (further to those offered by its original advocates), operationalizing its key concepts and demonstrating the credentials of network analysis for macro social analysis. We don't get much more macro than the world system! Indeed, the use of network analysis in these studies allowed for the first adequate operationalization of the key concepts of 'structure' and 'position' within world systems theory (ibid.). Though world systems theory is better supported, empirically, than many macro social models, the notion that individual nations occupy a position within a structure had only figurative significance in empirical analyses prior to these network studies. Network analysis gave those concepts empirical and operational meaning. Not only does network analysis of relations between corporate actors have 'macro' credentials, therefore, it allows macro sociology to more fully operationalize its key concepts.

Macro ties: media of exchange

The concept of corporate actors addresses the micro–macro problem by way of a focus upon the nodes of networks: networks of macro (corporate) actors constitute a social macrocosm. We might also address the problem by way of a focus upon relations and ties, however, or rather what some, including both Parsons (1979) and Habermas (1987), call 'media of exchange'. The idea of media of exchange is that face-to-face and linguistic exchanges are limited in terms of the number of participants they can involve on a direct basis, the length of the chains of inter-actors they can meaningfully hold together and their geographical spread, but that certain interactive media allow these limits to be overcome.

Technical innovations, particularly information and communication technologies constitute one example; voting systems and other political 'technologies' constitute another. Millions of actors cannot participate in a single conversation and on that basis decide upon a collective course of action but they can vote. Voting systems are political technologies or media of exchange which facilitate collective decision making amongst large populations. They connect actors in a (political) network. In what follows I discuss communication technologies, political technologies and money as 'media of exchange' in large networks.

Communication technologies

By means of newspapers, radio, television and more recently the internet and Web 2.0, millions of people can be connected in a communication web. The same message, information and ideas can be received simultaneously by millions of actors in vast networks which operate on a macro scale. Actors in these networks communicate by means of natural languages. In these respects their interactions are no different to those described earlier in this book. But these are interactions involving millions of actors. The capacity to do this rests upon four crucial factors.

First, it involves a physical–technical network of transmitters, receivers and cables which carry communications (and electricity) across distances, or alternatively, printing presses, distributors and outlets such as newsagents. Communication networks end where their technological–commercial infrastructure (itself a network) ends. Many social interactions in the contemporary world are mediated by such technological networks.

Second, to anticipate a theme which I return to, they tend to involve hubs. Millions of people do not directly communicate to one another, rather they are communicated to and increasingly communicate back with a central figure or figures within a network, whether a newspaper columnist, a radio DJ, television presenter or perhaps a celebrated blogger or tweeter. Moreover, this hub position is often also built into the aforementioned physical–technical–commercial network which functions as its infrastructure. There is often one transmitter to many receivers, e.g. one radio station to many radios – although that does not hold in cyberspace.

Third, communications are sent out from hubs in a relatively indiscriminate way. The term that is used to describe this in network science, 'broadcast network', could be misleading in this context. It does not refer specifically to the mass media. Viruses are sometimes said to spread through broadcast networks, for example, because carriers do not transmit them to anyone in particular but rather anybody in range, e.g. a cough on the bus might infect everybody on that bus. However, this does apply to the mass media. Journalists may have a target audience but they do not know exactly who is 'tuned in' and could not do so because of the size of their audience. They broadcast their message to anybody and everybody who happens to be tuned in.

Finally, broadcast networks, at least where they involve the communication of linguistic meanings between human actors, tend to be unidirectional. One individual actor can send out a message to millions of others and in theory they might receive a million responses but they could not process those million responses, at least not individually and 'communicatively'. They may have teams working for them, who sift through responses for them, spotting themes which they can respond to and identifying particular communications to respond to, or they may invite their audiences to respond to them by way of a vote, selecting from a narrow and pre-determined range of responses, but they can't read a million individual responses and respond to them all individually.

This may not be what we conventionally think of under the rubric of 'social networks' but it is a social network. It involves a set of actors and a set of meaningful connections between (some of) those actors. It is a fantastically complex and very big social network but a social network all the same: a macro-network. And conceiving of it as such allows us to render the social macrocosm in relational terms, demystifying it and revealing certain of its structures and mechanisms (e.g. hubs and broadcasts) in a manner which does not resort to overly abstract or reified constructs. If actors in a large population orient to similar points of interest and share common fashions and attitudes it is in no small part because they all belong to the same macro-communication networks and therefore receive the same information, stimulation and ideas. The early critics of the 'mass society' and 'culture industries' (e.g. Adorno and Horkheimer 1983), who believed that the mass media were manipulating and homogenizing the population, destroying indigenous culture and traditions, and replacing it with a commercial and ideological alternative, undoubtedly overstated the case and underestimated the critical capacities of social actors but they at least remind us that whatever degree

of cultural homogeneity we do find must be explained by reference to communication networks. 'Society' and 'culture' exist by virtue of social interaction and
extend only as far as that interaction. In mass societies this involves massive,
technologically mediated networks.

Political technologies

The concept of voting, briefly introduced above, points to further media of
exchange. It suggests that communication between actors may be simplified by
way of tokens which do not need to be processed in the same way that linguistic
'information' is processed in a one-to-one or small group exchange. Audiences
of a television programme who vote for one out of a pre-selected range of options
participate not only in a media network but also in a system of communication
which simplifies information exchange so as to allow millions of nodes to
communicate with and influence the behaviour of a single hub.

Voting in a political context, where authority is transferred from citizens to
a particular political party, is another example of this. Like the broadcast media
referred to above, 'the state' or government is a centralized hub in the political
networks (political world) of national societies. Insofar as it is a democratic
state it is supposed to communicate with its citizens and be accountable to them.
In societies where citizens number in the tens of millions, however, direct one-
to-one exchange is restricted. Individual citizens may write to their MP or to
a government minister but this only works as long as very few do so. Another
channel, generally pursued by big business, is the lobby. Lobbying firms broker
between businesses and governments, on behalf of the former. Finally, citizens
sometimes have recourse to the more direct and 'popular' mechanism of protest.
In the protest, collectives of varying sizes seek either to demonstrate their views
symbolically, in the hope of swaying a government which claims to represent
them, or they draw upon their (collective) power in an effort to force the government's hand, e.g. by denying government something which it depends upon them
for (e.g. their labour or taxation money) or threatening them coercively with
violence and damage to property. Beyond protest, however, which is a minority
pursuit (even in the case of 'mass' protests), most citizens 'communicate' with the
state only by voting in elections, paying taxes and perhaps less directly by way of
their compliance with laws, directives and appeals. They exchange votes for
policies which they believe will serve their interests.

Thinking of the state as a hub in a network, connected to its citizens through
exchanges of votes and tax payments for policies is perhaps an unusual way of
thinking about both networks and states. The political world, centred upon the
state, is a network, however. The actions of the state depend upon the flow of
revenue from tax payers. Without that flow there would be no state. Similarly,
there is a flow of legitimate authority from voters to the state which politicians pay
great heed to, fearing that a shift of allegiance will be damaging to their party or
worse still that a loss of belief in the state as a whole will plunge society into chaos
or revolution. The gesture of voting is small and infrequent but it causes

governments to fall and shifts the political direction of a society. Furthermore, citizens are connected to one another through this network. They enjoy a structurally equivalent position to one another vis-à-vis the state and indirectly affect one another through their interaction with it. Supporters of one party are stuck with government by another, for example, if their fellow voters vote in sufficient numbers for that party. Likewise services for one group might necessitate tax rises for another.

The political network within which the state is embedded, as a central hub, is sustained by more than just the transfer of votes during elections and money via taxation, however. As Elias (1984) notes, states tend only to find stability where they preside over a population whose members already enjoy a high level of interdependence and who therefore rely upon the state, to some extent, to arbitrate between them. Throughout the middle ages, Elias shows, attempts at state centralization failed due to a lack of economic interdependence between different localities and their indigenous networks. Kings and military leaders would send their deputies to govern conquered lands, only to find that those deputies established these lands as their own and claimed independence. Centralization gave way almost immediately to decentralization. The cycle was only broken when the areas involved became economically interdependent and thus acquired a material interest in the existence of a central power which would regulate and guarantee their economic transactions. Actors were only prepared to accept a transfer of authority from a local hub to a bigger and more distant hub, covering a bigger network and geographical area, when that bigger network had already come into being by virtue of increased interaction and interdependence between what had previously been separate networks. Centralized political authorities only achieved an enduring presence in territories whose denizens were already economically interdependent.

In a different but related argument Foucault (1979) claims that the centralized state, at least in its present form, belongs to and is sustained by a network of 'disciplinary power'. He is critical of theories of the state in both their liberal and their more radical forms. This critique has numerous facets, some of which I have discussed elsewhere (Crossley 1994, 2006a,b). The key point for our purposes is that traditional theories of political life paint a lofty and abstract picture of the state which fails to locate it within networks of everyday life and thereby fail to explain its influence. Liberal democracies and their voting systems presuppose a level of social order and compliance which is unexplained in conventional political theories, Foucault argues. There can be no liberal democracy in the absence of mechanisms which secure the order and compliance upon which it is based – which is not to say that this pre-requisite in any way explains these mechanisms. Moreover, states are only effective to the extent that they connect with those whom they govern – an issue largely ignored in most theories.

It is in this vein that Foucault (1979) explores the emergence, in Europe in the course of the eighteenth century, of a variety of interlocking practices and agencies which function both to generate knowledge and information about individuals, which is integral to modern forms of government, and also to secure their control and compliance. Throughout the course of the eighteenth century, he notes, new spaces opened up in the everyday lives of Europeans where their behaviour was subject to increased surveillance and regulation, from the school and factory to the workhouse and madhouse. In these spaces new techniques and practices for regulating social conduct were institutionalized. Moreover, new agencies such as police, teachers, social workers and psychiatrists emerged who were charged with administering populations and regulating behaviour at a local level, processing and attempting to correct it where it departed from norms which were both established and legitimated by the aforementioned new forms of knowledge whose emergence was interwoven with their own and that of their techniques of control. These agencies and practices, in contrast to the lofty figure of 'the state', directly touched individuals in their everyday lives. Children were and are monitored and trained in schools. Citizens were and are monitored in the streets. Criminals were and are incarcerated, monitored and trained in prisons etc. It is these practices, at the ground level, which connect individuals to the state, according to Foucault, and which generate the social order that allows liberal political regimes to function as they do.

The 'power' of the state, on this account, rises from the bottom up. Disciplinary practices and relations first emerged outside of 'the state' and the state as we know it was only possible on the basis of their convergence in a network. The modern state took shape as the various agencies and practices identified by Foucault connected and formed a single web of social control. Of course key agents of state, such as politicians, direct actors below them. Decisions pass 'downwards'. But this downward flow presupposes a network which secures control at the ground level. Without a police force, schools, social workers etc., the state or government as we know it would be completely ineffectual. *'The state' is a network and the power of its centre, insofar as it is appropriate to talk in those terms, is an effect of operations further out in its periphery.*

Foucault's analysis is extremely important. He refuses to take 'the power of the state' as a given and seeks rather to trace it back through networks which link this 'macro-actor' to the social microcosm. Talk of 'the state', he suggests, is often an unhelpful abstraction. The state is not a thing, a substance, but rather a vast network linking multiple social worlds, e.g. the school, the prison, the workplace, the mental hospital and (via social workers) the family. He asks how it is that members of political worlds are connected up so as to form a political world and by way of answering this question identifies the numerous practices which mediate and structure relations within political society. This disciplinary network, like voting systems and the mass media, is a mediated social network which binds the social macrocosm together. It aids our efforts to make sense of the macrocosm relationally.

In addition, Foucault's concept of power both suggests ways in which we might extend our conception of it, as developed in Chapter 7, but also falls short of adequacy and thus calls for the corrective which our account affords. This calls for a brief digression.

Foucault's 'power': a digression

Foucault adds to our understanding of power, as developed in Chapter 7, because he identifies various ways in which power relations are mediated by social practices and material culture in a way which enhances and extends their reach. Even if we disregard the many more rhetorical formulations for which he is best known and concentrate only upon his more precise and analytic moments, however, he remains very vague and fails to get to the very heart of power *qua relation*. His concern with *technologies of power* often obscures a proper focus upon *relations of power*.

His famous discussion of the Panopticon affords an instructive example to work with (Foucault 1979). In feudal society, he argues, power functioned by way of its visibility. Kings and queens threatened and intimidated their subjects into compliance by way of their castles, public ceremonies and by elaborate public rituals of torture and execution. Their subjects were left in no doubt as to what would happen if they transgressed the sovereign's will. In the modern regime, by contrast, power functions by making the individuals subject to it visible, that is, by means of surveillance. Many of the practices of power that Foucault explores in *Discipline and Punish* serve to make individuals visible and subject them to surveillance, the most famous of these being Jeremy Bentham's Panopticon prison design. In the Panopticon all cells are arranged in a circle around a central watchtower. From the watchtower it is possible to observe any prisoner at any time but an arrangement of lights and shutters prevent the prisoner from ascertaining whether or not he is being seen at any point in time. The prisoner is 'seen but he does not see; he is an object of information, never a subject in communication' (1979: 200). The Panopticon is 'a machine for dissociating the see/being seen dyad (ibid.: 202). This, Foucault claims, creates an 'anxious awareness of being observed' (ibid.) which serves to secure compliance. Moreover, as such, the prisoner is complicit in his own control:

> He who is subject to the field of visibility, and who knows it, assumes responsibility for the constraints of power; he makes it play spontaneously upon himself; he inscribes in himself the power relation in which he simultaneously plays both roles; he becomes the principle of his own subjection.
>
> (ibid.: 202–3)

And this extends beyond the prison and beyond any context where an external observer might be involved. Echoing Mead's (1967) arguments on the internalization of the perspective of the generalized other, Foucault argues that in modern societies:

> There is no need for arms, physical violence, material constraints. Just a gaze. An inspecting gaze which each individual under its weight will end interiorizing to the point that he is his own overseer, each individual thus exercising this surveillance over, and against himself.
>
> (Foucault 1980: 155)

This is a fascinating account, not least in the respect that it demonstrates how human relations can be mediated by technologies and conventions embedded in their physical environment. Our account of power, introduced in Chapter 7, must be embellished through reference to such mediations.

However, the mechanism effected by these practices, which associate them with *power* is unclear. Why does the other's capacity to observe me when I cannot observe them introduce an imbalance of power? Or rather it doesn't, not always. The kids who make rude gestures at CCTV cameras in city centres are apparently unmoved by an 'anxious awareness of being observed'; likewise actors on a stage or a set and the kings and queens in the feudal regime. All are observed in asymmetrical conditions where they cannot observe back without necessarily being disadvantaged in an imbalanced power relation. Being looked at might be unpleasant, as Sartre's (1969) famous discussion of 'the look' suggests, but the unpleasantness is often momentary and does not necessarily tip or even affect the balance of power in a relation. To understand power we must look beyond *technologies* to *relations*.

Foucault goes some way to doing this. He conceives of power as a relationship between actors: '[L]et us not deceive ourselves; if we speak of the structure or the mechanisms of power, it is only insofar as we suppose that certain persons exercise power over others. *The term 'power' designates a relationship between partners*' (Foucault 1982: 217, my emphasis). It is, he continues, 'always a way of acting upon an acting subject or acting subjects by virtue of their acting or being capable of action. A set of actions upon other actions' (ibid.: 221). His point is that power does not detract from the agency of the actor over whom it is exercised. It works only through and by means of their agency. Indeed, he goes so far as to suggest that it is only meaningful to speak of power where the actor on the receiving end is 'recognised and maintained to the end as a person who acts' and where 'a whole field of responses, reactions, results, and possible inventions' is open to them (ibid.: 220). But what is it in these situations that merits use of the term 'power'?

Foucault never answers this question but I suggest, following the argument of Chapter 7, that power derives from the respective capacities of parties to mobilize sanctions in relation to one another, whether by withholding a good that the other wants or imposing a bad that they do not. Both parties will have some sanctions at their disposal and neither is assured of achieving compliance but relations may be imbalanced or asymmetrical insofar as one is in a position to mobilize sanctions with a greater impact. The kids who moon at CCTV cameras do so because they know that it will have no negative consequences and do not care what those who see them think because, again, it is inconsequential. Surveillance matters and only matters when the observed fear the consequences of their transgressions becoming known, even if those consequences amount only to a sense of shame deriving from others' withdrawal of respect and recognition. In this respect, moreover, returning to a further argument from Chapter 7, power is therefore more likely and more effective in relations of interdependence where actors are invested in one another.

Returning to our central argument, however, and notwithstanding the need to embellish and deepen his work in this way, Foucault's account of the disciplinary network provides an invaluable way of linking the micro and macro dimensions of social and political life and of drawing out the networked dimension of 'macro' political order. 'The state', to reiterate, consists of a network of practices and agencies which take root in the fabric of everyday life: in families, schools, social service department, doctors' surgeries, hospitals etc. This network secures the social order upon which liberal democracy depends and provides the infrastructure which allows decisions of state to be implemented.

Money and economy

Money too is a medium of exchange which extends networks. In the absence of money, exchanges of goods and services tend to be highly circumscribed and discrete. Ego does something for alter and alter does something in return. Repayment may not be immediate but it is likely to occur shortly afterwards, lest one party either forgets the obligation or dies. Nobody else is implicated or involved, although such exchanges are most likely to occur in small, relatively closed networks in which trust has been cultivated, which will tend to entail a spatial concentration of actors. Money transforms this situation (Simmel 1990; Habermas 1987; Giddens 1990). If alter pays ego for her services then ego can use that money to pay a third party or several parties for further services which alter cannot provide, or she can save the money, adding it to money she has received from other sources and spending it many years later in a place far removed from where it was earned. Furthermore, if she trusts in the currency then she need not even know the individuals that she is trading with, thereby widening her sphere of (economic) interaction. She might earn her money in Cornwall and spend it in Aberdeen, in both cases exchanging with complete strangers.

In these ways money extends the spatio-temporal reach of economic trans-actions. It joins dyads into long chains and ultimately networks of interdependence as credit acquired in one relation is spent in another: i spends the credit (money) she earns from j in a transaction with k, who then spends it in a transaction with l, who needs it to pay m and so on. If i has no money to pay j then m may end up out of pocket, even though she is separated from i by 4 degrees. Money circulates through different transactions, linking them in a network of interdependence. It is for this reason, of course, that financial booms and busts cascade between eco-nomic sectors and geographical regions. Actors, regions and sectors rely upon one another for goods and services, of course. Money is just a token. But it connects dyadic partners into a connected whole, extending the reach of interdependence in a networked form.

If we accept this notion of money as a medium of exchange and social relations then it becomes possible to think of the economy, the macro-structure *par excellence*, as a network. Along with 'the state', 'the economy' is what many writers have in mind when they refer to the social macrocosm. But the economy is nothing more than a structure of interaction, or more specifically of exchange and interdependence between actors, both human and corporate. It is a big, complex and mediated (by money) network but it is a network all the same.

The networked aspect of the economy is obscured within the dominant, neo-classical conception of it. Actors exchange with one another and, to that extent, there is a network of interaction, but neo-classical economics conceives of actors as atomized, operating rationally with perfect information in a pure market. Social network analysts have made important steps in challenging this conception, however (White 1970, 2002; Granovetter 1973, 1974, 1983, 1985). They have sought to show that economic actors, whether human or corporate, are not atomized but rather 'embedded' in a network of relations which shape their perceptions, information, decisions and actions (ibid.). Moreover, they demonstrate that 'markets', the linchpin concept of neo-classical economics, do not work in the way that neo-classical economics suggests that they do, at least not completely. The notion that supply and demand meet one another through the free and independent action of multiple actors working with complete information is a myth. Producers and consumers form durable relationships and the information that brings supply and demand together is distributed unevenly and by means of established network channels.

Granovetter's (1974) classic study, *Getting A Job*, provides an important example of this. Employment markets do not work as a free and open competition, Granovetter shows. Prospective employers and employees alike depend and prefer to draw upon established ties to others when seeking out their counter-part. When they need a job or an employee they put out 'feelers' within their personal networks, and even when they don't actively do this they are still more likely to find a match by means of personal contacts. Employment markets are embedded in networks of informal contacts.

To give another example, it is increasingly recognized that consumer choices and preferences are shaped by a combination of loyalty (to a brand or outlet), habit (sticking with what and whom you know) and social influence (Becker and Murphy 2000). In itself this points to networks but network structure is further important by virtue of the documented influence of well networked 'taste makers' (Gladwell 2002). Preferences and thus demand within a market can be shaped by a small number of actors who are innovative in their practice and, by dint of a central network position, highly influential in shaping the tastes of others. At every level then, the economy, as a key element of what we ordinarily think of as the social macrocosm, is a network of interdependent and mutually influencing actors.

Blockmodels and catnets

So far we have considered how the social macrocosm might be understood in relational, network terms by focusing upon specific types of both nodes (corporate actors) and relations (media of exchange). A further strategy derives from the blockmodelling procedures introduced in Chapter 9.

Blockmodeling, as noted in that chapter, detects structure in networks by identifying relations (or the lack of) between blocks or clusters of nodes in equivalent network positions, 'equivalence' usually being defined in either 'structural' or 'regular' terms. It is also a method of data reduction. By clustering nodes in blocks, which then become the nodes of a secondary network, it simplifies networks by reducing the number of nodes they involve. A network of several thousand nodes may become a network of ten blocks. This affords a higher level, more abstract way of thinking about networks and their structure which can be more easily applied to large networks. We still conceptualize the social world as a network, however.

More importantly, central macro-level accounts of the social world can be rendered in terms of blockmodels. Consider, for illustrative purposes, the basic Marxist schema of class society. In effect Marx specifies a blockmodel, rooted in regular equivalence, in his account of class. He identifies two positions in society, the bourgeoisie and the proletariat, each defined by their relations to the means of production (i.e. ownership of resources) and to one another. Any given individual belongs either to the proletariat, in which case they enjoy a relationship to one individual in the bourgeois block, who owns the factory that they work in, or they belong to the bourgeoisie, in which case they enjoy relations with a subset of the proletariat, who constitute the workforce in their factory.

Whether members of the proletariat and bourgeoisie are connected within their own respective blocks (making those blocks 'complete') or not (making them 'empty') is an interesting question on which Marx wavers. In some of his comments on the bourgeoisie, for example, he suggests that they compete and conflict with one another, which is a type of relationship, but might, if we take cooperation as a measure of relatedness, suggest that their block is empty. Members of the bourgeoisie occupy an equivalent position, as they all employ members of the proletariat, but they do not necessarily enjoy relations amongst themselves. In other comments, however, he implies that the bourgeoisie are capable of acting in concert (e.g. in the context of their effective control of the state), which tends to suggest that they do enjoy cooperative relations and that their block is complete. For our purposes it doesn't matter as either is compatible with a blockmodel. What matters is that the Marxist model of class can be specified as a blockmodel, utilizing the notion of regular equivalence. This should not come as a great surprise given the emphasis upon relations in Marxist philosophy but it does at least help us to see how certain macro images of society are effectively network-based images and can be rendered in network analytic terms.

There are more concrete examples of this. I have already noted the studies of Snyder and Kick (1979) and Smith and White (1992), for example, which use blockmodelling of relations between nations to empirically operationalize and analyse Wallerstein's (2004) conception of 'the world system'. Likewise, Bearman (1993) uses blockmodelling to trace transformations in social relations in England prior to the 1642–49 civil war, arguing that the former facilitated the latter. The civil war can be explained, in some part, according to Bearman, by reference to structural changes in English society which can be tracked by way of blockmodels.

Pushing this further and sticking with Marx for illustrative purposes, we might interpret his prediction that the proletariat will form itself into a solid, revolutionary class, capable of collective action, as a prediction about their 'block' becoming internally connected. Initially, he maintains, members of the proletariat may be relatively atomized. They occupy an equivalent position to one another in the respect that each sells their labour to a capitalist in return for a wage, but this does not entail that they enjoy ties to one another. Over time, however, as they transmogrify from a 'class in itself' to a 'class for itself', the density of ties between them qua both social and equivalence class grows. Indeed the latter is a precondition of the former. To become a revolutionary force they must first connect to one another and develop ties of solidarity.

This example also touches upon what the pioneer of blockmodelling, Harrison White (1965/2008), calls 'catnets'. Catnets exist where a set of actors are both internally densely networked in a relevant and meaningful manner and also share a common 'category' or 'collective identity'. Actors can belong to a common category and even adhere to a common identity without necessarily enjoying meaningful and dense network ties: hermits are an obvious example. Likewise actors can be densely networked in a meaningful fashion without necessarily belonging to a salient category or sharing a collective identity: socially heterogenous friendship groups might be an example. Where both conditions come together, however, we have a catnet and catnets are important, according to White, because the combination of networks and identities is particularly conducive to collective action, including protests and social movement mobilization (see also Tilly 1978). Like Marx, White believes that networks can become a force for change when their members identify as a group. In a somewhat more flexible manner than Marx, however, he claims both that 'cats' can give rise to 'nets' and that 'nets' can give rise to 'cats'. Whilst either may exist in isolation the homophily mechanism discussed in Chapter 9 entails that actors who belong to a common category – particularly when it entails an identity which is important to them – are more likely to associate and form networks but by the same token actors who interact regularly and enjoy strong, transitive connections are more likely to generate collective identities for themselves. Dense friendship groups might form as gangs with collective identities, for example (Crossley 2008b).

Arguments about blockmodels and catnets do not preclude the possibility that actors may simultaneously occupy different positions, any one of which could, given the right circumstances, become their dominant collective identity in the context of political struggle. In a very important study of the Paris commune of 1871, for example, Gould (1991, 1993b, 1995) notes that the residential relocation of Parisians into mixed class neighbourhoods, following Haussmann's famous reforms, led to a relative decline of class consciousness, at least as manifest in political struggle, and a rise of cross-class neighbourhood ties and identification. The working class did not cease to be working class. Their position in the network of labour relations did not alter. But they were also involved in neighbourhood relations, which brought them into contact with members of other classes and these neighbourhood relations became more important to them as sources of collective identity. The network and identity (catnet) bases of the Parisian insurrection of 1871 was not rooted in class, according to Gould, but rather in neighbourhood.

I am not suggesting that Marx is right about proletarian revolution. I do not believe that he is and the historical record supports my scepticism. My point is simply that macro-level processes and transformations of the kind he describes and predicts can be tracked and modelled in network terms by way of block-models. Network analysis, in the form of blockmodelling, can address itself to the large-scale social changes that are often of interest to macro-sociologists and to the movements and collectives whose activities shape and influence such changes. Indeed a large and growing body of literature points to the importance of social networks in relationship to social movements (for reviews see Diani and McAdam 2003; Crossley 2008a). Not only are social movements usually conceived of as networks (of both activists and 'social movement organizations' (SMOs)) but it is argued that they tend to grow out of pre-existing networks, such that mobilization is much more likely where networks already exist. In addition, networks are deemed crucial to recruitment. I could continue but the point is clear enough. Social networks are crucial elements in the social movements that, in turn, play a crucial role in the conflict and transformation integral to our understanding of the social macrocosm.

It is important to add, however, that social movements are not 'corporate actors' in the sense discussed earlier. They might include corporate actors. Some SMOs and NGOs fall into this category. But movements as a whole tend to lack the apparatus of centralized decision making and implementation constitutive of corporate actors as we have defined them. Governments often cannot negotiate with 'social movements' as they might negotiate with a trade union, for example, because social movements generally lack a representative mandated to speak on their behalf and empowered to enforce the terms of negotiated agreements amongst their membership. Nevertheless, social movements are collective forces which can make a major social impact (e.g. environmentalism, feminism and the labour movements of the nineteenth and early twentieth centuries) and which, as such, again illustrate the significance of networks for a proper understanding of the social macrocosm.

The small world effect

A further way in which social network analysis can be brought to bear upon the social macrocosm centres upon the 'small world effect', a phenomenon popularly glossed with the claim that, on average, any two individuals within a national population are connected by a chain of just five acquaintances and thus 'six degrees of separation'. This idea has become something of an urban myth in Western societies (Kleinfeld 2002a, b). It was the topic of serious social scientific research in the 1960s, however, and has been revisited in recent years in the context of the so-called 'new social physics' (for sociological commentaries see Crossley 2005b, 2008e; Scott 2004; Urry 2004).

Social scientific evidence regarding the small world effect is far from conclusive. Although a series of studies, beginning with Milgram's classic work (Milgram 1967; Travers and Milgram 1969; Korte and Milgram 1970), support the 'six degrees' claim, all are dogged by serious methodological problems (see Schnettler 2009a,b for a review, and on Milgram's original work, also Kleinfeld 2002a,b). Furthermore, all tend to invoke artificial experimental conditions whose relationship to everyday networks of interaction and relations is questionable (Crossley 2008a). However, work in the natural sciences suggests that such networks do exist, both in organic structures and in such human constructs as the internet, World Wide Web and airport networks, and mathematicians have demonstrated both that and how such structures are possible; that is, how networks involving hundreds of millions of nodes can nevertheless be characterized by average path lengths of six degrees. Indeed, researchers have identified two quite different network architectures which each produce the small world effect: Duncan Watts' (1999, 2004) 'small world' model and Albert-László Barabási's (2003) 'scale free' model. Even if the empirical work on small worlds is inconclusive in the sociological case these models are important on two grounds.

First, they allow us to *conceive* of national and even international populations as integrated networks, to imagine how that might be possible, *theoretically*, thereby indicating the utility of network ideas for macrocosmic sociological reflection. The models suggest that members of large populations, numbering in the tens or hundreds of millions, need not be separated from one another by impossibly long chains of connection which, by virtue of their length, render the diffusion of culture and resources or the coordination and orchestration of social activity impossible. What happens on one 'side' of such networks might conceivably send ripples right across to the other. Second, the models are sociologically suggestive, resonating and seeming to fit with much that we already know or imagine with respect to social life.

Macro-patterns and trends become much more intelligible and much more reconcilable with what we know of human behaviour at the microcosm if, in theory at least, actors are only separated by, on average, six degrees of separation. From the sudden rise of social movements, subcultures and panics, through the cascading of economic crises or affluence, to the shifts in fashions and even the establishment of core aspects of a common culture (e.g. language and national identity), macro-trends become more intelligible by means of the concept of the small world effect. We can see that actors in a national population might be connected in a way which makes mutual influence plausible as a mechanism of their organization.

Of course 'smallness' is relative. Six degrees is, for many purposes, a long way. Milgram, for example, suggested that 'six degrees' be rendered as six structures or social circles:

> Almost anyone . . . is but a few removes from the President . . . but this is only true in terms of a particular mathematical viewpoint and does not, in any practical sense, integrate our lives with [his] . . . We should think of the two

points as being not five persons apart but 'five circles of acquaintances' apart – five 'structures' apart. This helps to set it in its proper perspective.

(Milgram 1967: 117)

Furthermore, he noted that the chain letters which lay at the heart of his research methodology[1] often traversed geographical space far more easily than social space. Status and ethnic gaps often seemed to slow the progress of letters as senders were unable to identify suitable receivers. Homophily in social relations meant that few actors had contacts in class or ethnic groups different to their own.

This way of framing it makes the relationship seem more distant, and appropriately so. Moreover, it is important to bear in mind that, even if the figure is correct, it is still only an average. I am, on average, six degrees away from anybody else in the population, meaning that I am closer than that in some cases but also further in others. These are important points. However, they do not alter the fact that six degrees is a relatively short average distance for nodes in a network numbering in the tens of millions, short enough to make a conception of the social macrocosm as a vast network plausible. In what follows I describe each of the two aforementioned models of the small world effect in turn, outlining where and why I believe that they speak to 'macro' issues in sociology.

Watts' small world networks

Watts (1999, 2004) bases his model around mathematical work on random graphs by Erdös and Rényi (1960). Their work demonstrated that the small world effect emerges in networks of any size, even if each vertex has only a proportionately small number of ties, if those ties are randomly assigned. Random networks very often manifest the small world effect. The reason for this may be relatively straightforward. As Pool and Kochen (1978/9) note, if each of us is assumed (not unrealistically) to 'know', in the loose sense used here, 500 people and each of the people we know knows a further 500 people, then we are connected to 250,000 people via only one intermediary (two degrees). Take that one step further by adding the 500 contacts of each of those we are connected to by our intermediary (three degrees) and the figure is 125,000,000 contacts, which is already much larger than the estimated 61,000,000 people who make up the UK population. Note also that the 500 contacts of each individual in this hypothetical example constitute only a tiny fraction of the 125,000,000 total (0.0004 per cent).

The obvious objections to these claims, as Watts notes, concern 'redundancy' and randomness. Many of our acquaintances would list one another as acquaintances and thus fail to reach out to new contacts. And they would do so because our ties are not random. Our alters are likely to know one another if only because of their common link to us. Positive human relations are often 'transitive': if i is connected to j and j to k then i is (more) likely to be connected to k too.

Watts explores this problem by reference to the work of Granovetter (1973, 1983), which shows that individuals who are strongly tied to one another tend each to have further sets of strong ties to the same people. Ties, Granovetter noted, are not random. They are structured. Actors are friends with their friends friends. Granovetter also provides Watts with his solution, however. In addition to strong ties of friendship, he argues, individuals have weak ties to others outside their immediate circle, ties which bridge cliques and provide a pathway to new contacts. Social structure has a dual aspect. It consists of 'clumps' of strongly tied individuals, linked by weak ties.

It is these weak ties which provide for small worldliness in Watts' view. If we regard weak ties as random ties, he argues, then they suffice to generate small worldliness both in (mathematical) theory and in simulation experiments which test this theory. These experiments show that the small world effect is not only a feature of randomly configured networks but also of networks which combine the orderliness of 'clumps' of strong ties with the randomness of weak ties. Furthermore, Watts conducted a series of empirical studies which identified this network structure in a variety of complex systems, including the US electrical power grid and the neuronal connections of the nematode worm. Watts' small world network model is both mathematically sound and empirically grounded.

Note, however, that this model is only superficially different to the one described by Erdös and Rényi. They describe a network of randomly configured relations between individuals. Watts describes a network of randomly configured relations between clumps of individuals. The difference lies only in the nature of the nodes (if we take Watts' clumps to be higher order nodes) and this difference is irrelevant in structural terms. It is no surprise that Watts finds small worldliness in his network figuration because its structure is the same as that described by Erdös and Rényi.

I do not mean to detract from the importance of Watts' work and I am simplifying. This point is important, however, as it reinforces a further point; Watts does not get round the problem of randomness that he criticizes in Erdös and Rényi. Randomness is not eliminated in his model. It is attributed to one type of tie (weak), with the concession that strong ties are not configured randomly. But this still suggests that some social ties are random and Watts himself questions whether relations really are ever random.

What does it mean to suggest that weak ties are random? I suggest that, at most, randomness of ties is generally nested within structure. We may not form weak ties in the same way that we form strong ties (although it is far from obvious that this is the case), but it is still reasonable to suggest that their formation is structured by social events (e.g. work, holidays, leisure activities) and by the variably distributed resources, dispositions and social positions that enable, incline or otherwise lead us to partake in them. There may be a level of randomness in terms of who exactly within a delimited pool of others we actually meet and form bonds with but which 'pools' or rather worlds we move in is much less random.

On a trivial level, for example, and returning briefly to issues discussed in Chapter 9, it is no accident that many of my ties, both strong and weak, are to other sociologists and more specifically to those sociologists working in the same areas as me. I tend to meet other sociologists because we all converge upon certain key 'foci' (Feld 1981, 1982), e.g. sociology conferences, workshops and seminars.

I don't set out to meet likeminded sociologists at these events, as such, and which sociologists exactly I meet might be random in some respects but it is not a random matter that I know a lot of sociologists. More to the point, if I really did meet people on a purely random basis it is highly unlikely that I would form ties, weak or otherwise, with them because I would be unlikely to have anything in common with them or any pretext for meeting. Hitting it off is no more a random matter than meeting people in the first place.

I do not mean to deny that 'randomness' is an interesting and important statistical concept nor to suggest that it may have a substantive sociological application in this context. As noted, there is perhaps a degree of randomness at work within structural parameters. But the concept of randomness and its applications are not clear and require further exploration and clarification.

Small worlds and social worlds

There is an alternative to the randomness argument, however, which Watts hints at and which we can develop further. Borrowing a concept from White (1995), Watts notes that networks are organized into 'domains', a concept which, for our purposes, overlaps with the concept of worlds discussed in Chapters 8 and 9. Any actor belongs to a number of discrete worlds and more specifically to the networks constitutive of these worlds, and their own personal network is partitioned in accordance with them. Any actor may, for example, have work colleagues, family, old friends from school, friends associated with a particular leisure activity and so on. We would expect most of their friends within a particular world to have ties to one another but we would not necessarily expect ties to cross worlds. Actors may keep their worlds relatively separate from one another, not least because it can be very difficult, logistically, to bring actors who belong to separate worlds together. If I work at a distance from where I live, for example, then my work colleagues and my neighbours are unlikely to ever meet. This is an argument which Simmel (1955) explored to some extent in his discussion of 'intersecting circles' and it was touched upon in Chapters 8 and 9 too. We all belong to and constitute the intersection between worlds which are, in other respects, quite distinct from one another.

This observation addresses the small world debate because it suggests that each actor belongs to a number of distinct clusters which they effectively link. There are clumps and connections between them, as Watts suggests, but this is not, as his model suggests, a matter of strong and weak ties. Rather, clumps reflect worlds that are kept separate in actor's lives and those actors, themselves, are the links between the worlds. Transitivity is not offset by weak random ties so much as by actors' involvements in multiple relatively discrete social worlds which are closed off from one another. And social space is 'compressed' because we know, in each of the social worlds in which we are involved, others who are involved in multiple other worlds in which we are not directly involved, wherein they know others involved in yet further worlds and so on. I belong to a gym, university, family and neighbourhood, for example. At my gym I know a man who works for a supermarket, belongs to a different family to mine and belongs both to a local political group and an orienteering club. In his political group he knows a solicitor who works for a large law firm and who is a member of both a knitting circle and a rugby club etc. There is order and transitivity here. Most of the people who I know at the gym tend to know one another because we all work out at the same time and introduce one another. But there is not complete transitivity because we each belong to a range of other, separate and different worlds too. Each actor bridges a number of worlds and connects those worlds to one another.

Moreover, many worlds operate on a national or international basis and, in this respect, afford actors meaningful long-distance ties. I have already discussed sociology, for example, which like many occupations involves conferences and other meetings which serve to bring its members from across the world together. Similarly, in my punk research, discussed in Chapter 9, I found evidence of ties and tie formation not only within cities but also between them. Quite how these distance-spanning ties form, diffusing worlds geographically and linking their various geographical bases, is an interesting question which I cannot take up here. There is at least some evidence in the case of the punks, however, which resonates with Watts' account. At least some ties had a contingent aspect suggestive of the randomness he refers to. For example, Roger Eagle, the owner of Liverpool's famous Eric's club (where all of the punk and post-punk bands of the day played and where most of Liverpool's own future stars met), had originally lived and run a club in Manchester. And he maintained Manchester links after setting up Eric's. He invited Tony Wilson, the famous Manchester punk impresario, to work with him, for example. Likewise Martin Fry, of Vice Versa (and more famously ABC), who was born in Manchester but went to university in Sheffield and became a major player in the Sheffield scene. In this case local scenes were initially linked by way of the prior time–space trajectories of their pioneers, trajectories which were not in any way shaped by the scenes in question and might therefore be treated as random.[2]

The aforementioned mediated ties are important too, moreover. Many important links were formed after network members in one city heard of the activities of network members in another, via media sources, and sought to make contact. The important links between the London and Manchester punk scenes, for example, which played a key role in launching the latter, were famously sparked when the instigators of Manchester punk, Howard Devoto and Pete Shelley, read about the Sex Pistols in the *New Musical Express* (*NME*) magazine and decided to travel to London to see them (Crossley 2008c, 2009). These ties are much less random, however, as only actors with a keen interest in popular music read the *NME*.

Even if the details of Watts' argument are questionable and insufficiently sociological, therefore, his notion of a network structure involving dense clusters of actors, which are themselves only relatively weakly tied, does have some resonance in relation to my account of society as a network of interconnected social worlds. Social worlds are the dense 'clumps' and the multiple affiliations of social actors constitute their interconnection.

There is a potential problem here in relation to the small worlds issue, however. I argued in the last chapter that worlds tend to cluster, such that people who share one world with me may belong to a range of further worlds to which I do not belong but they will not belong to just any worlds. They will tend to belong to a specific range of clustered worlds. For example, members of middle class occupational worlds may be more likely to gravitate towards certain leisure worlds rather than others, because they influence one another with respect to leisure activities. To the extent to which they do so, they constitute a counter-veiling tendency to the small world effect. Just how much of a problem this is can only be determined by further empirical work on social worlds. We need to ascertain just how much clustering there is in the network of social worlds. It is worth reiterating, however, that Milgram, in his foundational work, claimed that 'social distance' proved far more of an impediment to interaction than geographical distance, suggesting that, at his time of writing, there was a high level of socially stratified clustering. Observing that some chain letters more or less immediately arrived in the town of their target but then went 'round and round', he suggested that 'social communication is restricted less by physical distance than by social distance' (Milgram 1967: 117). A sociological appropriation of small world theory cannot afford to overlook these crucial sociological properties of networks.

Barabási's scale-free networks

Watts' model presupposes that all nodes in a network have the same number of contacts ('degree') or at least that degree is normally distributed. This is not necessarily so, however. In his work on the URL connections comprising the World Wide Web, Barabási (2003) found a scale-free distribution of degree. The definition of 'scale free' is complex and examples, including Barabási's own, are often contested. For our purposes it will suffice to say that Barabási is referring to highly degree centralized networks (in the network analytic sense) in which the vast majority of ties involve a small number of network 'hubs'; that is, more or less everybody in the network connects to one or more of a small number of hub nodes. This network configuration generates a small world too, Barabási argues, because most nodes in the network are connected to one another via the mediation of the central hubs. Barabási thus offers an alternative model of how a small world network might be configured. And, like Watts, he cites empirical examples which appear to match his model, i.e. the World Wide Web, the internet, food chains and airports.

Barabási's (2003) model requires us to identify large network hubs which link millions of otherwise separate nodes to one another. We are looking for centres and centralizing forces within the social world. An obvious example, which connects with arguments from earlier in the chapter, is 'the state'. All of the citizens in a given society (or polity) interact with 'the state' in a variety of ways, including payment of taxes and voting. And they are linked to and affected by one another through the mediation of this hub. A change of government or weak government, for example, is inflicted upon all of its citizens, irrespective of their individual voting behaviour, if a sufficient number of other citizens in the network vote (or fail to vote) in a way which brings this about. Likewise, the tax burden for some may rise as a consequence of the rising cost of outputs demanded or needed by others. Actions have effects at a distance in this structure in virtue of the network of connections between its parts, a network which is hub centred and small worldly in the manner described by Barabási.

In addition, the centralized state, qua hub, constitutes the network by spanning and 'compressing' distances which are not spanned by way of face-to-face acquaintance. The denizens of Liverpool are connected to and share a fate with those of London, forming a common, national political system, by way of their common connection to the British state. And international political bodies have the same effect in relation to nations. Citizens of different countries share a similar fate by virtue of the ties of their respective national states to international bodies such as the European Commission, the United Nations and the World Bank.

Note the overlap between this account and my earlier discussion of corporate actors and nested network structures. The state is a hub in a scale-free network of national political interactions but it is equally a corporate actor, representing the network as a whole in a wider network of international political transactions. It links to its citizens but also represents them in a global political network.

To give another example of hubs, the channels of the mass media, particularly television, radio and national newspapers, variously constitute or host societal hubs. Television has been identified as a cause of the erosion of social ties in contemporary debates on social capital (Putnam 2000), which it may be, but it belongs to a vast network of communication, linking large chunks of the population to one another through their common connection to it. And though audience relations to presenters and programmes assume a very specific form, they are relations and they increasingly play a role in individuals' lives and identities. In the case of my punk networks, for example, the radio DJ John Peel was a very central hub through whom many enthusiasts from across the UK and much wider were linked. Peel famously received hundred of demo tapes from bands, some of whom he selected for sessions. And he played records released on small, little-known labels, bringing the bands involved to a wider audience. In both cases this allowed members of one (geographically local) scene to hear about and get themselves known to members of another. Peel was a (much loved) hub of the punk and post-punk scene and a broker between its different local manifestations.

The models compared

Barabási's model differs considerably from Watts'. It is highly centralized where Watts' is decentralized. Figure 10.2, which offers simplified illustrations of what the two models can look like, illustrates this (the size of vertices in these illustrations is relative to their degree). However, these models should not be thought of in either/or terms. It may be that aspects of each combine in real world situations. I am inclined to treat them as ideal types which approximate real life social networks and can be used in analyses and theoretical discussions of them.

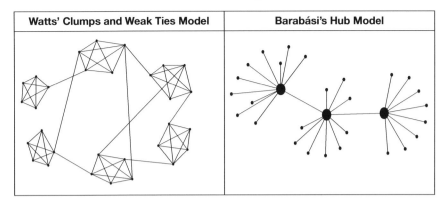

Watts' Clumps and Weak Ties Model	Barabási's Hub Model

Figure 10.2 Simplified illustrations of the network models suggested by Watts and Barabási, respectively

There are many problems with the work of Watts and Barabási, from a sociological perspective (Scott 2004; Urry 2004; Crossley 2005a, 2008e). Both approach social life from the perspective of physics, often with only a superficial grasp of work in social network analysis, let alone sociology. Failing to fully reflect upon the nature of social life and what distinguishes it from the other 'systems' of interest to them, their take upon it is often relatively crude. This should not deter us from engaging with what they have to say, however. As I hope I have shown, their models and ideas are, at the very least, highly suggestive and point to ways in which we might develop a relational approach to the micro–macro dichotomy.

Conclusion

I began this chapter with a relatively simple question: is the network conception of the social world really adequate to deal with so-called 'macro' structures, that is, structures which operate on national and global scales. My answer has been 'yes' and I have tried to substantiate it by pointing to three different ways in which network theory has thought about 'size'.

First, some networks and worlds involve macro or corporate actors. It is not only human actors who interact and form networks but also governments, trades unions, NGOs, business corporations etc. Second, relations can be mediated in various ways which facilitate 'mass'. Communication technologies, from the poster and printing press through to Web 2.0, are an obvious example but money, as a medium of exchange, and also political mechanisms, including voting systems and 'disciplinary practices', are no less important. We might not conventionally think of these phenomena in network terms but that says more about our conception of networks than the phenomena themselves. Finally, recent developments in network analysis suggest that the organization of networks may sometimes be such that very large numbers of nodes do not necessarily preclude the possibility of relatively short pathways between them, such that resources, influence etc. can flow easily between them. As the international spread of diseases indicates only too clearly, our world is a small world. It is connected or, rather, we are connected.

My argument in this book has been that connections matter. Indeed, for sociologists they are or should be 'what it is all about'. This is often recognized in relation to the microcosm but it is no less important in relation to the macrocosm. Social life doesn't cease being about what actors achieve together in interaction, whatever scale we choose to analyse it at and whatever abstractions we bring to bear. From children in the playground to the 'world economic order', societies are networks of interacting and co-constituting actors, orienting to conventions, exchanging resources and more generally 'being social'.

Notes

1 Introduction

1 Not that the story of Robinson Crusoe suggests atomism. Crusoe had parents, friends and crew-mates before being marooned and his interactions with those others made him who he was.
2 I am not denying that individual actors exist, have properties or are significant, only that they do not do so independently of their relations with one another.

2 Individualism, holism and beyond

1 Marx's intentions are famously subject to debate.
2 Thatcher actually said 'And, you know, there is no such thing as society. There are individual men and women, and there are families' (Thatcher 1987).
3 I borrow the 'in order to' and 'because' terminology from Schutz (1972).
4 They look for a good (satisfying) deal for themselves but not necessarily the best deal they could achieve.
5 Transitive preferences are ordered such that, for example, if I prefer i over j and j over k then I prefer i over k too.
6 That is, in terms of an evolutionary timescale.
7 As various writers, both sociological and biological, have suggested, the environment which selects for traits in the evolutionary process is not only natural but social (e.g. Hirst and Wooley 1982; Levins and Lewontin 1985). If collective living aids a species' survival, for example, then individual traits conducive to collective living will too and are more likely to survive.

3 Mapping the territory

1 Technically the space is n-dimensional but in practice Bourdieu's representations are always two-dimensional. Likewise, in theory they would include many of a range of forms of capital but, in practice, Bourdieu focuses on economic and cultural capital.
2 Bourdieu usually presents his correspondence maps in a format which focuses upon the location of practices/tastes and occupational categories within them (rather than individuals). The method (of multiple correspondence analysis) that he uses necessarily maps the positions of individuals too, however, and the statisticians who worked with him in his later work, as I note later in the chapter, tend to emphasize this 'cloud of individuals' in their own work and interpretations (Le Roux and Rouanet 2004). The necessity of both views derives from the fact that multiple correspondence analysis begins by decomposing a cases (individuals) by variables (practices and categories etc.) matrix.

3   Obviously actors do not reflectively debate which practices to adopt – although they may be aware of the social specificity of their preferences and collective 'taste formation' is an aspect of collective identity building. The consensus is in what actors do, not what they reflectively think. Later in the book I discuss Wittgenstein's (1953) conception of 'agreement in forms of life'. This is a very similar notion.

4   I have put scare quotes around 'internalize' because, at a philosophical level, there are considerable problems with the notion of an 'inner' world (Crossley 1996, 2001). What I mean, on one level, is behaviour that is taken over by the actor so as to become a disposition. In this particular case, moreover, I mean to imply both the world of the actor's imagination and a world which they perhaps keep private from (most) others.

5   Again I do not mean 'internal' in a heavy philosophical sense here (see note 4). I am referring rather to the set of others whose 'roles' have been internalized by the actor and are mobilized within their self-dialogues.

6   Such as convention, routine or habit.

7   My use of 'habit' follows that of Merleau-Ponty (1962) and Dewey (1988). Habits are flexible and intelligent pre-reflective dispositions, not mechanical reflexes. See Crossley (2001).

4 From strategy to empathy

1   The language is a little confusing because 'defection' involves cooperation with the police and cooperation involves not cooperating with the police. In each case, however, it reflects the relationship between the two prisoners. To defect is to 'do the dirty' on one's fellow prisoner. To cooperate is to cooperate with one's fellow prisoner.

2   Piaget (1961) argues that children are 'egocentric', by which he means that they are unaware of the subjective points of view of others. This is not to say that they are selfish, which would tend to suggest that they are aware of the perspectives of others but do not value those perspectives. They literally cannot see beyond their own perspective on the world such that, for example, their descriptions of events presuppose a background knowledge which only they enjoy. In Chapter's 5 and 6 I will discuss Mead's (1967) account of the way in which actors are lifted out of this egoistic state by way of social interaction and experience.

3   I touch here upon the definition of 'rationality'. Game theory, following RAT, defines rationality as the capacity to pursue goals in an efficient manner. Many other philosophical schools define rationality in broader terms such that, for example, it entails acting in ways which take the perspectives of others into account and which are understandable to others (e.g. Habermas 1991; Husserl 1990).

4   I confess that I cannot remember where I read this. But I did read it!

5   By my reading, White treats 'identities' as both the outcomes and the instigators of interaction and control. Identities are formed in the process of securing control but identities also seek control. I do not believe that my own position is substantively different to his but I believe that his manner of expression is unclear. I take this issue up again in Chapter 8.

5 Mind, meaning and intersubjectivity

1   As Mead (1967), amongst others, stresses, different organisms have different sensitivities and therefore perceive their environment differently. Human beings, for example, do not have the 'sonar' reception of bats and consequently do not perceive the world in the same way. By the same logic, viruses and bacteria which can prove fatal to some organisms might be beneficial or inconsequential for others.

2   As Leder (1990) suggests, however, awareness of our bodily sensations is more common when our body is dysfunctioning in some way – e.g. when we perceive blinding lights or very loud noises which are painful. Likewise, Ryle (1949) argues that

even pain tends to have intentional aspects: e.g. a stabbing pain is a pain which feels as if it results from our being stabbed. We can only make sense of it by relating it to objects outside of us with which we are engaged.

7 Exchange, sociability and power

1   That is to say, we tend to meet others similar to ourselves because our similarities will tend to draw us to the same places where we are more likely to meet. Film buffs have an increased likelihood of meeting and thus getting to know one another, for example, by virtue of their tendency to frequent cinemas.
2   Transitivity implies that we are, so to speak, friends with our friends' friends: if i is tied to j and j to k then i is more likely to be connected to k too. See also note 3.
3   Intransitivity implies an absence of any transitive tendency. It implies that i knowing both j and k does not increase the likelihood of them knowing one another. See note 2.
4   This work centred upon computer-mediated games where subjects bargain and exchange under different conditions and according to different rules.
5   2.5 times more likely, to be precise.
6   Following Heath (1976) I take the coercion theory to be an extension of the exchange theory such that the two can be treated as one.

8 Structure, agency and social worlds

1   Ownership can be separated from control, as critiques of the classic Marxist position regarding ownership and control of the means of production suggest. However, in the final analysis, owners are in a position to remove control rights from managers and take control themselves. Any separation of control from resources is conditional upon their consent.
2   To follow a rule it would seem necessary that we are conscious of it at some level and it makes no sense to say that we are unconsciously conscious of it.

9 Networks, conventions and resources

1   For example, the Sex Pistols, the Clash, the Damned, Siouxsie and the Banshees, Subway Sect, the Slits and the various infamous short-lived and 'bedroom bands' who preceded them.
2   I was unable to date all of the relationships in it, and thus used the smaller sample (whose relations I could date approximately), represented in Figures 9.2 and 9.3, to visualize and explore the process of network evolution.
3   Marco Pirroni, who played in the first line of Siouxsie and the Banshees and later in Adam and the Ants, is included in block one with the Sex Pistols. This seems odd – although he did play in the Banshees with Sid Vicious.
4   Two-mode networks are networks with two types of node. Each node can only connect to other nodes of a different type to itself. Consequently nodes of a given type are only connected to one another indirectly, through common links to a node of the other type.
5   The *Guardian* is a left-liberal newspaper in what is generally deemed the 'quality' sector of the newspaper market. The *Mail* is a right-wing newspaper, not usually perceived to be at the 'quality' end of the market but enjoying greater status than the *News of the World*, which is renowned for its sensationalist exposés of sex and scrubbing by famous people.

10 Big networks and small worlds

1   Milgram asked randomly selected subjects to initiate a chain letter which would eventually reach a selected target in another city, whose name and occupation they were

given. Subjects selected an alter whom they thought might know the target or might known someone who knew them, and sent them a letter. Alter then did the same and so on until the target was reached.

2   Of course in other respects they are not random at all. Both actors probably had very good reasons for moving cities, linked to other aspects of their lives. The point is that their trajectories are not in any way explained by the scenes we are analysing and, in this sense, might as well be random.

Bibliography

Abercrombie, N., Hill, S. and Turner, B. (1986) *Sovereign Individuals of Capitalism*, London, Allen and Unwin.

Abbott, A. (1997) Of Time and Space: On the Contemporary Relevance of the Chicago School, *Social Forces* 75(4), 1149–82.

—— (2001) *Time Matters*, Chicago, Chicago University Press.

—— (2007a) Mechanisms and Relations, *Sociologica* 2, http://www.sociologica. mulino.it/journal.

—— (2007b) Mechanisms and Relations: A Response to the Comments, *Sociologica* 2, http://www.sociologica.mulino.it/journal.

Adorno, T. and Horkheimer, M. (1983) *The Dialectic of Enlightenment*, London, Verso.

Althusser, L. (1969) *For Marx*, London, Verso.

—— (1971) 'Ideology and the State Ideological Apparatus', in *Essays on Ideology*, London, Verso, 1–60.

Archer, M. (1995) *Realist Social Theory*, Cambridge, Cambridge University Press.

Axelrod, R. (1985) *The Evolution of Cooperation*, Harmondsworth, Penguin.

—— (1997) *The Complexity of Cooperation*, Princeton, Princeton University Press.

Bachelard, G. (2002) *The Formation of the Scientific Mind*, Manchester, Clinamen.

Barabási, A.-L. (2003) *Linked*, New York, Plume.

Barnes, B. (2000) *Understanding Agency*, London, Sage.

Bateson, G. (1972) *Steps to an Ecology of Mind*, London, Picador.

Bearman, P. (1993) *Relations into Rhetorics*, New Brunswick, Rutgers University Press.

Becker, G. (1996) *Accounting for Tastes*, Cambridge, Harvard University Press.

Becker, G. and Murphy, K.(2000) *Social Economics*, Cambridge, Harvard University Press.

Becker, H. (1952) The Career of the Chicago Public Schoolteacher, *American Journal of Sociology* 57(5), 470–77.

—— (1982) *Art Worlds*, Berkeley, University of California Press.

Bennet, T., Savage, M., Silva, E. and Warde, A. (2009) *Culture, Class, Distinction*, London, Routledge.

Bentham, J. (1988) *The Principles of Morals and Legislation*, New York, Prometheus.

Berger, P. and Luckmann, T. (1971) *The Social Construction of Reality*, Harmondsworth, Penguin.

Bhaskar, R. (1979) *The Possibility of Naturalism*, Brighton, Harvester.

Billig, M. (1991) *Ideology and Opinions*, London, Sage.

Blau, P. (1986) *Exchange and Power in Social Life*, New Brunswick, Transaction.

Blumer, H. (1969) 'Collective Behaviour' in McClung-Lee, A. (1969) *Principles of Sociology*, New York, Barnes and Noble, 67–121.

—— (1986) *Symbolic Interaction*, Berkeley, California University Press.

—— (2004) *George Herbert Mead and Human Conduct*, New York, Alta Mira.

Bonacich, P. (1987) Power and Centrality: A Family of Measures, *American Journal of Sociology* 92(5), 1170–1182.

Boorman, S., and White, H. (1976) Social Structure from Multiple Networks II: Role Structures, *American Journal of Sociology* 81(6), 1384–1446.

Borgatti, S.P., Everett, M.G. and Freeman, L.C. (2002) Ucinet for Windows: Software for Social Network Analysis, Harvard, MA, Analytic Technologies.

Bott, E. (1957) *Family and Social Network*, London, Tavistock.

Bottero, W. (2005) *Stratification*, London, Routledge.

—— (2009) Relationality and Social Interaction, *British Journal of Sociology* 60(2), 309–420.

—— (2010) Intersubjectivity and Bourdieusian approaches to "identity", *Cultural Sociology* 3(3).

Bottero, W. and Crossley, N. (2010) Worlds, Fields and Networks, *Cultural Sociology* (forthcoming).

Bourdieu, P. (1977) *Outline of a Theory of Practice*, Cambridge, Cambridge University Press.

—— (1984) *Distinction*, London, Routledge.

—— (1987) What Makes a Class? *Berkeley Journal of Sociology* 32, 1–18.

—— (1992) *The Logic of Practice*, Cambridge, Polity.

—— (1993) 'Social Space and the Genesis of Classes', in *Language and Symbolic Power*, Cambridge, Polity, 229–51.

—— (1995) Public Opinion Does Not Exist, in *Sociology in Question*, London, Sage.

—— (1996) *The State Nobility*, Cambridge, Polity.

—— (1998) *Practical Reason*, Cambridge, Polity.

—— (2000) *Pascalian Meditations*, Cambridge, Polity.

Bourdieu, P. and Passeron, J.-C. (1996) *Reproduction*, London, Sage.

Bourdieu, P. and Wacquant, L. (1992) *Introduction to Reflexive Sociology*, Chicago, University of Chicago Press.

Breiger, R. (1974) The Duality of Persons and Groups, *Social Forces* 53, 181–90.

Burt, R. (1992) *Structural Holes*, Cambridge, Harvard University Press.

—— (2005) *Brokerage and Closure*, Oxford, Oxford University Press.

Carrington, P.J., Scott, J. and Wasserman, S. (eds) (2005) *Models and Methods in Social Network Analysis*, Cambridge, Cambridge University Press.

Cassirer, E. (1923) *Substance and Function and Einstein's Theory of Relativity*, London, Open Court.

Coleman, J. (1975) 'Social Structure and a Theory of Action', in Blau, P. (1975) *Approaches to the Study of Social Structure*, New York, Free Press, 76–93.

—— (1988) Free Riders and Zealots: The Role of Social Networks, *Sociological Theory* 6(1), 52–57.

—— (1990) *The Foundations of Social Theory*, Cambridge, Harvard University Press.

—— (2006) *The Mathematics of Collective Action*, New York, Aldine.

Cooley, C. (1902) *Human Nature and Social Order*, New York, Charles Scribner's Sons.

Crossley, M. (2000) *Introducing Narrative Psychology*, Buckinghamshire, Open University Press.

Crossley, N. (1994) *The Politics of Subjectivity*, Avebury, Ashgate.

—— (1995) Body Techniques, Agency and Intercorporeality: On Goffman's *Relations in Public*, *Sociology* 29(2), 133–49.

—— (1996) *Intersubjectivity: The Fabric of Social Becoming*, London, Sage.

—— (2001) *The Social Body*, London, Sage.

—— (2004a) The Circuit Trainer's Habitus: Reflexive Body Techniques and the Sociality of the Workout, *Body and Society* 10(1), 37–69.

—— (2004b) 'Ritual, Body Techniques and Intersubjectivity', in Schilbrack, K. *Thinking Through Rituals: Philosophical Perspectives*, London, Routledge, 31–51.

—— (2005a) Mapping Reflexive Body Techniques, *Body and Society* 11 (1), 1–35.

—— (2005b) The New Social Physics and the Science of Small World Networks, *The Sociological Review* 53(2), 351–58.

—— (2006a) *Reflexive Embodiment in Contemporary Society*, Buckinghamshire, Open University Press.

—— (2006b) In the Gym: Motives, Meanings and Moral Careers, *Body and Society* 12(3), 23–50.

—— (2007) 'Exploring Embodiment by Way of Body Techniques', in Shilling, C. (2007) *Embodying Sociology*, Oxford, Blackwell.

—— (2008a) Social Networks and Extra-Parliamentary Politics, *Sociology Compass*, http://www.blackwell-compass.com/home{_}sociology{_}compass.

—— (2008b) (Net)Working Out: Social Capital in a Private Health Club, *British Journal of Sociology* 59(3) 475–500.

—— (2008c) Pretty Connected: The Social Network of the Early UK Punk Movement, *Theory, Culture and Society* 25(6), 89–116.

—— (2008d) Social Networks and Student Activism: On the Politicising Effect of Campus Connections, *Sociological Review* 56(1), 18–38.

—— (2008e) Small World Networks, Complex Systems and Sociology, *Sociology* 42(2), 261–77.

—— (2008f) 'Bourdieu and Social Class', in Grenfel, M. (2008) *Bourdieu: Key Concepts*, London, Acumen.

—— (2009) The Man Whose Web Expanded: Network Dynamics in Manchester's Post-Punk Music Scene 1976–80, *Poetics* 37(1), 24–49.

—— (2010a) The Social World of the Network, *Sociologica* http://www.sociologica.mulino.it/journal (forthcoming).

—— (2010b) Networks, Interactions and Complexity, *Symbolic Interaction* (forthcoming).

de Nooy, W., Mrvar, A. and Batagelj, V. (2005) *Exploratory Social Network Analysis with Pajek*. Cambridge, Cambridge University Press.

Della Fave, R. (1980) The Meek Shall Not Inherit the Earth, *American Sociological Review* 45, 955–71.

Descartes, R. (1969) *Discourse on Method and The Meditations*, Harmondsworth, Penguin.

Dewey, J. (1896) The Reflex Arc Concept in Psychology, *Psychological Review* 3, 363–70.

—— (1988) *Human Nature and Conduct*, Carbondale, South Illinois University Press.

Diani, M. and McAdam, D. (2003) *Social Movements and Networks*, Oxford, Oxford University Press.

Durkheim, E. (1915) *Elementary Forms of the Religious Life*, New York, Free Press.

—— (1952) *Suicide*, London, Routledge.

—— (1964) *The Division of Labour in Society*, New York, Free Press.

—— (1965) *The Rules of Sociological Method*, New York, Free Press.

—— (1973) *The Dualism of Human Nature and its Social Conditions, in Émile Durkheim: On Morality and Society*, Chicago, Chicago University Press, 149–66.

—— (1974) *Sociology and Philosophy*, New York, Free Press.

—— (2002) *Moral Education*, New York, Dover.

Edwards, G. (2009) Mixed Method Approaches to Social Network Analysis, National Centre for Social Research, Methods Review Paper.

Edwards, G. and Crossley, N. (2009) Measures and Meanings: Exploring the Ego-Net of Helen Kirkpatrick Watts, Militant Suffragette, *Methodological Innovations On-Line* 3(2).

Elias, N. (1978) *What is Sociology?* London, Hutchinson.

—— (1984) *The Civilising Process*, Oxford, Blackwell.

—— (1986) *The Germans*, Cambridge, Polity.

—— (2001) *The Society of Individuals*, London, Continuum.

Elias, N. and Dunning, E. (1986) *The Quest for Excitement*, Oxford, Blackwell.

Ellis, B.E. (1991) *American Psycho*, London, Picador.

Elster, J.(1985) *Making Sense of Marx*, Cambridge, Cambridge University Press.

—— (1989) *Nuts and Bolts for the Social Sciences*, Cambridge, Cambridge University Press.

—— (1990) *The Cement of Society*, Cambridge, Cambridge University Press.

—— (2007) *Explaining Social Behaviour*, Cambridge, Cambridge University Press.

Emerson, R.M. (1962) Power-Dependence Relations, *American Sociological Review* 27, 31–40.

Emirbayer, M. (1997) Manifesto for a Relational Sociology, *American Journal of Sociology* 99(6), 1411–54.

Emirbayer, M. and Goodwin, J. (1994) Network Analysis, Culture and the Problem of Agency, *American Journal of Sociology* 99, 1411–54.

Erdös, P. and Rényi, A. (1960) The Evolution of Random Graphs, *Publications of the Mathematical Institute of the Hungarian Academy of Sciences* 5, 17–61.

Erikson, E. (1963) *Childhood and Society*, New York, Norton.

Feld, S. (1981) The Focused Organisation of Social Ties, *American Journal of Sociology* 86, 1015–35.

—— (1982) Social Structural Determinants of Similarity Among Associates, *American Sociological Review* 47, 797–801.

Fine, G. and Kleinman, S. (1979) Rethinking Sub-Culture, *American Journal of Sociology* 85 1–20.

—— (1983) Network and Meaning: An Interactionist Approach to Structure, *Symbolic Interaction* 6 (1), 97–110.

Fish, S. (1980) *Is There a Text in the Class?* Cambridge, Harvard University Press.

Foucault, M. (1970) *The Order of Things*, London, Tavistock.

—— (1979) *Discipline and Punish*, Harmondsworth, Penguin.

—— (1980) *Power/Knowledge*, Brighton, Harvester.

—— (1982) 'The Subject and Power', in Dreyfus, H. and Rabinow, P. (1982) *Michel Foucault; Beyond Structuralism and Hermeneutics*, Brighton, Harvester, 208–26.

Freeman, L. (2006) *The Development of Social Network Analysis*, Vancouver, Empirical Press.

Gadamer, H.-G. (1989) *Truth and Method*, London, Sheed and Ward.

Gambetta, D. (1988) *Trust*, Oxford, Blackwell.

Gibson, J. (1979) *The Ecological Approach to Visual Perception*, Boston, Houghton Mifflin.

Giddens, A. (1973) *The Class Structure of Advanced Societies*, London, Hutchinson.

—— (1984) *The Constitution of Society*, Cambridge, Polity.

—— (1990) *The Consequences of Modernity*, Cambridge, Polity.

—— (1991) *Modernity and Self-Identity*, Cambridge, Polity.

Gintis, H. (2009) *The Bounds of Reason*, Princeton, Princeton University Press.

Gladwell, M. (2002) *The Tipping Point*, London, Abacus.

Goffman, E. (1959) *The Presentation of Self in Everyday Life*, Harmondsworth, Penguin.

—— (1961) *Asylums*, Harmondsworth, Penguin.

—— (1969) *Strategic Interaction*, Philadelphia, University of Pennsylvania Press.

—— (1971) *Relations in Public*, Harmondsworth, Penguin.

—— (1996) *Frame Analysis*, Boston, Northeastern University Press.

Goldstein, K. (2000) *The Organism*, New York, Zone.

Goldthorpe, J. (2000) *On Sociology*, Oxford, Oxford University Press.

Gould, R. (1991) Multiple Networks and Mobilisation in the Paris Commune, 1871, *American Sociological Review* 56, 716–29.

—— (1993a) Collective Action and Network Structure, *American Sociological Review* 58(2), 182–96.

—— (1993b) Trade Cohesion, Class Unity and Urban Insurrection, *American Journal of Sociology* 98, 735–83.

—— (1995) *Insurgent Identities*, Chicago, Chicago University Press.

Goyal, S. (2007) *Connections*, Princeton, Princeton University Press.

Green, D. and Shapiro, I. (1994) Pathologies of Rational Choice Theory, New Haven, Yale University Press.

Granovetter, M. (1973) The Strength of Weak Ties, *American Journal of Sociology* 78, 1360–60.

—— (1974) *Getting a Job*, Chicago, Chicago University Press.

—— (1983) The Strength of Weak Ties: A Network Theory Revisited, *Sociological Theory* 1, 203–33.

—— (1985) Economic Action and Social Structure: The Problem of Embeddedness, *American Journal of Sociology* 91(3), 481–510.

Habermas, J. (1987) *The Theory of Communicative Action* (Vol II), Cambridge, Polity.

—— (1988) *On the Logic of the Social Sciences*, Cambridge, Polity.

—— (1989) *The Structural Transformation of the Public Sphere*, Cambridge, Polity.

—— (1991) *The Theory of Communicative Action* (Vol I), Cambridge, Polity.

Hall, O. (1948) The Stages of Medical Career, *The American Journal of Sociology* 53(5), 327–36.

Hall, P. (1987) Interactionism and the Study of Social Organisation, *The Sociological Quarterly* 28 (1), 1–22.

Hardin, R. (1982) *Collective Action*, Baltimore, Johns Hopkins.

—— (1993) The Street Level Epistemology of Trust, *Politics and Society* 21(4), 505–29.

Heath, A. (1976) *Rational Choice and Social Exchange*, Cambridge, Cambridge University Press.

Hedström, P. (2005) *Dissecting the Social*, Cambridge, Cambridge University Press.

Hedström, P. and Swedberg, R. (1998) *Social Mechanisms*, Cambridge, Cambridge University Press.

Hegel, G. (1979) *The Phenomenology of Spirit*, Oxford, Oxford University Press.

Heidegger, M. (1962) *Being and Time*, Oxford, Blackwell.

Hindess, B. (1982) Power, Interests and the Outcomes of Struggle, *Sociology* 16(4), 498–511.

—— (1988) *Choice, Rationality and Social Theory*, London, Unwin Hyman.

Hirst, P. (1979) *Durkheim, Bernard and Epistemology*, London, Routledge.

Hirst, P. and Wooley, P. (1982) *Social Relations and Human Attributes*, London, Tavistock.

Hobbes, T. (1971) *Leviathan*, Harmondsworth, Penguin.

Hollis, M. (1994) *The Philosophy of the Social Sciences*, Cambridge, Cambridge University Press.

—— (1995) *Reason in Action*, Cambridge, Cambridge University Press.

Homans, G. (1973) 'Bringing Men Back In', in Ryan, A. (1973) *The Philosophy of Social Explanation*, Oxford, Oxford University Press.

—— (1974) *Social Behaviour*, New York, Harcourt Brace.

Hume, D. (1984) *A Treatise of Human Nature*, Harmondsworth, Penguin.

Huizinga, J. (1950) *Homo Ludens*, Boston, Beacon.

Husserl, E. (1990) *Cartesian Meditations*, Dordrecht , Kluwer Academic Publishers.

Jackson, M. (2008) *Social and Economic Networks*, Princeton, Princeton University Press.

James, W. (1981) *Principles of Psychology* (Vol 1), Cambridge, Harvard University Press.

Jenks, C. (2005) *Subculture*, London, Sage.

Johnson, J. [pseudonym of Bruno Latour] (1988) Mixing Humans and Non-Human Together, *Social Problems* 35(3), 298–310.

Kant, I. (1993) *Critique of Practical Reason*, Upper Saddle River, Prentice Hall.

Kahneman, D. (2003) Maps of Bounded Rationality, *American Economic Review* 93(5), 1449–75.

Karinthy, F. (1929) 'Chain Links', reproduced in Newman, M., Barabási, L. and Watts, D. (eds.) (2006) *The Structure and Dynamics of Networks*, Princeton, Princeton University Press, 21–26.

Kennedy, J. (2003) *Space, Time and Einstein*, Chesham, Acumen.

Khodyakov, D. (2007) Trust as a Process, *Sociology* 41(1), 115–32.

Kleinfeld, J. (2002a) Could it Be a Big World After All? *Society* (available at http://www.uaf.edu/northern/big{_}world.html).

—— (2002b) Six Degrees of Separation: Urban Myth? *Psychology Today* 35(2), 74.

Knox, H., Savage, M. and Harvey, P. (2006) Social Networks and the Study of Relations, *Economy and Society* 35(1), 113–40.

Kojève, A. (1969) *Introduction to the Reading of Hegel*, New York, Basic Books.

Korte, C. and Milgram, S. (1970) Acquaintence Networks Between Racial Groups, *Journal of Personality and Social Psychology* 15(2), 101–8.

Krackhardt, D. (1999) The Ties That Torture, *Research in the Sociology of Organisations* 16, 183–210.

Kripke, S. (1982) *On Rules and Private Language*, Cambridge, Harvard University Press.

Latour, B. (2005) *Reassembling the Social*, Oxford, Oxford University Press.

Laver, M. (1997) *Private Desires, Political Action*, London, Sage.

Leder, D. (1990) *The Absent Body*, Chicago, Chicago University Press.

Le Roux, B. and Rouanet, H. (2004) *Geometric Data Analysis*, Dordrecht, Kluwer.

Levins, R. and Lewontin, R. (1985) *The Dialectical Biologist*, Cambridge, Harvard University Press.

Levi-Strauss, C. (1963) *Structural Anthropology*, New York, Basic Books.

—— (1966) *The Savage Mind*, Chicago, Chicago University Press.

—— (1969) *The Elementary Forms of Kinship*, Boston, Beacon.

Lewontin, R. (1993) *The Doctrine of DNA*, Harmondsworth, Penguin.

Lin, N. (2001) *Social Capital*, Cambridge, Cambridge University Press.

Lockwood, D. (1964) 'Social Integration and System Integration', in Zollschan, G. and Hirsch, W. (1964) *Explorations in Social Change*, London, Routledge.

Lorrain, F. and White, H. (1971) Structural Equivalence of Individuals in Social Networks, *Journal of Mathematical Sociology* 1, 49–80.

Manski, C. (2000) Economic Analysis of Social Interactions, *Journal of Economic Perspectives* 14(3), 115–36.

Martin, J.-L. (2009) *Social Structures*, Princeton, Princeton University Press.

Martin, P. (2006a) *Music and the Sociological Gaze*, Manchester, Manchester University Press.

—— (2006b) Musician's Worlds, *Symbolic Interaction* 29(1), 95–107.

Marx, K. (1959) *The Economic and Philosophical Manuscripts of 1844*, Moscow, Progress Publishers.

—— (1970) Introduction to A Critique of Political Economy, in Marx, K. and Engels, F. (1970) *The German Ideology and Supplementary Texts*, London, Lawrence and Wishart, 124–52.

—— (1973) *Grundrisse*, Harmondsworth, Penguin.

—— (1977) The Eighteenth Brumaire of Louis Bonaparte, in McLellan, D. (1977) *Karl Marx: Selected Writings*, Oxford, Oxford University Press.

Mauss, M. (1979) *Sociology and Psychology*, London, Routledge.

McAdam, D. (1982) *Political Process and the Development of Black Insurgency*, Chicago, University of Chicago Press.

McAdam, D., Tarrow, S. and Tilly, C. (2001) *The Dynamics of Contention*, Cambridge, Cambridge University Press.

McLean, P. (2007) *The Art of the Network*, Durham, Duke University Press.

McPherson, M., Smith-Lovin, L. and Cook, J. (2001) Birds of a Feather, *Annual Review of Sociology* 27, 415–44.

Mead, G. (1967) *Mind, Self and Society*, Chicago, Chicago University Press.

—— (1972) *The Philosophy of the Act*, Chicago, Chicago University Press.

—— (2002) *The Philosophy of the Present*, New York, Prometheus.

Merleau-Ponty, M. (1962) *The Phenomenology of Perception*, London, Routledge.

—— (1964) *Signs*, Evanston, Northwestern University Press.

—— (1965) *The Structure of Behaviour*, London, Methuen.

—— (1971) *Sense and Non-Sense*, Evanston, Northwestern University Press.

—— (1973) *The Adventures of the Dialectic*, Evanston, Northwestern University Press.

—— (1968) *The Visible and the Invisible*, Evanston, Northwestern University Press.

—— (2004) *The World of Perception*, London, Routledge.

Merton, R. (1957) *Social Theory and Social Structure*, Glencoe, Free Press, 19–84.

Milgram, S. (1967) 'The Small World Problem', reproduced in Carter, G. (2004) *Empirical Approaches to Sociology*, Boston, Pearson.

Mills, C.W. (1967) *Power, Politics and People*, Oxford, Oxford University Press, 439–52.

Milroy, L. (1987) *Language and Social Networks*, Blackwell, Oxford.

Mische, A. (2003) 'Cross-Talk in Movements', in Diani, M. and McAdam, D. (2003) *Social Movements and Networks*, Oxford, Oxford University Press.

Mische, A. and White, H. (1998) Between Conversation and Situation: Public Switching Dynamics Across Network-Domains, *Social Research* 65, 295–324.

Mitchell, J.C. (ed.) (1969) *Social Networks in Urban Situations*, Manchester, Manchester University Press.

Molm, L. (1997) *Coercive Power in Social Exchange*, Cambridge, Cambridge University Press.

Nadel, S. (1957) *The Theory of Social Structure*, London, Cohen and West.

Newman, M., Barabási, L. and Watts, D. (2006) *The Structure and Dynamics of Networks*, Princeton, Princeton University Press (Princeton Studies in Complexity).

Oliver, P. and Marwell, G. (1993) *The Critical Mass in Collective Action*, Cambridge, Cambridge University Press.

Olson, M. (1971) *The Logic of Collective Action*, Cambridge, Harvard University Press.

Ormerod, P. (2005) Crime: Economic Incentives and Social Networks, Westminster, Institute of Economic Affairs.

Pahl, R. (2000) *On Friendship*, Cambridge, Polity.

Parsons, T. (1937) *The Structure of Social Action*, New York, Free Press.

—— (1951) *The Social System*, New York, Free Press.

—— (1979) *Action Theory and the Human Condition*, New York, Free Press.

Piaget, J. (1961) *The Language and Thought of the Child*, London, Routledge and Kegan Paul.

Pool, I. and Kochen, M. (1978/9) Contacts and Influence, *Social Networks* 1, 5–51.

Popper, K. (2002) *The Poverty of Historicism*, London, Routledge.

—— (1992) *The Open Society and Its Enemies* (2 Volumes), London, Routledge.

Prell, C. (2009) Linking Social Capital to Small Worlds, *Methodological Innovation Online* 4(1), www.methodologicalinnovations.org.

Putnam, R. (2000) *Bowling Alone*, New York, Touchstone.

Radcliffe-Brown, A. (1952a) *Structure and Function in Primitive Society*, London, Cohen and West.

—— (1952b), 'On Social Structure', in *Structure and Function in Primitive Society*, London, Cohen and West, 188–204.

Rawls, A. (1992) Can Rational Choice be A Foundation for Social Theory? *Theory and Society* 21(2), 219–41.

Rogers, E. (2003) *The Diffusion of Innovations*, New York, Free Press.

Ryle, G. (1949) *The Concept of Mind*, Harmondsworth, Penguin.

Sartre, J.-P. (1969) *Being and Nothingness*, London, Routledge.

Saussure, F. (1959) *Course in General Linguistics*, New York, The Philosophical Library.

Savage, M., Warde, A. and Devine, F. (2005) Capitals, Assets and Resources, *British Journal of Sociology* 56(1), 31–48.

Schelling, T. (1981) *The Strategy of Conflict*, Cambridge, Harvard University Press.

—— (1995) *Micromotives and Macrobehaviours*, New York, W.W. Norton and Co.

Schnettler, S. (2009a) A Structured Overview of 50 Years of Small-World Research, *Social Networks* 31(3), 165–78.

—— (2009b) A Small World on Feet of Clay? *Social Networks* 31(3), 179–89.

Schutz, A. (1964) 'Making Music Together', in Schutz, A. (1964) *Collected Papers Vol 2: Studies in Social Theory*, The Hague, Martinus Nijhoff, 159–78.

—— (1972) *The Phenomenology of the Social World*, Evanston, Northwestern University Press.

Scott, J. (2000) *Social Network Analysis: A Handbook*, London, Sage.

—— (2004) Social Physics and Social Networks, paper presented at New Issues in Social Network Analysis, University of Manchester, October 22nd. 2004.

Searle, J. (1995) *The Construction of Social Reality*, New York, Free Press.

Shibutani, T. (1955) Reference Groups as Perspectives, *American Journal of Sociology* 60 (6), 562–69.

Simmel, G. (1902) The Number of Members as Determining the Form of the Group I & II, *American Journal of Sociology* 8(1), 1–46 & 8(2) 158–96.

—— (1906) The Sociology of Secrecy and Secret Societies, *American Journal of Sociology* 11(4), 441–98.

—— (1955) *Conflict and The Web of Group Affiliations*, New York, Free Press.

—— (1971) *On Individuality and Social Forms*, Chicago, Chicago University Press.

—— (1990) *The Philosophy of Money*, London, Routledge.

Smith, A. (1991) *The Wealth of Nations*, New York, Prometheus.

—— (2000) *The Theory of Moral Sentiments*, New York, Prometheus.

Smith, D. and White, D. (1992) Structure and Dynamics of the Global Economy, *Social Forces* 70 (4), 857–93.

Smith, J.M. (1986) *Problems of Biology*, Oxford, Oxford University Press.

Snyder, D. and Kick, E. (1979) Structural Position in the World System and Economic Growth, 1955–70, *American Journal of Sociology* 84 (5), 1096–1126.

Strauss, A. (1973) Social World Perspective, *Studies in Symbolic Interaction* 1 119–28.

—— (1993) *Continual Permutations of Action*, New York, Aldine de Gruyter.

Thatcher, M. (1987) Interview, *Women's Own* (October 31st).

Thibaut, J. and Kelley, H. (2007) *The Social Psychology of Groups*, New Brunswick, Transaction.

Tilly, C. (1978) *From Mobilization to Revolution*, Reading, Addison-Wesley.

—— (2002) *Stories, Identities and Political Change*, New York, Rowman and Littlefield.

—— (2006) *Identities, Boundaries and Social Ties*, New York, Paradigm.

Travers, J. and Milgram, S. (1969) An Experimental Study of the Small World Problem, *Sociometry* 32, 425–43.

Urry, J. (2004) Small Worlds and the New 'Social Physics', *Global Networks* 4(2), 109–30.

Volosinov, V. (1986) *Marxism and the Philosophy of Language*, Cambridge, Harvard University Press.

Vygotsky, L. (1986) *Thought and Language*, Cambridge, MIT.

Wallerstein, I. (2004) *World Systems Analysis*, Durham, Duke University Press.

Wasserman, S. and Faust, K. (1994) *Social Network Analysis*, Cambridge, Cambridge University Press.

Watts, D. (1999) *Small Worlds*, Princeton, Princeton University Press.

—— (2004) *Six Degrees*, London, Vintage.

Weber, M. (1978) *Economy and Society* (2 vols), New York, Bedminster Press.

Wellman, B. and Berkowitz, S. (1997) *Social Structures: A Network Approach*, Greenwich, JAI Press.

White, H. (1965/2008) Notes on the Constituents of Social Structure, *Sociologica 1* http://www.sociologica.mulino.it/journal.

—— (1970) *Chains of Opportunity*, Cambridge, Harvard University Press.

—— (1992) *Identity and Control*, Princeton, Princeton University Press.

—— (1995) Network Switchings and Bayesian Forks, *Social Research* 62, 1035–63.

—— (2002) *Markets From Networks*, Princeton, Princeton University Press.

—— (2008) *Identity and Control* (revised second edition), Princeton, Princeton University Press

White, H., Boorman, S. and Breiger, R. (1976) Social Structure from Multiple Networks I: Blockmodels and Roles and Positions, *American Journal of Sociology* 81(4) 730–80.

Winch, P. (1958) *The Idea of a Social Science and Its Relation to Philosophy*, London, Routledge and Kegan Paul.

Wittgenstein, L. (1953) *Philosophical Investigations*, Trans. G. E. M. Anscombe, Oxford, Blackwell.

Wouters, C. (1986) Formalisation and Informalisation, *Theory, Culture and Society* 3 (2), 1–18.

Wrong, D. (1961) The Oversocialised Conception of Man in Modern Sociology, *American Sociological Review* 26, 184–93.

Index

Printed in Great Britain
by Amazon